The Making of the 20th Century

This series of specially commissioned titles focuses attention on significant and often controversial events and themes of world history in the present century. Each book provides sufficient narrative and explanation for the newcomer to the subject while offering, for more advanced study, detailed source-references and bibliographies, together with interpretation and reassessment in the light of recent scholarship.

In the choice of subjects there is a balance between breadth in some spheres and detail in others; between the essentially political and matters economic or social. The series cannot be a comprehensive account of everything that has happened in the twentieth century, but it provides a guide to recent research and explains something of the times of extraordinary change and complexity in which we live. It is directed in the main to students of contemporary history and international relations, but includes titles which are of direct relevance to courses in economics, sociology, politics and geography.

The Making of the 20th Century

Series Editor: GEOFFREY WARNER

PUBLISHED TITLES

David Armstrong, Lorna Lloyd and John Redmond, *From Versailles to Maastricht: International Organization in the Twentieth Century*
S. R. Ashton, *In Search of Détente: The Politics of EastWest Relations Since 1945*
V. R. Berghahn, *Germany and the Approach of War in 1914*
Raymond F. Betts, *France and Decolonisation 1900–1960*
John Darwin, *Britain and Decolonisation: The Retreat from Empire in the PostWar World*
John F. V. Keiger, *France and the Origins of the First World War*
Dominic Lieven, *Russia and the Origins of the First World War*
Sally Marks, *The Illusion of Peace: International Relations in Europe 1918–1933*
Philip Morgan, *Italian Fascism 1919–1945*
A. J. Nicholls, *Weimar and the Rise of Hitler,* third edition
R. A. C. Parker, *Chamberlain and Appeasement: British Policy and the Coming of the Second World War*
G. Roberts, *The Soviet Union and the Origins of the Second World War*
Alan Sharp, *The Versailles Settlement: Peacemaking in Paris, 1919*
Zara Steiner, *Britain and the Origins of the First World War*
Samuel R. Williamson, *Austria–Hungary and the Origins of the First World War*
Robert J. Young, *France and the Origins of the Second World War*

FORTHCOMING TITLES

Saki Dockrill, *Japan and the Origins of the Second World War*
J. E. Spence, *South Africa in International Society*
Glyn Stone, *Great Powers and the Iberian Peninsular 1931–1941*
Jonathan Wright, *Germany and the Origins of the Second World War*

France and the Origins of the Second World War

Robert J. Young

St. Martin's Press
New York

FRANCE AND THE ORIGINS OF THE SECOND WORLD WAR
Copyright © 1996 by Robert J. Young

St. Martin's Press, Scholarly and Reference Division,
175 Fifth Avenue, New York, N.Y. 10010

First published in the United States of America in 1996

Printed in Hong Kong

ISBN 0–312–16185–9 cloth
ISBN 0–312–16186–7 paperback

Library of Congress Cataloging-in-Publication Data
Young, Robert J.
France and the origins of the Second World War / Robert J. Young.
p.   cm. — (The Making of the 20th century)
Includes bibliographical references and index.
ISBN 0–312–16185–9 — ISBN 0–312–16186–7 (pbk.)
1. World War, 1939–45—Causes.   2. France—Politics and
government—1914–1940.   I. Title.   II. Series.
D742.F7Y68   1996
940.53'11—dc20   96–10410
                                                          CIP

FOR KATHRYN
Of Stanhope Road and the Rue des Fossés Saint Jacques

Contents

Introduction

An American journalist once remarked on the difference between France and the English-speaking world. The French, he noted, did not assume that one had to teach history in order to write it. Here is the first simplification with which this book must deal. He was right to sense a certain distrust of the 'amateur' on the part of the 'professional', that is to say the university-trained historian. He was wrong to suggest that this was a peculiarly Anglo-Saxon myopia, for in France, too, there are reservations about journalists 'doing' history. There are fears that they are drawn to the sensational, not to say the scandalous, and that editorial deadlines encourage rushed and incomplete research. The fact that they are often accomplished writers, who address mass markets, earn public acclaim and accumulate personal fortunes, only heightens the anxiety and fans the resentment of the Academy.

As a Canadian member of that institution, I am sometimes party to such misgivings. If History is to instruct, as well as entertain, what goes into it should be the product of industry and reflection. It cannot afford to be premature, something hastily assembled to satisfy an arbitrary timetable. Therein lies the most common charge against the journalist-historian. That said, his critics are not entirely innocent. There are, of course, the research lapses, the narrow conceptual constraints, the occasional bias which professional historians regularly discern in the work of colleagues. But among the general public, it is our speech impediment which too often distracts. As a rule, we do not communicate as well as the best of our popular writers and journalists. Exceptions apart, we are inclined to rely on technical jargon, or on a more traditional but esoteric vocabulary. Too often, the result is a prose that either intimidates or suffocates – and that is a mistake. At least it is a mistake if we intend to retain some literary role in public education.

No one knows that more than the university students who fill our classrooms and, eventually, our positions. It is to them that I address this book, to them and to other non-experts whose curiosity and interest have survived their formal education. I write as a teacher of history whose task it is to explain France's role in the origins of the Second World War in 1939, and to offer some ideas about why she collapsed so suddenly in 1940.

It may seem an odd choice of assignments, as that war and its importance recede in our collective memory. Have we not already said everything that is going to be said, or can be said, about its origins? The question is not purely rhetorical, for the truth is that the invitation to write this volume brought it immediately to mind. And the answer was less obvious, less quickly forthcoming, than the presence of this book might suggest. So much has been written on the origins of the Second World War, by popular and academic historians alike; and if France has attracted proportionately less interest than Germany, the United Kingdom, or Russia, the fact remains that much capable work has been done on the domestic and international history of the Third French Republic. So again, that pertinent, potentially discomforting question: why another book on France and the Second World War?

There are three reasons why, each progressively more specific. The first is that this book affords a chance to improve the dialogue between students and teachers. Too often for the former, history is static, something finished with, an accumulation of answers. For the latter, at least for those who practise history, it is dynamic, something continually subject to revision and reinterpretation. And the reason for this, let us be clear, is not only because new documents come to light, but because new minds have been set to work. In fact, the documentation may remain relatively unchanged, what changes is the observer, the perspective. Thank goodness. How many generations of students have pondered what were the origins of war in 1914, or of the revolution in 1789? Questions like these are so important, and so familiar, but how many generations of teachers can bear posing the same questions and soliciting the same answers? The truth, of course, is that they do not. The questions may be the same, but the answers vary with the work and insight of every single student. Therein lies the novelty and the freshness of a discipline that is often misunderstood.

Every week of the teaching year, I warn my students against writing a 'story'. In truth, what story can an undergraduate in Winnipeg write about European history that is anything more than a repotted version of things written earlier by others? But if Ms

Brown and Mr Lebrun ask themselves 'why' something happened, then the essay becomes *their* answer, whatever other problems of execution may arise. Thus framed, this is my essay, my attempt to explain to myself and others how and why France got involved in the Second World War.

The second reason for undertaking this book can be expressed more briefly. The reader needs to know that 25 years of work have raised me an inch or two above groundlevel in the historiography of interwar France. Not so much a landmark as a small stone over which the careless might trip. In short, mine is not quite the new mind of which I spoke earlier. Indeed, it would be fair to admit that I have already developed some sympathy for the often abused Third Republic. No doubt that experience constitutes a mixture of asset and liability. At least it is undeniable, and therefore it seems best to come clean at the start. The fact is that I have been a student for many years and, in my better moments, sometimes think that I have learned something. Whatever that is, I have set out in the ensuing pages.

The third reason goes to the interpretive heart of the matter. I have said that history is dynamic rather than static, and acknowledged my own stake in the history of pre-war France. Together, these explain my fascination with the interpretive tension which slowly has arisen over the character of France between the two world wars. That tension would leave few unmystified. Is there anyone who does not know that France was defeated in 1940 because the French were lulled into a state of complacency by the much publicized defences of the Maginot Line? Is there anyone who has not been told that the French were beaten because they lacked confidence and sensed defeat? Is there anyone who can read these consecutive analyses and not be struck by their apparent incompatibility?

Here is my point of departure, this uneasiness with two ostensibly inconsistent interpretations of interwar France. What this volume offers, however, is not as reassuring as one might hope. For no choice is made between the two constructions sketched above. Instead, the view presented here accepts them both. Wrong-headed though it may be, it is not, at least, a simple argument, for it allows that contradiction, or ambivalence, is inherent in the human condition. Indeed, the argument itself is based on ambivalence, for that is precisely the quality which seems to me most characteristic of France between the wars. Did the French anticipate another war? Yes. Did they wish it to come? No. Did they do anything to instigate it? No. Were they prepared to do anything in their power to prevent it? No. Did they wish to settle things once and for all with Germany? Yes. Did they fear war? Yes. Did they anticipate victory? Yes. Could they imagine defeat? Yes. Did they all think the same way, share the same fears and the same promises? No, and no again. No more than the people of Germany, or Italy, or the United Kingdom.

Enough about the underlying concept and the interpretive direction of this book. Now it might be useful to say a word about source materials, and then to provide a guide to the structural apparatus upon which this exploration relies. As for the former, I draw the reader's attention to the select bibliography at the end of the volume. Caught between the opposing constraints of space and utility, I have limited myself to some of the key pieces of secondary literature which have appeared in English or French since 1985. Part of the argument for doing so is to take advantage of scholarship which is particularly well informed by unpublished archival material. Otherwise expressed, while my own direct references to such material have been kept to a minimum, it is important for readers to know that this work of synthesis is heavily dependent upon archival work which I and so many others have done for the past decade.

The objective of this work, to reiterate, is an explanation of why France opted for war in 1939 and, since defeat so swiftly undercut that decision, why the government accepted a war for which it seemed so badly prepared. Indispensable to that explanation, but as a prelude rather than an organic part, is an account of *what* happened. Such is the intent of Chapter 1. It is designed to introduce the reader to the key events of the interwar period, from a French perspective – that is to say, in a manner which highlights that nation's interwar ambivalence. And it struggles to record this *histoire événementielle* as matter of factly and impartially as possible. Here is the 'story' part of history, in one sense the easy part, however indispensable it is to the subsequent analytical effort. In quite another sense, however, it is the most difficult of the lot. For this is a story that should satisfy the informational needs of the novice, without exasperating the initiated with versions which are either too simplistic or, worse, erroneous. No easy matter this, to get everyone's accord without being tryingly pedestrian.

Chapter 2 addresses the relevant historiography, that is to say the range of historical interpretations upon which studies from the 1990s will be based. This seems to me important for two reasons. First, it is a concrete illustration of the dynamic quality in history to which I have several times referred. The fact is that we have not always looked at the same historical problem in the way we may look at it today. To think otherwise is to commit the error of believing that history begins with one's birth. Second, the essay in Chapter 2 also acknowledges a collection of debts which historians acquire from antecedents and peers. Beyond the spoken word of the lecture hall, there is a world of silent discourse, a world of scholarly exchange among academic historians, of which their students in Manitoba and Manchester, Kansas and Kent, too often remain ignorant. It is not only right, it is imperative, that they come to know their teachers' teachers.

Chapters 3 to 6 represent the core of the study, by which I mean the chapters where the *why* question is pondered from a variety of angles – diplomatic, strategic, political, ideological, economic, and psychological. Why did France accept a war in 1939 for which, evidently, she was so ill-prepared in 1940? The answer is elusive, rather like trying to define in the singular a river of many currents. At any rate this seems to me as useful a metaphor as I can think of to express the complexities and contradictions inherent in 40 million people. And if that were not difficult enough – just to make sense of one river's changes in depth, speed of passage, even direction, or its change from tranquil to turbulent – somehow one also has to be mindful of the river-watchers themselves, for ultimately it is they who chart it, and try to confine it within their measurements.

Chapter 7 is one of conclusion – the conclusion of the peace in 1939, the conclusion of the war in 1940. Simply expressed, it is an essay designed to relate the conduct of France's war in 1940 to the government and society which had accepted that war only months before. That ambivalence should again be used as an interpretive tool will surprise no-one. Few may be grateful. Many prefer to be confounded by simplification than by contradiction, and so will continue to opt either for France too much at ease or France catatonic. It is by no accident that proponents of either will find something to harden their arterial views in this volume. There is something to be said for both, but not simply either. Instead, I argue that choosing one over the other is like mistaking one current for the river.

Speaking of rivers, this work is the product of a long voyage which has taken me from the South Saskatchewan to the Thames, and from the Seine to the Assiniboine. A work of synthesis, it could fairly contain pages and pages of acknowledgements to the assistance I have received over the years from teachers, colleagues, students, librarians and archivists. Wherever I have been, I have found benefactors. But pages of sustained thanks would prove tedious to most readers and, worse, possibly incomplete to a few. Rather than run either risk, I will confine my acknowledged debts to two. The University of Winnipeg has been generous in its support of my work. I take pleasure in expressing my indebtedness and my gratitude. Kathryn has given more, and for longer. It seems fitting that you should know of her.

1 France Ambivalent, 1919–40

Sartre was among the first to say it, during the bitter German roundup of 1940. He has a French sergeant, a veteran hero of 1918 and now a prisoner of war, revenging himself upon the young lads under his command – 'explaining', as he put it, 'how it comes we won our war and you lost yours'. Marc Bloch was another, he too a veteran of the First World War, convinced by the anger of 1940 that 'something had been lost' since 'the old 1914 days'. More scathing still was Jean Dutourd: 'Our fathers, the *poilus*, who pulverized the redoubtable army of the Kaiser, would have made short work of those young Nazi guttersnipes'.[1] Ever since, it has been commonplace to contrast the two experiences, the hard-earned victory of 1918 with the easy defeat of 1940. From what happened then, it has been simple enough to trace the way back, through recalled premonitions of one sort or another. What more natural than a victor entering war with enthusiasm, or a loser faltering at the starting line?

So the fathers went to war confidently, with enthusiasm, cheered on by flag-waving wives and sweethearts. Twenty-five years later their sons departed for the front line glumly, doubtful of victory, unnerved by distraught and fearful women. So it is said, as if it were so. They went to war 'worried, dumbfounded and resigned'. 1939? No, 1914! They faced the prospect of war 'magnificently', with 'self-confidence and resolution', and 'noble determination'.[2] 1914? No, 1939! Then black is white, and white black. No, not that either. Rather it is the starkness, the lack of ambiguity and ambivalence that is confounding. In fact, it seems now that the French people went to war in 1914, as in 1939, with very mixed feelings, driven by a single overriding sentiment – to get it over with, to settle things once and for all with Germany. 'Il faut en finir!', or 'Let's get it over with!' was as much a rallying cry in 1914 as in 1939.[3] It was not a desire to conquer, nor even a desire for revenge, only a desire to be left alone, free from menace and harassment, and from the jarring impact of successive international crises. That there was more excitement in 1914 cannot be doubted, the product of a naïveté which had yet to be chastened by the carnage to come. Conversely, and given that carnage, it should not surprise that the sons of 1939 were less child-like and far more sober than their fathers had been in 1914.

And the truth was that even those fathers had put down their arms in 1918 with more enthusiasm than they had shouldered them. The famous wartime *union sacrée* had many times worn thin. Remarkable as it was, to think that citizens of differing ideology and social *formation* could unite in common cause, the union never did paper over all of the pre-war schisms. At least not for long. As the promises of quick victory turned sour, as the casualties mounted and the destruction got out of control, there were soldiers and there were civilians who began to doubt the very concept, as well as the probability, of victory. With that, the angry pre-war dialogue resumed between wartime patriots like Maurice Barrès – who had been uplifted by the heroism, sacrifice and nobility of war – and patriots of another stamp, like Henri Barbusse – who had been appalled by the mud and excrement, the pieces of flesh, the vacant expressions of half-crazed soldiers. In the dailies, weeklies and monthlies, in the form of novels, poems, and short-stories, celebrated French writers publicly traded blows over the subject of modern war in general and this incessant and rapacious war in particular. Looking across the divide, in one direction, protagonists like Romain Rolland saw the killing as a by-product of capitalist greed, and people like Barrès, to use the words of Jean Guéhenno, as being the 'national director of funerals'. Looking the other way, the movement for a negotiated peace was at bottom treasonous, and Rolland – 'Herr Professor Rolland' – little better than a fifth columnist and a defeatist.[4] Clearly, the contrasting portraits of a France spiritually united in 1914–18, and divided in 1939–40, need some touching up at the early end.

The ambivalence and apprehension which were part of the reality of 1914, the acknowledged fragility of the celebrated wartime unity and the attendant concerns for both military and civilian morale, all became prologue to the nation's response to the peace settlement of 1919. For that, too, was mixed and ambiguous. Even within the government, and among its advisers, there were different opinions and different emphases.

The premier, Georges Clemenceau, slowly and successively bowed to the inevitable. Between January and June 1919 he abandoned any thought of dismembering the defeated Germany, of creating a separate Rhenish state, or of securing a permanent French occupation of the left bank of the Rhine. Instead, he accepted an assurance from the American and British governments to defend France from any future acts of wanton aggression. In the last analysis, he believed that this was the best he could do for French security. Not all agreed, certainly not the government's chief military adviser. Ferdinand Foch, *maréchal de France*, and supreme allied commander, believed that Clemenceau was making a mistake, and was indiscreet enough to say so. In his view, at the very least, France had to insist upon permanent control of the Rhine bridgeheads and unrestricted military access to the left bank of the Rhine. It was over this critical difference of opinion that relations deteriorated between the marshal and the premier, two men who had done so much to see France through to victory. At the same time, circles within the foreign ministry were exploring other avenues in 1919, avenues towards more cordial and cooperative Franco–German relations. Such certainly was the intent of discussions which took place between March and May 1919, precisely as the allied governments were busy fashioning the forthcoming treaty of Versailles with Germany. In this case, however, the gist of these unpublicized contacts – from the French side – was to underline the possibilities for treaty revision and extended economic cooperation.[5]

From the start, therefore, the treaty of Versailles became the subject of controversy. Some saw it as so punitive, so inspired by the belief in the 'bad German', that it was itself a guarantee of future animosity. For evidence, they drew upon such treaty provisions as the enforced, unilateral disarmament of Germany, the prohibition against a German air force, the 15-year allied occupation of the German Rhineland, the effective hiving-off of east Prussia by means of the Polish Corridor, the heavy reparations payments Germany was expected to make for war damages, and finally the involuntary acknowledgement by Germany of her responsibility for causing the war in 1914. But some saw it quite differently, not as a harsh but as a lenient peace, the work of statesmen who had been deceived into thinking they could distinguish between guilty German leaders and the 'innocent' German people. Thus deceived, they had spared the Boches the ignominy of having allied troops march down Berlin's broad Unter Den Linden, and they had declined to treat the Kaiser and his entourage as war criminals. More substantively, they had left the Reich territorially intact, had backed off from immediate reparation payments, and had delayed the date by which the German army had to be scaled down to 100 000 men. Why, they asked, this kid-glove treatment of an enemy who had made a practice of invading France?

So if the Germans disliked this treaty from the start, so too did the French, albeit for more disparate reasons. The mood in France was one of resignation. Parliament ratified the treaty in September, with little enthusiasm, and despite misgivings. The feeling was that the work had been done, for better or worse, and that France could not now assume the consequences of reneging on accords concluded by the government. But the Commission which appraised the treaty made no bones about its shortcomings – including the way in which Clemenceau had negotiated without reference to parliamentary opinion. The result, its *rapporteur* said, was a compromise devoid of a governing ideal. Having conceded so much, Clemenceau had nailed what was left to the Anglo-American guarantee of French security. If the American Congress failed to ratify the treaty, the guarantee went with it. If so, France would be thrown back on her own devices.[6]

Parliament, at least in this instance, seemed to mirror public opinion. Although the treaty was not signed until June, and ratified three months later, everyone knew as early as March that Germany was not going to be fully disarmed and that France was not going to secure a permanent foothold on the Rhine. Clemenceau may have done his very best, but it was clear that this was going to be no 'paix française'. From that all else flowed. Best to get it over with, accept the treaty for what it was, and then try to forget about it by studying the racing forms at Longchamps, or following the crime reports on the mass-murderer Landru. More probable still, most ordinary men and women were too preoccupied by unemployment and rising prices to have time or inclination to monitor international politics. And when politics of the domestic kind intruded, as it did with the autumn general election of 1919, not much attention was paid to the recent war or its troubled treaties, or to foreign policy matters in general. In all, therefore, the country's mood was one of resignation, but a resignation alloyed with 'bitterness, disappointment and worry too'. By late 1919 the French public were convinced that this last war was not the last, that the peace was not a peace but an armistice.[7]

It was irony at its finest, yesterday's victor already alarmed by tomorrow's menace, already uncertain of its own *sécurité*. Few, of course, believed that the threat to peace was imminent, as is evidenced by the domestically focused general election campaign of 1919. By then, the French armed forces enjoyed a decisive military preponderance over the stripped-down and demoralized army of Germany's new Weimar Republic. But from the beginning, from the early months of 1919 when it became clear that this was not going to be an out-and-out victor's peace, there was widespread recognition that the 'German problem' had not been resolved. Therein lay the idea of the temporary armistice or, in Foch's famous and prophetic words, a 'twenty-year truce'.

The roots of this misgiving will require subsequent and more careful exploration, for it is somewhere in this tangle that there lies the explanation of how and why France returned to the battlefield in 1939. For the moment, however, it is enough to outline the most salient reasons for the Third Republic's undiminished fear of Germany. At base, it was a matter of economics and demographics. Germany's population, in excess of 60 million people and rising, overshadowed France's almost static 40 million. There was a similar edge, overall, in industrial capacity – metallurgical, chemical, electrical, and transport. In an age of modern warfare, with mass armies equipped and moved by industrial technology, this did not bode well for the smaller of the two. It was not quite the look of David and Goliath, even without invoking French imperial assets, but there was no mistaking which was the more powerful. And from that imbalance arose calculations of another order. If France could not contemplate a strictly bilateral war with Germany – save in the years immediately following the peace treaty – it would be necessary to recruit assistance. But in that hope lay much despair, certainly when it came to the 'great' powers. Russia, France's principal continental ally on the eve of 1914, was a wasteland, ravaged first by the war with Germany, then by communist revolution and civil war. Left in a shambles, the new Soviet government had neither the resources nor the inclination to assist a capitalist, and overtly unsympathetic, French regime. So it was that Clemenceau had sacrificed much in 1919 for the all-important, but finally elusive, Anglo-American guarantee. And so it was, too, that the fundamental problem of

France's security was as transparent by the end of 1919 as it had been in 1914, as if the Great War had solved nothing.

It should be stressed at this point that there was little ambivalence in France about the substance of the security threat or about its provenance. Although France had international competitors elsewhere in the world, several of which represented security concerns, the number one issue was Europe and the threat from Germany. Where the ambivalence arose, as it had done during the treaty-making and the treaty-evaluation process, was how best to address the issue. Even here, one is reminded of that opening metaphor by which French opinion was likened to a river of several currents, rather than a haphazard and unrelated collection of streams running this way and that. For instance, throughout the entire interwar period there was really no serious, significant advocacy of a preventive war against Germany – the sort of argument for squashing Germany before she had a chance to recover fully from the defeat of 1918.[8] There were instances of such thinking, it is true, both public and private, but it was given little credence. By the same token, if no very powerful case were made for a pre-emptive strike, neither was there one for abject surrender to the strongest of France's neighbours. True, there were some absolute pacifists who said nothing was worth a war. But not many.[9] Later, in the 1930s, there were some who thought they could live more happily under Hitler's Reich. But not many. Most pacifists drew the line when it came to defending their country from attack; and most of those whose ideology took them closest to European fascism were also nationalists who had never aspired to foreign rule.

The fact is that we have allowed our recognition of some deep-seated domestic disagreements, to obscure what was a fairly coherent, mainstream response to the problem of national security. Most French commentators seemed to approve of a strategy of negotiating from a position of strength, which is another way of insisting on the compatibility of deterrence and conciliation. Some, of course, the self-seen realists, were more pessimistic, arguing that Germany should not be trusted until every clause of Versailles had been fulfilled – and most particularly those relating to reparations and disarmament. Others, self-seen realists in their own right, were more optimistic. The future of the peace, they believed, lay within a spirit of conciliation and at least modest compromise. Too much emphasis upon deterrence, too rigid a refusal to consider treaty revision, would only inflame relations between France and Germany and thus make war more, rather than less, likely. Nevertheless, the 'pessimists' were treaty enforcers, men determined to uphold the law, not warlords resolved to use capricious violence as a form of social control. Conversely, few among the 'optimists' believed that the peace of Europe depended on unilateral disarmament, and unilateral concessions, by France.

The point is that these two broad currents coexisted within the same body politic. Did in 1919, did in 1939. In other words, while recognizing these differences, we should not overlook what they have in common, no more than our interest in change should blind us to continuity. And in this case, the point is of particular importance, for overdoing the animus and divisions of interwar France is one way of making 1940 not only explicable but predictable. That is why the concept of ambivalence seems to me more appropriate. By ambivalence I mean to distinguish between the symptoms, such as 'indecisiveness', and the condition of interwar France within which, from the beginning, there competed two legitimate and credible approaches to the German problem. Recognizing that condition means recognizing that all French men and women did not think alike. But this is an internal ambivalence within something whole and identifiable. Unless we accept that, the notion of a mainstream, a single river, and unless we distinguish between symptom and condition, we are thrown back *a priori* to the language of division and discord, and to the expectation of defeat.

Surveying the 1920s, even with the broad brush strokes required here, it would be difficult to miss the doubts and uncertainties which confronted the people of France. Having been left strong enough in 1919 to effect a hasty recovery, Germany never lost her status as national enemy number one. On that, most French opinion was agreed; but it became frayed by debate over possible solutions – and frayed very much along the lines of the preceding analysis. For instance, several times in the course of 1920–1, French troops were sent across the Rhine with a view to ensuring German compliance with reparation obligations. The last of these stiff measures was in March 1921, one undertaken by the government of Aristide Briand, the same Briand who, by the end of that year, was suspected by members of his own government of paving the way for reparation concessions to Germany. Instead, he paved the way for his own fall from office in January 1922. His successor, Raymond Poincaré, a former President of the Republic during the war years, had never been suspected of being soft on the Germans. Indeed, in 1919 he had been especially critical of Clemenceau's compromises and concessions. Still, it took him the best part of a year to act. Angered by German treaty violations, with respect to both disarmament and reparations, the 61-year old Poincaré was torn between his fear of Germany and his belief that the Weimar Republic was the key to any European defence against Anglo-American financial hegemony.[10] No more the hawk of legend than was Briand the dove, he finally got in place – at least to his own satisfaction – the legal foundation for sending a large military force into Germany's industrially rich Ruhr valley. That was in January 1923; and there that force remained for a year – gradually securing a grudging compliance from the German government, but offending much of world opinion into the bargain and adding to what France was already owed, the costs of the occupation itself.

Controversy surrounded Poincaré's action in 1923, and has been kept dense and impermeable by decades of ensuing scholarly debate. Still, what is clear is that once again, another experiment in force was to be succeeded by new initiatives in the name of European appeasement. By mid-1924 there were new circumstances and new faces. The continental economy was showing undeniable signs of recovery, and with that promise came a new spirit of political optimism. At the same time, it looked as if the new German Republic had weathered a series of economic and domestic political crises; and in France, general elections had brought to power a coalition of centre-left parties which were a little more inclined to compromise in international politics. Chief among the latter was the new premier and foreign minister, Edouard Herriot. So ensued one of the most famous periods of the interwar years, that ephemeral 'golden' period of the mid-to-late 1920s when there seemed some chance of fulfilling a widespread commitment to make World War One the war to end all wars.

The foundations of this period were economic in nature, specifically the modified approach to reparations which was laid out in the form of the Dawes Plan of 1924 and further refined with the Young Plan of 1929. In brief, those powers most directly interested in the issue of reparations agreed to a series of measures which facilitated such transactions – partly by lightening Germany's actual burden, partly by easing her payments schedule. The end result was a tonic for an already recovering economy, and a revived conviction that peace and prosperity were indissolubly linked. It was this improved atmosphere in turn which allowed for the next major political démarche, that known as the Locarno agreements of 1925. Concluded between Aristide Briand, now foreign minister in the Painlevé cabinet, and Gustav Stresemann, his German counterpart, this agreement officially recognized the disposition of Germany's western frontiers with both Belgium and France. Otherwise expressed, it meant that Germany accepted as permanent her loss of Alsace and Lorraine, but that in return France recognized the inviolability of Germany's western frontiers – frontiers which, in 1925, the Weimar Republic was hardly in a position to defend. While Locarno has been criticized for its ambiguity – the Germans seeing it as the first of France's compromises, the French seeing it as among the last – the fact remains that nothing more was likely to be built without the kind of foundation it provided.

For awhile, there was plenty of evidence of construction, as befitted a time of economic prosperity and the optimism it generated. In 1925, Germany was finally admitted to membership in the League of Nations, a status which reflected the Weimar Republic's claim to being among the democratic and peace-loving countries of the world. As such, her delegation to Geneva could work with that of France in addressing a familiar range of challenges to international harmony – including problems associated with world hunger, illiteracy and refugee relief, and substandard conditions of labour, health and justice. Even in the General Assembly, where the glare of publicity was more intense than in the backrooms of the working committees, former enemies like France and Germany could try to surpass themselves in mutual toleration. For awhile. As long as Briand could inspire League attenders and League watchers with passionate speeches for peace, or leave them momentarily enthralled with schemes to stamp out war by making it illegal.

In many ways Briand was a marvel. Sixty-nine years of age in 1931, when he finally retired from the foreign ministry, he was a veteran politician in a society where *politicien* meant nothing good. He was a parliamentary street fighter, a bare-knuckles man and a master cynic, on whom sainthood in Geneva rested uneasily. It is doubtful that he ever fully believed the peaceful professions of faith which regularly emanated from Berlin, where successive German governments just as regularly violated the terms of the Versailles treaty. But there is no doubt, romanticist as he was, that he had caught some genuine vision of world peace, and that it had pleased him. He did not offer to scrap the treaty there and then, did not try to erase every German grievance with some French concession, but he certainly did associate himself with the notion that the security of France rested ultimately on reconciliation with her most powerful neighbour.[11] It was that vision which he sought to realize between 1925 and 1931, in the face of obstacles which loomed larger and larger. First, there were the 'realists' on both sides of the Rhine who said 'security first'; in other words negotiate only from a position of armed strength. Second, there was the death of Stresemann in 1929, the German statesman with whom Briand had shared the Locarno-earned Nobel Peace Prize. Third, that autumn there was the collapse of the Wall Street Stock Exchange – at once a symptom, a signal and a cause of the economic Depression which would settle on the world for most of the 1930s. Converted by the outset of that decade to the equation of peace and prosperity, the European community now looked ahead with mounting unease.

Well before then, of course, indeed within the shadows of the Paris Peace Conference, other kinds of negotiations had been initiated with a view to addressing France's security problem. These were not of the order later associated with multi-lateral agreements, the League of Nations and peace apostles like Briand. Rather, they were of a more traditional cast – bilateral accords, alliances and military conventions. In a word, here were the familiar devices by which nations, had traditionally conspired in the interests of mutual se-curity. To be sure, such agreements were not welcomed by all, especially those who believed that World War One had been caused by precisely these sorts of entangling conventions. Nevertheless, to traditionalists, the old ways were still the best, or at least still the most reliable. They included armaments as well as alliances. So it was that while one important current picked up speed within the French government and tried to carry opinion towards the vision and ideals of the League of Nations, another coursed towards the opposite bank. It is this latter current that now requires some attention.

Diplomatically, a succession of French governments in the 1920s engineered a series of bilateral agreements, including governments of which Briand was either premier or foreign minister. Although such agreements sometimes are said to have betrayed France's desire to establish a form of European imperium, and thus to have reflected her unbridled post-war confidence, the truth seems rather different. What had happened in Paris in 1919 derived from the French government's unallayed anxiety about the country's future security. Much had been sacrificed in order to secure the best guarantee possible – the joint assurance from the United States and Great Britain. When that assurance turned to dust, alternate guarantees had to be found. Or so it was argued by officers, diplomats and statesmen thoroughly convinced of German barbarism, duplicity and desire for revenge. It was because they believed their country vulnerable that they concluded a collection of disparate agreements with the governments of Belgium, Poland, Czechoslovakia, Rumania and Yugoslavia.[12]

These agreements were certainly not of a piece. The first, concluded in September 1920, was a semi-secret, Franco-Belgian military accord. It was not an alliance, and it fell short of compelling either party to assist in the other's defence. However, the product of Marshal Foch's persistence, this accord was certainly intended to link each other's military forces in an active defence against some future German attack; and it did make provisions for annual staff talks. Indeed, it even set out the possibility of joint military mobilization in the face of German aggression anywhere in Europe.[13] French enlistment of Polish assistance took longer to finalize, partly because the new Polish state was as concerned about the threat from the Soviet Union as from Germany – a dual concern which doubled France's potential liability – and partly because the original alliance and military convention of 1921 had to be formally associated with a Locarno-inspired, League-registered mutual assistance treaty of October 1925. Notwithstanding such delays, or French apprehensions about the reliability and judgement of the Poles, the fact was that France had secured one truly bona fide ally in eastern Europe.

Next in importance came the Czechs, and behind them the Rumanians and Yugoslavs. The Franco-Czech agreement dated from January 1924, and was accorded the status of an alliance. But unlike France's accord with Belgium, which was only a convention, that with the Czechs was more vague on the matter of joint staff planning and pledged the two signatories only to consult in the event of possible aggression. It was not until October 1925, with the conclusion of another Locarno-associated, League-registered treaty, that the two parties committed themselves to mutual assistance against aggression. But if the fate of the Polish and Czech treaties now could be seen to depend on the survival of the Locarno accords, the same was not true for those with Rumania or Yugoslavia. If anything, they were more fragile. The Franco-Rumanian treaty of June 1926 held out the possibility of consultation in the event that either country seemed likely to become the victim of aggression, and the possibility of joint staff talks. But it shied away from a commitment of mutual assistance, as did the Yugoslav treaty of November 1927. In fact, the latter was even more vague in its wording, less precise in its obligations and bereft of any provision for staff talks.[14]

Stripped to its essentials, this was the French 'alliance system'. It was more than a figure of speech, as the range of agreements makes clear, but it was certainly far less than what the language implied. The government in Belgrade was not committed to defend Paris, neither was that in Bucharest. Those in Prague and Warsaw were, but only under the obscured auspices of the Locarno-driven treaties of 1925. Ironically, the Belgians, who were the least committed in a formal sense, remained the most engaged of France's 'allies'. But they were never prepared to go to war for the sake of the new Polish state, or for any other state in eastern Europe; the Polish and Czech governments heartily disliked each other, as well as the conditions under which the other had been created in 1919; finally, the cooperative accord which associated Czechs, Rumanians and Yugoslavs in the so-called 'Little Entente', was primarily aimed at preventing a restoration of the old pre-war Hapsburg monarchy. While broadly sympathetic to France, for a host of political and economic reasons, these states were not yet in a position to counter a German attack on France with a unified military front in the east. In all, neither they alone, nor in an improbable combination with the Poles and Czechs, were going to be enough to compensate for France's great pre-war ally, Czarist Russia. Accordingly, given the recent collapse of the Anglo-American guarantee, and the implicit but unmistakable reluctance of either power to return to another continental war, it was clear enough that something more was called for.

Many thought that this was a job for the soldiers, even those who wanted no more war of any kind. Apart from the most aggressive of pacifists, many of whom saw armaments as a cause rather than a symptom of war, mainstream France rallied to the standard of national defence. To the majority, the anti-war slogan 'Never Again' meant something different. It was fine to hope that never again would there be another war, but it was imperative to ensure that never again would France fall victim to an unprovoked German attack. If deterrence through multilateral combinations should prove deficient, then the least the Republic would have to do was defend its own frontiers. To do less would be to betray the millions who had died or been wounded defending France in the last war.

Precisely how this was to be done became a matter of intense debate throughout the 1920s. But slowly there emerged a strategic design which promised to reconcile the competing demands of what may be called the 'active' versus the 'passive' components of the national defence system. For the better part of the 1920s the French army planned to meet any German threat with early offensive action in the Rhineland and towards the Ruhr. Not really an offensive strategy – given that it was reactive rather than preemptive – this was rather one of 'forward defence'. In its interests a succession of military plans was developed, each one ordered to offensive require-ments, if not to that of the alphabet – Plan T in 1920, Plan P in 1921, Plans A and A bis in 1924 and 1926 respectively. Nevertheless, even by the latter date there were signs of revised thinking, signs that more attention was being paid to the defensive capacities of the armies initially committed. By 1929 the entire orientation had changed. Plan B of that year was expressly defensive in nature, symptomatic of Briand's peace campaign in Geneva but even more of some recent far-reaching changes within the French military establishment: the reduction of military service from 18 months to 12, the restrictions on the number of career soldiers, the cut from 32 to 27 infantry divisions in the peace-time standing army, and the imminent evacuation by French and allied troops of the most northerly zone in the demilitarized Rhineland.[15]

It was neither by accident nor coincidence that in the late 1920s, just as the 'active' component of the French armed forces was developing defensive operational plans in accord with its new defens-ive strategy, there should have been a major development on the 'passive' side. Precisely at a time when the army was shifting to a predominantly defensive stance, France's parliament was approving the opening of tenders for the construction of what came to be called the Maginot Line. Work began in 1929, the same year as Plan B came into force; and it was nearing completion by 1932, the year Briand died and the year the Depression started to hit France in earnest.[16] It was not, therefore, an economy measure designed to save money. Indeed, it was exceptionally expensive, even for the prosperity-buoyant days of the mid-1920s. But it was designed to save lives, partly in deference to the bloodbath of 1914–18, and partly to the shrunken conscription roles, which from 1935 would halve the number of soldiers available for annual training. There is something else that the Line was not designed to do. It was not built to protect the whole of France from German attack and therefore did not extend from the North Sea to the Swiss border. Instead, the principal fortifications of the Maginot Line were constructed in eastern France, with a view to protecting the industrially-rich provinces of Alsace and Lorraine and thereby to shutting off one key invasion route into France. Finally, these static Maginot defensive works were intended to permit, not to preclude, a mobile thrust into Belgium with a view to joining forces against an actual, even an imminent, German attack. In short, whatever impact these static defences eventually may have come to have on French concepts of mobile warfare, conceptually the two were never anticipated to be mutually exclusive.[17]

Thus, in summary, one has the background to the Disarmament Conference which convened in 1932 after years of preliminary discussions. On the one hand, there was still that current of opinion which believed that French security had much to gain from both the rhetoric and the substance of conciliation. Briand was at its fore, followed closely by Pierre Laval, a protégé of sorts and premier from January 1931 to January 1932. Once again, these were not men who believed that peace depended solely on French concessions to Germany. But they did believe that the greatest threat to European peace lay in Germany's undiminished resentment of the Versailles treaty, and therefore that a rigid insistence on the application of the Versailles conditions was probably counter-productive. Especially at the outset of a new decade. On the other hand, there remained that other familiar current, one which neither ruled out nor wished to depend upon negotiation. If Germany truly wished to be accepted at face value, a nation which had learned the costs of naked aggression and which was now committed to defending the peace, then she would feel honour-bound to respect the terms of the treaty signed by her government in June 1919. If not, she should be made to do so and, for good measure, France should continue to prepare diplomatically and militarily for a revived menace from east of the Rhine.

By 1932, it would be fair to say that this latter current was probably the more powerful of the two. It was more than simply Briand's ill-health, retirement and subsequent death, or the publication that year of Stresemann's memoirs, in which his nationalism seemed more apparent than his internationalism. It was more too than the international disillusionment generated by the League of Nations' failure to punish Japan for its rape of Manchuria in 1931. From France's point of view, the timing of the long-awaited Conference on Disarmament was anything but propitious. At least for those who saw armaments as a cause of war. Essentially freed from its reparations obligations, thanks to the Hoover Moratorium of 1931, the German government continued to flaunt the arms restrictions imposed by Versailles. War materiel was again being produced in German factories, the forbidden German air arm was in the process of being reborn, the expansion of paramilitary forces was shortcircuiting the restrictions on the size of the German army, and the Russo-German agreements of the 1920s were continuing to provide useful fields of collaboration between the Red Army and the Reichswehr. For its part, the French army was already well on the way towards adopting an increasingly defensive mentality and an attendant set of operational plans. Its own standing strength was still subject to reductions, and its stellar attraction was an expensive, largely subterranean network of concrete fortifications.

One measure of the strength of these anxieties was the response of a series of centre-left governments. Between June 1932 and October 1933 the Quai d'Orsay had as its minister either Edouard Herriot or Joseph Paul-Boncour. Both, philosophically, were internationalists, men temperamentally inclined to welcome the newer precepts of collective security through the League of Nations. Yet like the real Briand, not the starry-eyed Briand of legend, neither was comfortable with the stark choices before him. Given Germany's inherent industrial and demographic superiority over France, it seemed perilous to throw away the Versailles restrictions and concede outright arms parity with France – whether this meant German rearmament or further French disarmament. The fact was that 'parity' was a minefield of definitions. How should the French empire and its resources be balanced against those of continental Germany? How to balance tanks against anti-tank weapons, bombers against fighter aircraft and anti-aircraft artillery, infantry divisions against naval squadrons? And yet continued resistance to the concept of parity was not only certain to further antagonize Franco-German relations, but also to set France apart from other key members of the international community – notably Great Britain. Unhappy with the choice before them, and mindful of the stakes involved, neither minister rushed to leave the fence.[18]

But it was an uncomfortable position to be in, even more so after acute economic distress delivered the Chancellorship of Germany to Adolf Hitler in January 1933. Within a matter of months the parliamentary regime of the Weimar Republic was swept away by 'enabling' legislation for the Führer's dictatorship, and the German armed forces were sworn in loyalty to Adolf Hitler personally. In some respects, of course, the new National Socialist regime only promised more of the same – more determination to rid the country of the Versailles *diktat* with all of its humiliating constraints. That included a restoration of the Saar valley and the Rhineland to full German sovereignty, and the right to rearm Germany to a level consistent with the requirements of its own national defence. Ostensibly, it was the latter commitment which led to the German delegation's abrupt departure from the Disarmament Conference in October 1933, and to the simultaneous announcement that Germany intended to leave the League of Nations as well. There were other differences. For one, if the celebrated *Mein Kampf* were any guide, Germany was now led by a man who had earmarked France as his principal enemy. For another, the new regime was much more outspoken about Germany's need for greater living space, *lebensraum*, in eastern Europe. But it was the two in tandem that proved particularly disconcerting for governments in Paris. If Germany were to fulfil its ambitions against France and attack in the west, any military relief offered by Poland and the countries of the Little Entente was in the nature of an asset. If, however, the Nazi regime first expanded eastward, then French commitments to Poland and Czechoslovakia in particular were likely to compel France's entry into war with Germany. For a country which wished to avert war, and which had concluded its various treaties with that in mind, those commitments became inherent liabilities with the coming to power of Adolf Hitler.

1933 thus marked a bend in the river of French opinion, and for awhile the two currents seemed to run much closer to each other. It is this narrowing which has led to some controversy, as so many observers have tried to separate out something that was inherently heterogeneous and ambivalent. That controversy is most obvious when it comes to a reading of the policies of Paul-Boncour, Louis Barthou and Pierre Laval. Joseph Paul-Boncour was foreign minister from December 1932 to January 1934, in a series of centre-left Radical-Socialist cabinets. In that period he accomplished two things of note. Somewhat gingerly, he led the way to his government's recognition in principle of Germany's right to arms parity with France. In that, he might be seen as a dove of sorts. At the same time, however, he began the process of repairing relations with the Soviet Union, potentially the first step towards some kind of Franco-Russian entente. Assessed traditionally, it might look like the work of a hawk. But again, it is the language that impairs. What seems on the surface to be disingenuous and inconsistent may be otherwise interpreted. Begin the appeasement of Germany by acknowledging the principle of parity, begin a broader-scale continental harmonization by preparing the way for Russia's membership in the League of Nations and by regularizing the national frontiers of eastern Europe under the auspices of something akin to the Locarno accords of 1925. If fulfilled, a strategy of this sort could lead to a general pacification of Europe. If unrealized, it might offer the foundation for fuller Franco-Russian cooperation – eventually in ways that might temper the ambitions of the Nazi regime in Berlin.

If then, there is an inherent ambivalence in the policy of Paul-Boncour, a man of quasi-socialist persuasion, the same may be said for Louis Barthou, a man more clearly associated with centre-right politics. Foreign minister in a cabinet of that ideological complexion, one formed by Gaston Doumergue in February 1934, Barthou has also become a figure of some controversy – lauded by some, pilloried by others, for being an old man from an old school. Chronologically, at 72 years of age he was certainly the former, despite a level of energy envied by many much younger. But it is arguable how much of a traditionalist he was. Having inherited the diplomatic initiatives of Paul-Boncour, Barthou pursued with vigour the opening to Moscow and completed the process of securing League membership for the Soviet Union in September 1934. He also did what he could to reinforce France's ties with Poland, and the countries of the Little Entente, and began tentative discussions aimed at some kind of Franco-Italian entente. Thus assembled, one might well detect the trail of a traditionalist, a man bent on constructing new editions of the pre-war and wartime alliances of an earlier generation.

But Barthou was also a close friend of Briand and a publicly acknowledged admirer of his foreign policy. Indeed, he rejected any suggestion that he was undoing the work of his deceased friend, and claimed the exact reverse. As in the case of Paul-Boncour, once more the controversy can be reconciled – especially if one is not blinded by the radiance of Briand the peacemaker. A father who had lost an only son in 1914, Louis Barthou nursed a great deal of animosity towards the Boches. But who better qualified to understand the price of war, and the importance of averting it? That is why he was quick to seize any opening for further dialogue with Berlin, why he was personally inclined to keep disarmament discussions alive, why he was anxious to cooperate with German authorities over the Saar plebiscite scheduled for early in 1935. And if such overtures failed, if Hitler could not be enlisted in the cause of Franco–German reconciliation, then – like Paul-Boncour – Barthou was prepared to develop the deterrence potential of France's new relations with the Soviet Union and Italy. No more a narrow nationalist than was his predecessor a naïve internationalist, Louis Barthou was also a student of tactical ambivalence.[19]

Bluntly put, the same can be said of Pierre Laval, Barthou's successor from October 1934 to January 1936. But put more gently, it would still offend. Of all the politicians of interwar France, Laval has been the most reviled, largely because of what he did after 1940, partly because of what he was suspected of wanting to do in the 1930s. Contrary to Barthou, whose conservatism has been allowed to conceal his flexibility, Laval has been attacked for the opposite reasons. More accurately, he is customarily seen either as a man of dubious principles – a German-lover and a pre-war collaborationist – or a man of no principles at all, lest these be personal power and the craven avoidance of war at any cost. Nevertheless, while it is certainly true that Laval spoke passionately about his commitment to defuse Franco–German antagonisms, never in the 1930s did he negotiate a deal with Hitler's Germany. He was cooperative on the matter of the Saar plebiscite in March 1935, he spoke to journalists of both nationalities about his desire for peace, and there is reason to believe that he hoped to use France's developing ties with Mussolini's Italy as an entrée to the Führer. At the same time, however, it was Laval who in May 1935 concluded the mutual assistance treaty with Stalin's Russia – albeit with limited enthusiasm. And it was Laval who, as premier, approved the opening of

Franco–Italian staff contacts in the spring of 1935. In both cases, the Russian and the Italian, it was clear that the most probable enemy would be Germany. So like Paul-Boncour, in his way, and Barthou in another, Pierre Laval was also in the mainstream of French ambivalence – not because he, any more than they, was chronically indecisive, but because he was more of a pragmatist than many have been willing to acknowledge.[20]

By 1936 Hitler was testing the patience of pragmatists and men of principle alike. He had dropped his earlier, reassuring guise of a man of reason, an aggrieved moderate. In March 1935 he had begun to boast about the power of the Luftwaffe, the air force prohibited by Versailles and the very existence of which hitherto had been denied. In the same month he announced the return of military conscription to Germany, yet another flagrant repudiation of the Versailles conditions. And it was not long afterward that he started conditioning the rest of the world to anticipate an early remilitarization of the Rhineland. When it happened, in March 1936, it came as no surprise and caused no great consternation in France.[21] The entry of German troops into a region of unquestioned German sovereignty was interpreted nowhere as a signal for an invasion of France. But it was a signal for something. Before long fortifications would be built, and with every installation the avenue for any kind of French offensive operation would be further narrowed. From this, it followed that there were fewer opportunities for French military action in the west, in the event that Germany should choose to threaten the security of either Czechoslovakia or Poland. From that, in turn, one could anticipate the escalation of doubts in France, as to whether the eastern allies were more liability than asset, and doubts among those same allies as to whether they had been backing the wrong horse. As early as 1934 the Poles had concluded a non-aggression pact with Germany, and the Czechs had turned to the Soviet Union in 1935. Once Germany was secure in the Rhineland, and able to turn her back on a French army already in a defensive posture, there was no telling where the Führer's dreams of *lebensraum* would take him.

General elections in the spring of 1936 brought a new government to power in Paris, new and apparently different. At least it was different in the sense that the coalition of parliamentary forces which it represented was called the Popular Front, a loose grouping of left and centre-left parties which were committed to the struggle against fascism at home and abroad. Its premier was Léon Blum, a Socialist, its foreign minister was Yvon Delbos, one of the many liberals who fooled no-one by calling themselves Radical Socialists. It was fitting, for nothing very dramatic or radical was going to happen in terms of French foreign policy. Indeed, while bankers saw red whenever they could bring themselves to look at the new 'socialist' regime, the foreign policy efforts of this and successive Popular Front governments were very much within the familiar mainstream.

As always, there were the two currents, two points of view, one a little more inclined to conciliation, the other slightly more towards deterrence – but neither dismissive of the other. Blum, an intellectual and a man of great refinement, was the archetype of a single individual within whom both currents competed for attention. In 1936 and 1937 he twice received in Paris Hitler's favourite economic adviser, the shrewd German banker, Hjalmar Schacht. During those conversations there was talk of the mutual benefits which could be drawn from increased Franco–German economic cooperation. There was even talk of French concessions in the colonial field, should there be some promise of a genuine political détente in Europe. In other words, Blum, and with him Delbos, principals in an anti-fascist Popular Front, were perfectly prepared to talk to Hitler's agents, prepared to discuss ways of accommodating their differences in the interests of peace. Indeed, in a less public fashion, it seems that they were anxious to both retain and actually expand their economic links with Germany and Italy – despite apprehensions about Hitler and the severe injury Franco-Italian relations had suffered following Italy's aggression against Ethiopia in 1935.[22] Briand, who had no sympathies for fascism, would not have been disappointed, nor Paul-Boncour, Barthou or Laval.

But it was the summer of 1936, the German economy was fully recovered from the Depression, the armaments industries were flourishing, and Hitler's behaviour seemed more and more obsessive. Indeed, there were doubts about his mental as well as his physical health. Blum was in better shape, but not so the country which was beset by a depressed economy and an over-valued franc, and unsettled by the chasm which had opened between ideologues of right and left.[23] On the foreign front there was no better news. Earlier that year the Belgians had revoked their military accord with France, and returned to what they called a policy of 'independence' – what everyone else called neutrality. Italy was drifting towards Nazi Germany, a process which would accelerate through their collaboration in the Spanish Civil War that erupted that summer.[24] The Soviet Union remained at arm's length, largely, so it seemed, because many French officials preferred it that way. The eastern allies were restless – the Poles alert to the Russians and the Germans, the Czechs principally to the Germans and the Poles, the Rumanians to the Russians, the Yugoslavs to the Italians. And above the fray remained the United Kingdom, the one ally the French really wished to recruit,[25] it too ambivalent about how to preserve peace without making war inevitable.

So it was that the Popular Front governments, first that of Blum and then of Camille Chautemps, did more than court the dictators. In ways reminiscent of their predecessors, they courted but they also conspired. In particular, they made some effort in 1936 and 1937 to advance relations with Stalin's Russia, principally by encouraging conversations between appropriate diplomatic personnel and especially between French and Russian staff officers. And no longer was much care taken to frame such contacts under the League of Nations, so that something very traditional might appear as something progressive. In fact, little came of those efforts thanks, primarily, to the particularly deep-seated ideological distrust which too many officials nourished in Paris including – it should be said – certain members of Blum's own cabinet.[26] Reticence of another sort constrained the government's potential for strengthening France's ties with the eastern allies. Belatedly, and with limited energy, Yvon Delbos explored the possibilities of concluding a single mutual assistance pact between France, on the one hand, and the three Little Entente countries, on the other. Nothing came of that either, again primarily because the government in Paris was reluctant to pay for the asset of strengthened alliances with the liability of increased French commitments to eastern Europe. Curiously, the only example of ostensible success in the east came with Poland – to which the Blum government actually increased its financial and armaments commitments, without reciprocally increased commitments from Warsaw.[27]

Overall, if familiar enough in outline, the incidence of ambivalence in Popular Front foreign policy was even more marked than that of previous administrations. Like the latter, it continued to draw a blank in London, where British governments were prepared to do little more than commit themselves to the principle of assisting France in the event of unprovoked aggression. Franco-Italian relations experienced no thaw, those within the Franco-Russian alliance had barely started to defrost, and the smaller eastern allies were perceptibly unnerved by the contrast between France's reticence and Germany's increasing political and economic vigour in the region. Indeed, given the latter, the increased French ambivalence should not surprise in the least. Germany's military capacity to alter the 1919 map of Europe was now infinitely greater than what it had been in the 1920s when France had brought those small states into its constellation, greater too than in the early Nazi period when Paul-Boncour and Barthou had confronted a German strength more potential than real. For that very reason, perhaps, we also have a clearer illustration of direct Franco-German conversations than had been the case earlier.

More ambivalent diplomatically, the Popular Front government was much less so when it came to issues of national defence. In the autumn of 1936, it launched the first serious and substantial rearmament effort in interwar France; and in that very fact lay another, more basic. The threat to French security had become more imminent, in ways long since forecast by many of Clemenceau's critics in 1919. The German army was certainly the qualitative equal of the French, and the German air force had secured a comfortable margin of superiority. The fact was that Hitler had built well on the foundations constructed by the Weimar Republic, and had stolen a march on France. In response, the French governments of 1936–7 undertook some familiar and modest diplomatic initiatives, but threw the armaments industry into third gear.[28] The firepower of the existing frontier fortifications was to be enhanced with more modern weapons, and new fortified works were to go in further north, staggered near the border with Belgium. Additional money was to be allocated to the army, for the development of a more modern and expanded armoured force, and to the air force, for lighter and faster bombers. Again, and as always, no-one seriously proposed using the existing arsenal to pre-empt the German buildup. French weaponry, including the bombers, was intended to be used only for defensive, or at the most, counter-offensive, purposes. Again, as always, no-one seriously proposed throwing in the towel, conceding that France was no longer a great power and offering Hitler whatever he intended to take, anything to avoid a war.

Far from offering any relief, 1938 brought more and more tension with each ensuing month. As one succeeded another, as war seemed more imminent than ever, and as the desperation to avoid it grew more intense, the river that was French opinion became more turbulent. Between the spring and autumn of that year the competition accelerated between the two familiar currents. It began with the long-anticipated German annexation of Austria in March 1938, yet another Versailles restriction tossed away like chaff in the wind. The French government protested, like other League members, and promptly forgot about the Austrians. Whatever had been said in the past about defending Austria's independence, few in France were perturbed when Austrian Germans seemed to welcome becoming part of Hitler's Reich; and certainly no prominent military or civilian official advocated going to war over this *Anschluss*. Besides, it was clear to anyone who followed the papers or could read a map that this was little more than a prologue for something more dramatic. The moment Hitler owned Austria he had the opportunity to outflank Czechoslovakia's western fortresses by deploying his forces along the southern Austro-Czech frontier. And of course it was not long before the Führer intensified his campaign to incorporate the Sudetenland into the Reich – that predominantly German-speaking, western region of Czechoslovakia. It was, he promised, his final territorial demand in Europe. Peace hinged on his satisfaction.

French opinion, characteristically, wanted to believe the latter, but did not necessarily believe the former. Still, there was a case to be made, or so some now argued. In the past three years Hitler had reclaimed the German Saar, the German Rhineland, and German Austria, each a violation of the 1919 treaty, yet each consistent with the peacemakers' tributes to national self-determination. Although Czechoslovakia would protest the loss of its German territories, was there not something to Hitler's grievances? Besides, what could Czechoslovakia possibly do against the armed forces already being marshalled by the Nazi regime? It could not stand on its own. It would get no help from the Poles, or from the Russians unless – by the terms of the Russian–Czech treaty – France first came to the aid of Prague. And therein lay the rub. Unless one were prepared to argue that Hitler's previous violations had effectively put an end to the 1925 Locarno accords, and that all parties were henceforth free of commitments assumed then, France was committed to defend Czechoslovakia from unprovoked aggression.

From March 1938 to the autumn of 1939 the conduct of French foreign affairs was in the hands of two men, the premier, Edouard

Daladier, and the foreign minister, Georges Bonnet. Under them, the ambivalence of French foreign policy became further clouded. Colleagues in the same cabinet, they were associated with quite different currents of opinion. As a result, they could not help but further the sense of ambivalence which for so long had characterized the policies of successive French governments. At the same time, one need underscore the fact that the landscape of 1938 was not that of 1933 or 1936. Circumstances had changed, indeed worsened, and consequently the implications of deterrence and the motives behind conciliation were no longer what they might have been in an earlier period.

Georges Bonnet is one reason why appeasement has become a dirty word. It had been used before, even in the 1920s, by people with whom he had been associated – notably Briand and Laval – without acquiring negative overtones. Indeed, it was no more offensive a word than pacification or peace itself. Under Bonnet, however, it came to mean peace at any price. No real vision of differences peacefully settled by mutual compromise and concession, only a desperation-induced tactic which would excuse any ruse, any dishonour, in the name of peace. However he may be judged, in 1938 Georges Bonnet did everything in his power to free France from any obligation to go to war for the Czechs. It was this very quest for peace *à outrance* that further separated the foreign minister from his premier. For his part, Edouard Daladier was no sabre-rattler. A 54-year old veteran of the Somme, he had had his war, and wanted no part of another. But he doubted that Hitler intended to stop at the Sudetenland, and feared that bowing to his demands would only encourage his appetite; and while Bonnet lived only for the moment, at least where peace was concerned, Daladier wondered why a greater and more powerful Reich would be anymore inclined to peace, and how it would be stopped if someone did not soon curtail its growth.

Tormented by such doubts, Edouard Daladier put on a brave face as the Czech crisis mounted through the late summer and early autumn of 1938. France would go to war if Germany attacked Czechoslovakia; and to that end he used his joint authority as premier and minister of national defence to order the mobilization of the French armed forces. At the same time, he continued to promote an even greater rearmament effort and took some stiff and controversial steps to ensure that work stoppages were kept to a minimum. On the international front, he several times implored the British government to call Hitler's bluff by threatening him with a war Germany could never win. True to form, however, his own foreign minister would have none of this tactic. Instead, Bonnet played very effectively on dubious and unnerved British ministers, and strengthened their indecision. The risks of war were now indeed too great, and thus the Prime Minister, Mr Chamberlain, should be encouraged to make his own mark in the history of European appeasement. That he did so is beyond doubt, for his name will forever be linked with the famous Munich Conference of late September 1938.

What happened there and before is well known. The Czechs were brow-beaten by the British and French to surrender the territory that Germany wanted. Chamberlain returned to London, jubilant. Daladier flew back to Paris, disgusted, even more so when he saw Bonnet all smiles. The minister thought the peace had been saved, the premier believed war had been postponed.[29] Hitler, cynically, pronounced that Germany was now a satisfied power. The British and French governments, cynically, pronounced that they would guarantee the new Czech boundaries – just in case. Neither pronouncement was meant to be serious. In the middle of March 1939 the German army occupied the remainder of Czechoslovakia. There were grumbles from London and Paris, no more than that. And again the peace was saved, this time more easily than the last.

But there was another difference. There was less relief in March 1939 because there was less uncertainty about Hitler's satiability. By seizing Czech and Slovak lands the Führer had dropped any pretence of legitimacy. The question now was who would be next on his list – the Poles with their hated Corridor and their grip on the port of Danzig, the Rumanians with their oil, the French for their past and for their ability to constrain Hitler's full ambitions for eastern Europe? Stripped of any remaining illusions, the French government further intensified its rearmament programme, especially in the critical area of fighter aircraft and anti-aircraft artillery. At the same time, in concert with a bitter and more tough-minded British cabinet, the Daladier government reaffirmed its commitments to Poland and Rumania and was quick to agree to preliminary contacts between its own high command and the British Chiefs of Staff. Equally telling, this same government resisted external and internal pressures – including those applied by its own foreign minister – to sweeten Mussolini's mood with a collection of proposed concessions; and it led the way in seeking to bring the Soviet Union into some form of tripartite pact with Britain and France. All of this, of course, suggested that the current favouring deterrence had triumphed at last over that which for so long had flowed towards compromise.[30]

Still, the latter had by no means been subsumed by the force of its rival, and certainly not that part of it which had sprung from desperation. Indeed, as tensions accelerated and war became more imminent in late August 1939 – when Germany succeeded in negotiating a pact with the Soviet Union – those inclined to do anything to avert it began working overtime. None was more indefatigable than Georges Bonnet, who was convinced that Hitler was about to roll over Poland, that Poland was not worth a Franco-German war and, a matter of secondary importance, that the French war machine was not ready for such a war. For his part, Daladier thought that Hitler might yet be deterred by an unflinching Anglo-French coalition, and that Germany would certainly become unstoppable if she were allowed to seize all the resources of eastern Europe by simple forfeit. As for the nation's war machine, he knew that it was in far better shape than it had been the previous autumn, and was prepared to believe the assurances of his commanders that France could at least defend herself. Even then, however, it should be said that, like Blum and others before, he was not insensitive to the arguments and especially the apprehensions of those who maintained that this was not the time nor the cause, for France to go to war.[31] Indeed, even after the German attack on Poland had begun on 1 September, even as the ensuing British and French ultimatums to Berlin were ticking down on 3 September, the prime minister joined forces with Bonnet in exploring the possibilities of an Italian-initiated peace conference. And when he went to parliament for approval of vastly increased wartime spending, he avoided reference to any declaration of war; indeed, his speech to the Deputies was more full of references to peace than to war.[32] It is with this in mind that one observer has likened France's entry into the Second World War to that of a timid bather, afraid of the cold, perhaps even of the water.[33]

If so, it might also be fair to say that this was a swimmer who had come close to drowning several times, during the last war. And no-one had forgotten, no-one could forget, those four terrible years during which farmlands and villages, mines and factories, soldiers and civilians, the young and the elderly, had been swallowed whole and in pieces. Few were the towns that did not have a war memorial by August 1939, past which the new uniformed generation now marched in regiment; and, given that, few would have felt comforted had this new crop of men been giddy with the prospect of testing its valour against the enemy. It was not cowardice that sobered them, for the placing of the country on a war footing proceeded almost without protest. It was not defeatism either for, unsurprisingly, public and official opinion agreed that Germany could not win the long war which seemed in the offing. The combined resources of France and Britain, together with those of their empires, gave them a sustaining power that Germany could not match. Slowly, over a period of years her economy would grind down, her soldiers and civilians would become demoralized, and thus the way would be paved either for a successful internal coup against the Nazi regime, or for a sweeping and irresistible allied offensive. Providing, of course, that Germany was denied a successful short war. That rather critical proviso, together with the preceding strategic calculations, does much to explain the mood of quiet, guarded optimism that prevailed in August–September 1939. No-one anticipated a quick victory, next to no-one anticipated an early defeat.

From the start there were some, foreigners especially, who saw too much passivity in this the French response; and their numbers have grown by leaps and bounds in the intervening 50 years. Informed by the sudden defeat of May–June 1940, and the historian's prescience, they are convinced they 'saw it all a'coming a long time ago'.[34] And so they might. Quite apart from any misgivings about the readiness of the French armed forces, there was evidence aplenty that some Frenchmen could see next to no good reason for a new war with Germany. Again, and as ever, people of this current had no wish to leave the key in the lock of France's security. Rather, with varying degrees of effort and desperation, they had convinced themselves that Germany's complaints against Versailles were largely warranted, and that her right to some kind of imperium in eastern Europe was sustainable. Thus the seizures first of Czechoslovakia and then of Poland were no legitimate *casus belli* for France. More tragic than such losses, in their view, was the failure of Premier Daladier to respond positively to the publicly staged peace offer that Hitler issued on 8 October, or to do whatever had to be done to ensure that Italy stayed indefinitely neutral. The Daladier cabinet, like those of his predecessors, was split on such issues: some members, including Bonnet, pleading with the premier to ensure that war did not lead to fighting; others, like the Finance minister, Paul Reynaud, trying to stiffen his resolve by reminding him of where the trail of conciliation and concessions had led.

The ambivalence that such competing arguments produced – and had produced for two decades – was at no time more clear than in the period from September 1939 to May 1940. This was the 'Phoney War', a war of necessity but not necessarily a war. In response to the German attack on Poland, the French army conducted a careful, early offensive in the west – one that was tentative, localized, brief and unproductive. It ended with a careful, unforced retreat to the defensive lines from which the soldiers had recently departed; and from there the French army watched the German and Soviet armies quickly devour the Polish state.[35] Thereafter, Hitler offered peace, again, and France's soldiers settled down to a life of boredom and inactivity, punctuated only by training exercises and private soul-searching to explain why they were there and not at home. If anything, the civilians were busier: industrialists and workers offering an accelerating stream of tanks, planes and guns; cabinet ministers and bureaucrats implementing a host of new decree measures, including those which created an Armaments ministry and those which paved the way for an Information ministry. It could not be said, therefore, that nothing was being done. What could be said, and Daladier said it in December, was that French casualties were less than 2000 dead – compared to the 450 000 corpses of December 1914.[36]

The pace quickened on 10 May 1940, when the German offensive began in the north – against Holland, Belgium and France. Having altered its plan of attack that very spring, by redirecting its *Schwerpunkt* further to the south, the German high command capitalized on the element of surprise. In two senses. First, the Wehrmacht opened its offensive with powerful thrusts towards Holland and northern Belgium, and with sufficient armour to be fully credible. By so doing it confirmed the allied expectation that here was the centre of attack – an expectation that triggered a rapid Anglo–French counter-thrust into northern Belgium. Second, what proved in fact to be the main German attack force started its forward advance the following day, in Belgium's southern-most corner, through rough terrain which many European military experts had regarded as problematic for heavy armoured vehicles. For that very reason, because natural obstacles of forest and steep ravines seemed almost sufficient in themselves, it was in this sector that the French high command had installed its less substantial fortifications and its less powerful divisions. It proved to be an unequal contest, as a far more powerfully armed force swept over a locally inferior and surprised defence. Within a few days the Germans had bridged the river Meuse at Sedan, and by so doing had split the Allied defences. Thereafter, and moving at a pace unanticipated by the less mobile defenders, they were able to open a breach wide enough to permit a northward sweep of allied forces backed up along the English Channel and, eventually, a southern sweep behind the eastward facing guns of the Maginot fortresses.

There are arguments over precisely when the French high command did appreciate the gravity of its situation.[37] As early as 10 May, as late as the 15th? Thereafter, at any rate, no schoolboy could have been under any illusions. Scholars may disagree on whether or not the situation was by then irreparable, but none would maintain that the country had suffered only a minor flesh wound. Certainly before the end of May, there were numerous pockets of military and civilian officials in Paris who believed the battle was over, and a growing number who said the same for the war as a whole. Already there was talk of an armistice, amid angry demands for silence. Already there were advocates of carrying on the war from the empire, as well as a vocal army of opponents. Having been forced to resign as premier in mid-March – ostensibly for lack of vigour in conducting the war – Edouard Daladier watched his successor resign in protest against the cabinet's reluctance to press on. That was on 16 June when Paul Reynaud, a civilian, gave way to the elderly Philippe Pétain, a marshal of France and by now an advocate of armistice.[38] By then, the Germans were in full control of northern France, including Paris, and the French government had been a week-old refugee in Bordeaux. Under the circumstances, and whether or not one agrees with this still controversial decision, it came as no surprise when the Pétain government signed the armistice of 22 June. Three weeks later, on 10 July, the same government effortlessly induced parliament to bring down the curtain on the Third Republic. In its place stood the Marshal's new presidential regime, one soon to be known as Vichy France: constitutionally authoritarian, ideologically conservative and increasingly collaborationist. For a time at least, the bulk of the French population had been carried to peace, not on the current of resistance but rather that of its opposite.

So much for this abbreviated and abridged story of France and its early experience in the Second World War. With luck, it has fulfilled its intended purpose – that of offering an uncluttered narrative for the inexpert. With more, it might satisfy the already initiated, those scholars who will find it easier to tolerate the errors of commission than all I have chosen to omit. That is understandable, indeed even inevitable. Like the French, I too have been subject to competing currents, one for telling 'it all again', the other for providing something leaner and more economical. And like the French, I have had to make my own choices. In this case, for this chapter, what had to be kept central was the story of what happened. Or at least my version of it. For the simple fact is that pure narration is next to impossible, if by that term we imply something independent of the narrator. So if confessions are in order, now is the time to admit that this chapter is the work of a story-teller, which is not quite the same thing as saying it is a fabrication. I have taken what I consider to be 'facts', and assembled them in a way not done before. As usual, Sartre said it better, when he judged the historian as one who formulates 'honest hypotheses which take the facts into account. . . . Slow, lazy, sulky, the facts adapt themselves to the rigour of the order I wish to give them'.[39] That is good advice for students writing about history, and fair warning for their readers.

2 Ambivalence Revisited: History and Historians

The preceding chapter is based on the work of many, many historians who have pondered the collapse of the Third Republic. That may not be readily apparent, given the fact that most of my source citations come from the 1980s and 1990s. I have selected them deliberately, partly as a way of highlighting where recent scholarship has taken us, and partly as a way of illustrating what I earlier called the dynamic quality of history. Broadly speaking, what distinguishes these works from those of previous decades is the breadth of their archival base, for it was not until the mid-1970s that the French state started opening its official archives – including those of the foreign, finance and defence ministries. Thus, it would be fair to suggest that the previous chapter could not have been written as little as fifteen years ago – in the absence first of the primary evidence and second of ensuing scholarly analysis. In other words, amid all the variables which come into play whenever historians notice, record and employ certain data, one of those variables is the source base itself. However unappetizing the idea may seem to some, this is the historical equivalent of 'we are what we eat'.

The principal interpretive idea of the current chapter is to suggest that today's scholars and, appropriately their readers, still have something in common with interwar France. For we are no more in full agreement about why events unfolded the way they did in the 1930s, than the French were in anticipating their future. To be sure, there are scholars about who see it as their duty to dispel the last whiff of doubt, rather like conjurers and religious zealots. Possibility is simply elbowed out of the way by certainty. Especially when the evidence is frail, and needs a few tonic drops of exaggeration. Fortunately, those who fall prey to such temptation come from no single group, gender, generation or nation. They have only a methodology in common, not a cause. Yet despite the rock-hard debris some have left on the interpretive terrain of interwar France, it would be difficult to miss the constant movement underfoot. The simple, disturbing, satisfying fact is that we are no closer to unanimity on France in the 1930s, than we are on Napoleon, or the Reformation, or the Punic Wars.

This is not, I suppose, the sort of thing that historians should boast about. For there are some who think that we ought to have much of it completely straight by now. Worse, there are many who think we do, which explains the tradition of historical pedagogy based first on the recording of 'fact', and second on the memorization of that record. But it is this, not interpretive discord, that can give history a bad name, make it seem not only tedious but petrified. And it is precisely this sort of history that has provoked the formulation of the current chapter.

In this instance there are two objectives, each of which demands a word or two of explanation. The intention here is to bridge the gap between the previous chapter – with its interpretive narrative – and the succeeding chapters where a more intensive explanation is offered for why France went to war and defeat in 1939–40. Put more explicitly, this chapter on the historiography of interwar France introduces the reader to some of the scholarly debates which are so central to the ensuing analysis. Second, and on a more personal level, this chapter is a acknowledgement of the scholars whose work has contributed to my own *formation*. I have learned much from them all, even in those cases when I have been doubtful of their arguments. Many I know personally, acquaintanceships founded on encounters in archives, libraries, conferences and colloquia. Some go beyond that. They are friendships based on personal as well as professional rapport. That is why I sometimes include snippets of personal information about them, for it is a useful way of reminding readers that in this day of mass production, books are still hand-crafted, the products of individual insight and temperament.

Enough about good intentions. Now it is time to confront some of the thornier issues associated with the conceptualization of this chapter. First, however informed I have been by the works of others, the constructions I place upon their work may be different from what they intended. If so, it is out of misunderstanding rather than malice or perversity. The point is, that the reader is going to get an interpretation of an interpretation. In that sense, it is an impressionistic copy, which is no more valuable than the original and certainly is not intended to be a substitute for it. Lest there be any doubt on this score, it should be said that many of the works cited in this and the previous chapter do not explicitly address the problem of France's collapse and the reasons behind it. That said, it would be fair to add that many of them do situate themselves within an interpretive context which is – very broadly expressed – either critical of or sympathetic to the plight of the Third Republic.

Second, historiographical essays not only risk provoking the ire of scholars who believe their work has been misrepresented, such essays are glowing targets for those who feel under-represented. I make the point, partly in order to explain, partly to apologize. As for the explanation, readers should know that reference to one's work by others is an important part of the historical profession. No doubt there is an element of vanity involved; but underneath, there is a need to know that our work is taken seriously by other experts. There is nothing untoward about this, nothing shameful in the least; however, the student intent on securing a professor's approval ought to know that the professor, too, is on a similar quest. It is for this reason that I have also used the language of apology. Persuaded by several decades of reading that no single book can ever invoke *all* of the relevant and worthy literature, I regret but am not embarrassed to say that this is no exception. I have read much, but not everything; and, in turn, I have selected only from what I have read. Someone else no doubt would have included other works, perhaps discarded some, and certainly would differ with me over what is important and what not. Quite apart from any other consideration, scholars more familiar with work in German, Italian and many of the east European languages would necessarily have perspectives that are essentially closed to me. Anything that true, can afford to be said in print.

It was in the 1940s that the first layers of truth were applied in rapid succession, one over the other. Having promptly proclaimed De Gaulle a traitor and the Free France movement treasonous, the Vichy regime of Marshal Pétain set about constructing its own explanation for the collapse of the Third Republic. Knowing the truth as it did, knowing that responsibility could not be sloughed off either on the people of France or, by extension, on its armed forces, the Vichy government concentrated its attack on two already prostrate targets – the left-wing Popular Front governments of the mid-1930s and, more broadly, the discredited and displaced Third

Republic. That, essentially, was what was behind the infamous Riom trials of 1942, in the course of which defendants like Blum and Daladier were tried for disloyalty and incompetence. As defendants, however, they proved themselves to be anything but inept. With each deposition and testimony, they relentlessly associated some of the key officers of the Vichy regime – notably Pétain himself – with the decision-making of the 1930s. In short, if the language of guilt and innocence were to be maintained, clearly there were far more guilty men than had been rounded-up as defendants at Riom. And if one of the aims was to discredit the Socialists and Radical-Socialists of the Popular Front era, it was only embarrassing and counter-productive to give such men a stage from which they could demonstrate the depth and pace of French rearmament after 1936. The trials were called off.

Eventually, so was the war, but not before a victorious General De Gaulle had returned to France in the summer of 1944. It was time for new truths, and new trials. Laval was tried, and executed. Pierre Flandin was tried, and condemned to national disgrace. Pétain was tried, sentenced to death, and imprisoned for life. All of this, it should be said, had little to do with their pre-war records, at least expressly. Their sentences were mainly reflections of opinion about their activities and ambitions between 1940 and 1944, notably in connection with Hitler's regime and the German occupational forces in France. The horrors of those years, with their deportations, their bloody civil war, their retributions, far overshadowed the errors and omissions of the 1930s. At the same time, state prosecutors did not fail to support their charges with references to Laval's shady dealing with Mussolini in 1935, Flandin's public exhortations against resisting Germany in 1938–9, and Pétain's unrivalled influence on defence planning in the 1920s and 1930s. By implication, these post-war trials left an impression reminiscent of what had been intended at Riom. A guilty few needed to be purged. The defeat of 1940, and the attendant humiliation of Vichy, were only extensions of the servile appeasement policies pursued by a few men in the 1930s.

It was in the late 1940s that another layer of truth was applied. This one, diluted and thinner, spread further and seeped into whatever cracks remained unfilled. This was not the work of the court, but rather of parliament. In 1946 the French National Assembly created its own investigative commission. The two volume report which appeared six years later, accompanied by nine volumes of testimonies and depositions, addressed itself to the French experience between 1933 and 1945.[1] It was a huge undertaking and, perhaps predictably, there seems to have been an underlying determination to get it over with. Some key witnesses were never asked to appear before the commission, some did not accept the invitation to testify, others failed to answer questions put to them. The end result was a superficial report of sweeping dimensions, prepared hurriedly by commissioners who seemed relieved to put all this behind them. There was no intention to prosecute, no wish either to condemn or exonerate. Instead, what was paramount in the late 1940s was the need for some form of national reconciliation under the new Fourth Republic. That goal would not be met by further revisitations to the most painful period in modern French history, by fresh recriminations against or apologies for the buried Third Republic. Accordingly, the blurred but powerful impression left by the report itself was that responsibility for the collapse was so widespread as to be indeterminate. It was a condemnation with which almost anyone could live, suggestive as it was of a discredited but mercifully defunct collective past.

This publicly conducted shift away from the earlier notion of a guilty few had counterparts of rather different genres. One of them, unmistakably, was L'étrange défaite (1946), that extraordinary, introspective work by Marc Bloch. Written in 1940, before the era of truth-by-trial, these are the reflections of an historian caught-up on the tide of current events. He is not dispassionate, he is angry and humiliated by what has befallen France. But to his credit, he does not look for simple explanations of the disaster. He is certainly critical of the operational and intellectual shortcomings of the French high command, but he exonerates no-one – not the politicians, the civil servants, nor the workers, not pacifists, teachers, nor the middle-class. So it was that well before the efforts of the post-war parliamentarians, a single historian, and a patriot already wanted by the Gestapo, had offered a sweeping indictment of the society which had produced the defeat. And what was strange about that defeat, was its complexity, not its simplicity.[2]

Five years after Marc Bloch's execution by the Gestapo, Jean Paul Sartre completed the last volume of his trilogy Les chemins de la liberté. It was 1949, in the middle of the hearings being conducted by the parliamentary commission of inquiry. Like the latter, and even more like Bloch, Sartre declined to make one institution any more culpable or incompetent than any other. This third volume, translated as *Iron in the Soul*, deals expressly with the 1940 collapse, out of which Sartre himself emerged a German prisoner of war. It is that circumstance, a prison camp, in which he has a priest pronounce that the defeat was divinely ordained, the end result of a society gone degenerate. While it is unlikely that Sartre personally subscribed to that explanation, it seems clear from other evidence that he detected other forms of spoliation in the Third Republic and considered its collapse warranted if not inevitable. The same is true for the dialogue he weaves between the imprisoned sergeant and the men formerly under his command. They, representatives of an entire generation, had betrayed him and France. Somehow, they had lacked the fortitude and endurance which their fathers had shown in 1914. And they retort, predictably: No! It was his generation that had stumbled through the interwar years, making a new war inevitable by their collective incompetence.[3] Either way, the truth of fathers, the truth of sons, it seemed clear enough that the collapse of France could not be chalked up to a handful of pre-war *dirigeants* and wartime commanders.

So it was that by the end of the 1940s, all of France and much of the world was convinced that the collapse of the Third Republic had had something unavoidable about it. And it was a conclusion which neither the Fourth Republic nor the Fifth Republic of 1958 had any incentive to refute. Rival interpretations abounded, some of them remarkably fine-tuned, most of them coloured against the inept *Troisième*. These ranged from works which detected deep-penetration conspiracies on the part of both fascist or communist sympathizers. Some were convinced that Catholicism had finally brought down its long-time nemesis, the secular Third Republic, while others were as alive as ever to the clandestine manoeuvrings of free masonry. One need not have been religious to have recognized the debilitating effects of interwar materialism, any more than one had to have been a drunk in order to believe that alcoholism was at the root of the French condition in 1939–40. The propertied classes were more certain than ever that the restrictive practices of French unions had suffocated French rearmament efforts in the 1930s, but no more than the urban working class which knew that the problem had been the flight of capital from France. Suggestive of a belief that the causes of a great defeat need be correspondingly great, and complex, the combination of all this political, historical, literary, and ideological effort left something nearly indelible – the image of a sick, divided and demoralized France. Looking back from the late 1940s, there were not many who had failed to see it coming a long time ago.

Hence, there were not many inclined to re-examine the findings of this early post-mortem report. Especially not those luminaries of the little-lamented Third Republic. What they intended to do was sometimes explain themselves, always exonerate; and brief moments before judicial or parliamentary inquiries were not enough to do themselves justice. Memoirs were the answer; and thus the stream of memoirs which sprung suddenly from the rock in the 1940s, became a torrent in the 1950s. Politicians, diplomats, officers of army, navy and air force, intellectuals, and people from the world of journalism, all hurried to save their reputations – often at the expense of others. It was that latter process which further extended the stain of the war and the sudden defeat, rather like contractors who warn home owners about the dishonesty and incompetence of all their competitors. Single-handed attempts to assert singular innocence only heighten cynicism and spread scepticism. Besides, many of the earliest memoirs came from the most discredited of the pre-war French leadership: the serpentine Bonnet, the disgraced Flandin, General Maurice Gamelin upon whom the weight of the military defeat was cheerfully piled, Pierre Laval who spoke posthumously from a traitor's grave. Once more, as in the case of the trial procedures, men desperate to pull themselves from the pit would use anything that came to hand. Their own miscalculations – were they even to be acknowledged – were of minor importance compared to the blind and deaf world in which they had tried to operate.[4]

French scholars in the 1950s, men, mainly, who had adult memories of the war, were not much moved by this spectacle. Except, perhaps, by a feeling of disgust. The defeat, the occupation, even the Anglo–American led Liberation, invoked varying degrees of embarrassment. Not even the legend of a widespread and early Resistance, a legend with its own indelicacies, could compensate for what had happened between 1940 and 1944. There were other constraints as well. French academic historians, like those elsewhere, were chary about working on twentieth century subject matter – on the grounds that the events were too recent, the perspective too shallow, the documentation too incomplete. The latter, certainly, became a consideration of very legitimate proportions in post-war

France. The upheavals caused by the war had wreaked havoc on the state's archives; and what fire and bombs and careless storage had spared, various defendants, witnesses and memoir-writers further dishevelled. Finally, scholars anxious to make a career under the Fourth and Fifth Republics were not noticeably intent on exonerating the Third. In no sense was it a popular cause, either in the eyes of public opinion which already knew what it knew, or in that of regimes which controlled appointments to university posts as well as an arsenal of honours for intellectual and public service.

To be sure, there were an exceptional few, exceptional by ability as well as numbers. These included Georges Castellan, who was the first post-war scholar to look closely at the question of French military intelligence in the 1930s. Having done so, and informed by his remarkable access to the official files, Castellan made one thing clear. French intelligence had had more information than it needed to appreciate the military threat which had been mounting east of the Rhine.[5] But unmistakably, the principal impulse for the study of contemporary history in the 1950s came from the Sorbonne, and its diplomatic historians. Three of them, in particular, came to dominate the field: Pierre Renouvin, who turned 60 in 1953, was still very much at the helm, assisted by a younger Maurice Baumont, and a younger still Jean-Baptiste Duroselle.[6] Between them, they produced volume after volume, article after article, on the history of French foreign policy between the wars. And through that entire decade, these three, further sustained by the work of their respective graduate students, really began an in-depth exploration of what they called the *forces profondes*. In other words, it was not enough to understand the mechanics of diplomacy; one had to understand the inter-connectedness of diplomacy with strategy, and economics, and domestic politics, and ideas and social psychology.

Pierre Renouvin led the way or, perhaps more precisely, was among the first and few post-war scholars to pursue the intricate set of leads provided earlier by Marc Bloch. It was Renouvin, for example, who perceived the tension latent in France's entire interwar foreign policy – that between the arguments for deterrence and those for conciliation – and thus indirectly inspired my own preceding observations on ambivalence. So too was it he who pointed out the contemporary sense of France's genuine impotence in the 1930s, that induced by a growing appreciation of the constraints on the country's demographic and economic resources. Indeed, the general conclusion to his principal work on interwar international relations amounts to a short but masterful essay on the multitude of variables which condition a nation's foreign policy.[7] Like Bloch and Renouvin, Maurice Baumont also understood that the coming of war was too complex a phenomenon to be addressed with pat answers, conspiratorial or otherwise. A man who had spent the 1930s in Geneva as a member of the League secretariat, Baumont's views were informed by a great deal of direct experience. As early as 1945 he had concluded that France had been out of her depth since 1919, cast in an international role for which she had lacked adequate resources. The problem was not so much that she lacked the will to play the part, an unwillingness suggestive of some kind of 'décadence'. Rather, she was unable to. Indeed, the real problem was that of an international community too blind and deaf to understand the disparities which had arisen between the respective power bases of France and Germany.[8] Professor Duroselle agreed. France's apparent inertia had to be placed within the general failure of the western democracies to grasp the threat from Hitler and to summon up the requisite energies to contain him.[9]

What was happening of course, as passions started to cool, was that scholars, old and new, were appearing with fresh insights. Many of them were trained in the United States, where an historical interest in France had been sustained for generations. Some of them had had interest reinforced by military service in Europe in the latter years of the Second World War. Such was the case of Philip Bankwitz whose doctoral dissertation on General Maxime Weygand, written in the 1950s, appeared later as a celebrated book on civil–military relations. It was also true of John McVickar Haight Jr, whose post-war doctoral work became an important book on American aeronautical assistance to France between 1938 and 1940.[10] Both men enjoyed distinguished teaching careers long after the war, Bankwitz at Trinity College, in Hartford, Connecticut, McVickar Haight at Lehigh University in Pennsylvania. Other examples of early, and invaluable, post-war scholarship were the dissertations done by Fred Greene, Alvin Coox and Donald Harvey, the first at Yale, the second at Harvard, and the third at Columbia. Each was a variation on the theme of the French military collapse or, more accurately, on the organizational and doctrinal shortcomings which might have led to that collapse. For work done in the 1950s, when archives were closed and private papers at a premium, these were studies of the highest quality. And not surprisingly, they uncovered a host of deficiencies in France's pre-war planning – including a halting dialogue between military and civilian planners, an excessive concentration on defensive strategy and tactics, and a particularly glaring failure to coordinate air power and armour. Whatever their archival limitations, these works were too sophisticated to employ conspiracy theories for the collapse of 1940, and too measured to confuse explanation with incrimination.[11]

This fascination with the stunning French defeat continued unabated in American graduate schools, a fascination doubtless reinforced by the research done by that first generation of scholars in the 1950s. Whatever the explanation, new work was undertaken despite the continuing problems of securing access to official archives. Such problems served only as a spur, judging by the impressive range of secondary materials that were found, as well as by the instances of special archival access that were accorded to them. Such was certainly true of Judith Hughes, whose doctoral work on the origins of the Maginot Line was published in 1970. It was true also of Robert Krauskopf's study of the interwar French air force, a dissertation completed at Georgetown University in 1965; and the same could be said of Jeffery Clarke's work on technology and the French armoured force between the wars, a doctoral work supervised by Theodore Ropp at Duke University and completed in 1969.[12] What is interesting about these studies, undertaken from a distance of more than two decades from the defeat, is that they too eschew any temptation to invective. Krauskopf offers careful and measured explanations for the weaknesses which plagued the French air force in 1940 – without beating the drums of incompetence, indifference or treason. So too Clarke who, rather than mocking the French army and the dullness of its officers, sees the lack of command centralization as a critical factor in the slow development of the French armoured force. Even Hughes, who sees the 1930s as a decade of capitulation for the French, and partly because of their own half-heartedness, concludes that they were destined by the stars to be crushed between the ambitions of Hitler and the interests of the United Kingdom.[13]

These, to be sure, are but samples of some of the work done by American scholars in the 1950s and 1960s. They have two elements in common. First, they concern themselves with the military side of French attempts to avert, prepare for and fight the Second World

War. Second, they are indeed works which contributed to my own doctoral research at the London School of Economics in the late 1960s, and to the preparation of my first book ten years later. That extended venture was addressed precisely to the relationship between French foreign policy and military planning in the 1930s, and therefore was considerably informed by the findings and insights of these American scholars. They were among the very few experts in the field, and as such were so much better informed than the vast majority of teachers and scholars whose knowledge of France came from the writings of Winston Churchill, Alexander Werth, A. J. P. Taylor or – given their ominously translated wartime works – André Géraud (*The Gravediggers of France*) and Pierre Cot (*The Triumph of Treason*).[14]

It was only in the late 1960s that the tempo of scholarship on interwar France noticeably quickened. Some of it had to do with a momentary satiation with works on Hitler and the Nazis, some of it with the appearance of the early volumes of French diplomatic documents from the mid-1930s[15] and, no doubt, with the interest and reaction provoked by the flood of French memoirs. Whatever the explanation, before the decade was out there were suddenly three large, eminently readable volumes on the French collapse, one from the American journalist William Shirer, and one each from the British historians Alistair Horne and Guy Chapman. Although none was path-breaking from a documentary point of view, each made an effort to place the military defeat in some kind of broader context, and each was sympathetic to France's plight in the 1930s. But it was difficult to avoid the sense of foreordination. Horne, for example, resisted the fatalism that spelled out defeat even before battle had begun; however, in the end, he concluded that the odds against any other outcome in 1940 were 'enormously high'. Shirer had even greater difficulty in concealing his old conviction that what happened in 1940 had been in the works for 20 years. As he says on his opening page, even in the 1930s he had known that France was going 'downhill', 'sapped by . . . division, by an incomprehensible blindness in foreign, domestic and military policy, by the ineptness of its leaders, the corruption of its Press, and by a feeling of growing confusion, hopelessness and cynicism'.[16]

Familiar enough in outline, this was not going to persuade everyone. Such was certainly the case of the Canadian scholar John Cairns, at the University of Toronto. By then, Cairns had published two important papers on the subject of the fall of France or, more accurately, on the history of its history. In both, he had dismissed the already considerable pile of simplistic explanations – including those which played on the corruption of the Third Republic – and had stressed the need to keep the French collapse in some kind of perspective. It was, after all, an allied defeat, and the errors committed, the misjudgments recorded, were by no means exclusively French in origin. That is why this so widely admired, gentle scholar betrayed flashes of impatience with Horne and Shirer in particular. New works though they might have been, these were not new perspectives, or not new enough for one who already had an unrivalled knowledge of *la grande chute*. Neither, in his view, had been sufficiently cautious about the published works on which they had been obliged to rely. The fact was that many of those sources reflected a conditioned animus for the Third Republic, whether that which reflected a pro-Vichy bias or that of the Resistance.[17] More striking still was the contribution Cairns made in an article of 1974, for it was here that he addressed the problem of cultural bias. Could it be, he wondered, that Anglo-Saxon historians have been unduly influenced by contemporary English misgivings about interwar France? Is not part of the problem English indecisiveness over when the French should be compliant and when they should stand firm?[18]

Three years before Shirer's work first appeared in the United States, a young doctoral candidate at Leeds University completed his study of French foreign policy in 1938–9. Currently professor of international history in Berkeley, California, Anthony Adamthwaite came to the conclusion that French policy had been far more shrewd than anyone thus far had discerned. Cynical though it may well have been, and arguably dishonest, the policy of Georges Bonnet had been one of feigning indecision in order to let the British government carry responsibility for whatever concessions had to be made under appeasement. Although that was not an argument which I adopted for my own dissertation, it would be fair to say that both Adamthwaite and I detected more ability, and more calculation, in French foreign and military policy than most scholars had been inclined to accept.[19]

It was at this point, in the early 1970s, that scholarship on interwar France got its second wind. Following recent British and American examples, the French government replaced its 50-year archival law with one that allowed access to documents older than 30 years.

Suddenly, at least *en principe*, government archives were open for research on the 1920s and 1930s. Of course, *en réalité*, things were rather different. Only slowly, through the 1970s and 1980s, were the documents made widely available; and thus the familiar process of securing exceptional access, for special reasons, remained much in vogue. Still, research in France was becoming increasingly possible as parliamentary archives opened, as well as those of the foreign, finance and defence ministries, and as special collections of private papers became available at the National archives and elsewhere. Accompanying this new openness was a related trend in academic cooperation throughout the 1970s, especially among French, British and German scholars. International colloquium followed colloquium, and in the wake of each came a published volume of papers – most of them based on archives still closed to private scholars. The end result of these gatherings, as in the case of the French colloquia addressed to the governments of Léon Blum and Edouard Daladier, was a huge increase in the primary and secondary documentation available to scholars from around the world.[20]

With the exception of one key publishing event towards the end of that decade, there was a perceptible trend in this mounting body of historiography. By and large, it was away from the very old standbys – conspiracy and treason – and even from the familiar language of incompetence, stupidity, paralysis and degeneration. Instead, we derived new insights into the complex nature of France's dilemma between the wars. Speaking of foreign policy, Pierre Renouvin – as dominant a figure as ever in the early 1970s – concluded that France's apparent 'timidité' had stemmed from a realization that she could not risk war without assurances of British military and economic support. Firmly behind that conclusion was the work produced by various members of the historical sections in the army, navy and air force – including Colonel Pierre Le Goyet, Patrick Fridenson, Philippe Masson, Patrice Buffotot and General Charles Christienne. Their respective studies suggested clearly enough that by the mid-1930s France had lost the balance of military superiority and had neither the time nor the resources at its disposal to make good the gap between itself and Germany.[21]

What was particularly encouraging about the trend of the 1970s was the addition of new or at least relatively unexplored perspectives. Given the obviously military nature of the collapse in 1940, it was not altogether surprising that so much attention was still being addressed to questions of strategy, tactics, materiel, doctrine and intelligence gathering. But what was newer was the work done for many of these colloquia by economic historians like René Girault, Jean Bouvier and Robert Frank. Thanks to them, in particular, we derived a much better understanding of the relationship between the battery of constraints on France's financial and industrial resources and the cautious, 'timid' foreign policy with which we associate the Third Republic in the mid to late 1930s.[22] The same is true, though from a very different perspective, of the connections between that foreign policy and the turbulence of French domestic politics. Here, for example, there were two papers from Professor Duroselle, one presented to an Anglo-French colloquium in 1972, and one to a Franco-German colloquium in 1977. Neither the legendary instability of French cabinets, he concluded, nor the ideological fissures in parliament or press did anything to promote firmness in diplomacy.[23] The same needed to be said when it came to important currents within French public opinion: those of French veterans, as explored by Antoine Prost; of the socialist and communist parties, as canvassed by Professors Droz and Bruhat; or those of French pacifists, as surveyed by Henri Michel. And along similar but broader lines was James Safford's doctoral dissertation at Cornell, a work that specifically addressed the subject of French attitudes to the prospect of a new war.[24]

In fact, Americans were very much in the vanguard of scholarship on interwar France, despite continuing frustrations over archival access. Of particular importance, they did much to uncover the motivation behind French foreign policy in the 1920s. 1975 saw the completion of two strong doctoral dissertations, that of Vincent Pitts at Harvard, and that of Edward Keeton at Yale. Both disparaged the familiar representations of Briand as the naïve internationalist, and of the 1920s as – in Pitts' words – 'a period of . . . self-deception, paving the way for France's defeatist attitude in the 1930s'.[25] The following year Stephen Schuker and Sally Marks published their first books on post-war international politics, works in which they extended our appreciation of the multiple constraints on French diplomacy in the 1920s and sharpened our understanding of the relationship between the pre-and-post Hitlerian periods. Much the same could be said for the ensuing books of Walter McDougall and Marc Trachtenberg, books which highlighted the association between French economic resources and foreign policy in the early

1920s. Thus assembled, and derived solely from American scholars, these works suggest a sudden and welcome effusion of interest in France's situation in post-Versailles Europe.[26]

As sketchy and incomplete as these examples are, they are sufficient to illustrate the ever-widening ripples on the investigative pool. Part of that process were three books which appeared in English in the late 1970s, one by a Briton, one by an American, and one by a Canadian. The latter was my own, a work which extended the doctoral research on the relationship between French strategic calculations in the 1930s and the conduct of French foreign policy. The first was Anthony Adamthwaite's revised and extended dissertation, a very substantial piece of work which has particular strengths on the side of domestic politics. The second was Jeffery Gunsburg's revised dissertation from Duke University, a work which is especially strong on the conduct of the campaign in May–June 1940.[27] Interpretively, were I to categorize them, Gunsburg's work is an aggressive defence of the conduct of the French government and high command in 1940 as well as in the 1930s. If blame is to be apportioned, much of it should go to France's realized and unrealized allies – an idea earlier developed by Professor Cairns. Adamthwaite is tougher on the French, mindful of the obstacles before them and yet still inclined to find them too timid and supine. Rightly or wrongly, but as befits a Canadian, I see my own work as falling somewhere in between.

The same could not be said for Professor Duroselle's next major sortie into the world of French diplomacy in the 1930s. It was 1979. He awarded it the powerful title *La Décadence*, two words which instantly refilled the room with the dust of several decades. Why he did so remains unclear, for this thick volume made almost no effort to argue or illustrate that suggestive theme, and in fact introduced much evidence to contradict it. Nevertheless, with a final and cursory reference to Montesquieu's famous study of decadence within the Roman empire, the reigning doyen of French diplomatic history closed his text, and waited.[28] Reaction was mixed: part praise for the breadth of his knowledge and his grasp of the forces which underlay the public manifestations of foreign policy; part discomfort with the sparse but inflammatory language of his central argument – or at least the argument suggested by the eye-catching title.

To be sure, it was not entirely unexpected, for in his previous book on France and World War One he had warned his readers that the ensuing 20 years would prove to be quite different from 'la grandeur' achieved between 1914 and 1918. Not given to understatement, he summed up the 1920s and 1930s as decades of 'illusion, mediocrity and weakness'.[29] Still, it must have seemed hyperbole at best to Jacques Néré who, from his chair at the University of Brest, had recently judged French foreign policy in the 1930s to be no more subject to error and miscalculation than that of many other nations. So too it should have struck Jean-Pierre Azéma at the Institute for Political Studies in Paris who, remarking on the revival of French productive energies in 1939, warned against seeing France as down and out on the eve of war. As for Henri Michel, the long-time director of the French commission for the History of the Second World War, he was quick to speak out against the language of decadence and to reject any suggestion that France was beaten the moment it declared war.[30] Even René Girault, Professor Duroselle's successor at the Sorbonne, came to qualify his earlier subscription to the concept of decadence. In a paper delivered in 1982 he intoned that 'decay was in the air'. His antecedents of the 1930s had been 'preparing for defeat'. But the following year he published a paper which disputed the utility of any concept of national decline, and expressly cast doubt on the language of French 'décadence' – however 'remarkably' it had been used by Professor Duroselle.[31]

Interpretively, one would have to say, *Décadence* was a setback. It confirmed a host of prejudices within and beyond France, without the compensating virtue of sustained argument. Nevertheless, far from running dry, scholarly inquiry in the 1980s continued to flow around this newly raised and formidable obstacle. The 1920s fell under further scrutiny, with results that proved much more sympathetic to France's post-war position and much more laudatory of its foreign policy. In 1980, Marc Tractenberg repudiated earlier notions that French reparations policy had as its exclusive goal vengeance against Germany. Indeed, France's attempted hardline stemmed directly from the collective failure to agree on allied economic cooperation. As for the reputedly intransigent Poincaré, of Ruhr occupation fame, he acted only in desperation 'and hardly knew what he wanted to do once he got there'.[32] This is not far removed from the conclusions reached by Dan Silverman who, two years later, denied that French reparations policy was 'intransigent, aggressive, ignorant and incompetent'.[33]

A similarly interpretive line was extended into the 1930s, notably again by American-based scholars made uneasy by the simplistic clarity of a peculiarly inept France. Eleanor Gates and Nicolas Rostow, in their perceptive studies of Anglo-French relations, both came to the conclusion that for too long the English had enjoyed the interpretive equivalent of the Dunkirk escape. It was they who had refused to acknowledge the legitimacy of French security anxieties, they who had refused entreaties from Paris for greater economic and military cooperation, and thus they who had contributed mightily to the escalation of the German threat. Thus, to cite Gates, the British 'consistently weakened the one continental power with whom they were ever likely to be in alliance again'. Thus, to cite Rostow, British policy was 'poisonous [and] xenophobic', and 'sapped French strength, morale and will'.[34] Of a different order, but of similar interpretive genre, was the work of Colonel Robert Doughty, professor of history in the United States Military Academy at West Point. Addressing the subject of French military doctrine in the interwar period, Doughty arrived at one unsurprising, but very refreshing, conclusion. The French army was not well enough prepared for the conditions of 1940; but neither had it expected those of 1919, as if it had remained frozen in time, unchanged, and indifferent to weapons like tanks and planes. There had in fact been a substantial evolution of French military doctrine and the attendant technology. One could talk of errors, misjudgments, even failures, but not of 'stupidity, incompetence or decadence'.[35]

French university scholars of the 1980s found it more difficult to be quite as direct. But if there was a noticeable reluctance to dispute the interpretive simplicity of decadence, there was also little inclination to adopt it. Colonel Henry Dutailly did not do so in his official history of the French army in the 1930s. He did not deny the shortcomings, the intellectual conservatism, the lack of imagination in adapting more quickly than it did to the changes in modern military technology. But he was careful to document the substantial evolution and revival that had occurred by 1939, and careful to disavow any suggestion that the interwar army never thought beyond defensive strategy and tactics. Moreover, he was particularly careful to explain the connections between the anticipated future war of attrition, France's limited economic and financial resources vis-à-vis Germany, and her acute need for allies.[36]

Two other exposés of the French predicament quickly followed that of Dutailly, both from scholars whose reception of foreign visitors has been particularly cordial. The first came from Maurice Vaïsse, currently professor of international history at Reims, but formerly a doctoral student of Professor Duroselle. 1981 saw the publication of Vaïsse's monograph on French policy towards the Disarmament Conference between 1930 and 1934. In it, Vaïsse did next to nothing with the concept or language of decadence. Instead, while acknowledging the 'hésitations' which plagued French policy, he attributed the ambivalence to the genuine uncertainty which had long since arisen between proponents of deterrence and those of conciliation. Furthermore, rather like Gates, Rostow and others, Vaïsse attributed ultimate blame for the collapse of the Disarmament Conference, not to French, but rather to British and American policy.[37] The second monograph was that of Robert Frank, one which addressed the subject of French rearmament between 1935 and 1939. In it, Frank destroyed one shibboleth after another. France, in fact, had begun the financial preparations for rearmament as early as 1935; the left-wing Popular Front had launched the first serious programme for industrial rearmament; the delays in production had been occasioned as much by the flight of capital as by the limitations of a 40-hour-week for factory workers; and the proof of all these efforts and investments was just starting to become obvious in the last few months before war broke out in 1939.[38]

By then, by the early 1980s, French scholarship on the 1930s was experiencing a rapid acceleration; and without any doubt, much of the impetus came from Professor Duroselle's centre for international relations at the Sorbonne, and from the related founding of the indispensable journal *Relations Internationales*. Very little of the work was inspired by the notion of decadence, unlike other ideas first broached by the *doyen* himself. For instance, however uncomfortably it fit with his decadent society, there was the notion of a major economic and psychological revival in 1938–9. In *Décadence* he had even referred to it as a 'miracle'. For that reason, his students and colleagues obviously felt more free to expand upon ideas such as this than to confront directly the issue of decadence. So it was that Elisabeth Du Réau uncovered France's renewed diplomatic initiatives in 1938–9, particularly with respect to the Soviet Union and Italy, and much to the consternation of Whitehall. Christine Sellin discovered that French school textbooks were still saturated with notions of the glory and invincibility of France and that, by in-

ference, the youth of the interwar period neither expected nor
were prepared for the collapse of 1940. Maurice Vaïsse revealed that
French opinion in 1939 was essentially united on the subject of war,
that there were few signs of defeatism, and that the prevailing
sentiment towards Germans in 1939 – as in 1914 – was 'il faut . . .
en finir avec ce peuple'.[39]

These, of course, are but a few examples of what has happened in
recent years within the historiography of interwar France. And what
they illustrate is a common desire to expose as many corners of the
interwar tableau as possible, without getting hung up on the *tricorne*
of decadence, defeatism and inevitability. That there are exceptions
is certainly true. In 1983 the senior German scholar, Gilbert
Ziebura, picked up on Marc Bloch's idea of a 'selfish and self-cen-
tred' society; uncomfortable though he may have been with the
language of decadence, he had no compunctions about using that of
'blindness' and 'paralysis'.[40] Serge Berstein, of the Institut d'Etudes
Politiques, also remains convinced of the intellectual and moral crisis
which he says made the 1930s so different from the 1920s. In his
book of 1988, he does not recoil from the language of 'décadence
nationale', or from the conclusion that 1940 could be chalked up to
the 'inanité' of French military policy throughout the entire interwar
period.[41] It was in the same year that Piotr Wandycz of Yale
University rather more reluctantly subscribed to the vocabulary of
decadence in order to explain the failure of French diplomatic policy
in eastern Europe.[42] And three years later Nicole Jordan, of the
University of Illinois at Chicago, summarized French strategic planning in the 1930s, if not in the language of decadence at least of
Simone de Beauvoir's 'blood of others'. The whole cynical and
ignoble idea was that France should have its battles fought by others,
and elsewhere. Planning for war in the wrong place is what explains
1940.[43]

More recently, the Ottawa-based historian, Michael Carley, has
offered us a new impression of French policy in the 1930s, what he
and others before him call that 'low, dishonest decade'. As in some
of his other work, Carley argues that the peace of Europe was
undermined by sectors of the French business and bureaucratic elite
who conspired against Franco-Soviet cooperation.[44] And most recently, Anthony Adamthwaite seems to have settled lightly among
those reluctant to give the French too much credit. True, he rejects
the concepts of decadence and inevitability. But in their place, at the

'heart of the matter', he finds that the French simply lacked the 'courage' to say 'No!', or worse, to Adolf Hitler.[45]

But then again, against this surge of the last half-dozen years have come other lines of inquiry and other doubts about France's alleged moral incapacity. For instance, unlike Nicole Jordan and Piotr Wandycz, who see the collapse of France's eastern alliances as a French failure, William Shorrock writes of the 'stupefying... blindness' of the allied governments in the east and attributes part of France's reputation for indecisiveness to the uncooperative posture of successive British governments. The latter is not far removed from John Cairns' observation that France was 'rebuffed repeatedly' by its one 'indispensable ally', namely Great Britain.[46] Another variation on the same theme has come in 1991 from John E. Dreifort, professor of history at Wichita State University. He, like Cairns and Shorrock, does not deny the vacillation and hesitation in French foreign policy, but attributes much of the uncertainty and caution to unhelpful responses from the United States and Great Britain. Ambivalence, for him, is the key word; and it is an ambivalence inspired not by moral lethargy but by the lack of options.[47]

Neither do moral judgements play a role in Colonel Doughty's most recent book on the French army. Examining the course of the battle in May 1940, Doughty acknowledges the strategic, tactical and doctrinal miscalculations that led to the collapse of the French front at Sedan. But that collapse, he says, 'did not occur because of the decadence of French society'.[48] This is a judgement with which Martin S. Alexander concurs. Alexander, who has a doctorate from Oxford and currently holds a chair at Salford University, rejects the vision of a decadent France, 'irredeemably condemned by drift, demoralization and indecision'. Indeed, amid the mistakes that were made, there were also some successes, just as there were moments of foresight and vigour as well as shortsightedness and inertia. Take, for example, the forlorn Maurice Gamelin, that commander turned to stone, rendered immobile in May 1940 by a lassitude typical of the decrepit Third Republic. But Alexander says 'No!' For him, the general's handling of the decisive battles that spring testifies to 'vigour and imperturbable self-control'.[49]

William D. Irvine is another dissenter. Professor of history at York University in Toronto, Irvine recently has argued that France was both materially and morally ready for war in 1939, that the national morale was 'excellent' and that there was no sign of any domestic plot against the Republic. The problem, as he sees it, is not that decadence occasioned the collapse of 1940 but that the collapse itself simply demanded some sweeping, graspable, single explanation. By and large, this is a view which sits comfortably enough within the meticulously researched and fair-minded study of Jean-Louis Cré-mieux-Brilhac. Married on the eve of the German breakthrough at Sedan, this retired public servant seems to have exposed every blemish of the country's complexion in 1939 and 1940. Not to apportion guilt but to explain it. And it is precisely because he is committed to the latter that he insists on including evidence which is troublesome, which demands more of our ability to understand the defeat: the exceptional industrial recovery of 1939–40, and the attendant surge in French rearmament; the technical superiority of some of the modern French tanks over the German; the tenacity demonstrated, and the casualties sustained, by many of the fighting units in 1940. Decadence and its verbal siblings claim too much, and offer too little, to explain what happened in 1940.[50]

And so the debate continues, which is not only the principal point of this chapter but the way it should be – if History is to remain dynamic. Working backwards from that sudden collapse of 1940, many witnesses have found compelling the idea that the Third Republic was on its last legs even by the time of the 1919 peace conference. Materialism, alcoholism, sexual depravity, secularism, sloth, godlessness, communism – individually or in combination – had gnawed on the vitals of French society and made it vulnerable to the recklessness of Hitler. By and large, this perspective is a little too morally laced for most academic scholars, a little too convenient and, possibly, a little too deterministic. Philip Bankwitz, for example, believes that as late as June 1940 the French people, 'healthy and capable . . . in the depths of its soul,' still had what it took to stave off defeat.[51]

But if there are some who feel uneasy about the attribution of decadence to an entire society, that may not mean that they foreswear the concept entirely. The defeated General Gamelin, Bankwitz can still see as a product of 'moral decline', just as Professor Duroselle, like Marc Bloch and Léon Blum before him, could attribute much of the problem to the self-centredness of the bourgeois *classes dirigeantes*. Professor Berstein is in accord, eager to apply the vocabulary of decline, decay, and decadence to the intellectual leadership of interwar France. And if the intellectuals, one may ask, why not to the ranks of politicians called third-rate, or of senior officers called washed-up? Or better still, why not to the discredited and the dead? It is not difficult to hold up defeated generals, exiled marshals, assassinated admirals and executed politicians as the once rotten apples in the barrel. In short, we can have selective rather than wholesale decadence. It is easy, therefore tempting, and therefore commonplace.

Less common is an interpretive route which, without addressing the issue of decadence directly, turns it on its head. We find it in a certain depiction of France's peace-at-any-price leadership. To so many, Georges Bonnet was a conniving, spineless intriguer, not a moral pacifist but a moral coward. A few, however, have seen him as the one man in France in 1938–9 who was utterly, unequivocally, implacably committed to averting war. Daladier, and most of the cabinet were indecisive, fearful of war but fearful of the future without a war. Bonnet never wavered, and to that end undermined domestic French resistance by encouraging Neville Chamberlain to take the initiative to Hitler. And the responsibility of dealing with the German Chancellor. One need not like Bonnet, even approve of his means and objective, in order to appreciate his singular commitment and the 'skill and determination' which he brought to the task.[52] If indecisiveness is some sign of moral uncertainty, and that, a mark of decadence, then Bonnet was among the moral minority in the late 1930s.

That, in itself, ought to be enough to make one wonder whether morality has a future in historiography. But there is another, more powerful example. The morally-couched criticisms of interwar France are so often ignited with familiar verbal wormwood: rot, malaise, paralysis, corruption, dishonesty, blindness, indifference, defeatism and, the favourite, decadence. These are not neutral terms, as befit judgements which are anything but neutral; and they therefore provoke reactions which – however temperate by contrast – can produce comparably exaggerated impressions. How often in the preceding pages have we been aware of interpretations which, in trying to expose the predicament of interwar France, may come close to sounding like ungenerous indictments of the United Kingdom, the United States, and any or all of France's potential allies. Predictably, tempers rise another degree, as Poles and Belgians, Italians and Russians are diagnosed as having the same visual, auditory, visceral and mental afflictions as the French. That is one of the reasons why many historians, of many nationalities, really would prefer to escape from the textual world of right and wrong, good and bad, courageous and cowardly, blind and insightful. The problem is that we do not always agree when explanation has jumped the line to indictment, when exposition has slipped into apology.

There is another reason. One of the most difficult philosophical problems for historians is knowing where to draw the line between exposition and determinism. Are we not trying to explain why things happened the way they did? Yes. If that explanation is thorough and honest enough, does that not mean that what happened had its own strict logic, that it could not have happened any other way, that it was in fact inevitable? No. At least most members of the historical profession would say no: partly because they recognize that even one significant difference in response – of substance or timing – might have triggered a chain-reaction of other different responses, and partly because they accept that men and women sometimes respond unpredictably. For that reason, most eschew the language of inevitability, even when the vocabulary is only that of human error, misjudgment and ignorance. But the problem is greater when the vocabulary is morally-laced, when it attributes some kind of inherent defect to a whole people – or even to classes or to generations of a people. It is then that we have inevitability in its most extreme form.

So it is for several reasons that the ensuing pages decline the interpretive device of national decadence which has been with us for over 50 years. I doubt its accuracy, fear its potential to inflame, and distrust its association with the inevitable. Instead, and to recall an earlier metaphor, I would like to track the competing currents in the river of French ambivalence. Ultimately, I believe that it is here where we should seek explanations for how France became embroiled in war in 1939 and why she collapsed so suddenly in 1940. The trick is not to turn that defeat into some kind of victory, or even to argue that either was equally possible in 1940. It is to explain ambivalence, to portray rather than resolve uncertainty and confusion.

3 Accord and Discord: Diplomacy and National Defence in the 1930s

There are two kinds of responsibilities which relate directly to the approach of war. There are the diplomatic efforts which are made to preserve the peace and, should these fail, to then isolate one's enemy. There is the strategic planning which is designed to ensure the security of the nation, by deterrence in peacetime and by the application of military force in wartime. In short, we should distrust the old dictum that war is the extension of diplomacy by other means. The two are not sequential, they coexist. In fact, both the foreign ministry and the defence ministries have as their primary task the assurance of the nation's security in peace and in war.

In the case of France after 1933, there was little discord over the direction of the principal foreign menace: Nazi Germany. As witnessed earlier, this did not mean that all hopes of Franco-German entente had collapsed, any more than it meant that all Frenchmen remained immune to the appeal of the Nazi regime's social conservatism. Neither did it mean that Frenchmen could see no other enemy on the horizon. For those on the centre and the right, there was always Stalin's brooding, bloodthirsty regime. For those on the left, Mussolini's Italy offered a less ominous target for derision than the irascible regime in Berlin. And for those who continued to see France's future in imperial terms, Japan's ambitions in China and South-East Asia were as alarming as Italy's ambitions in North and East Africa.[1] At no point, therefore, did France's citizenry ever conclude that all but one of the dragons had been slain. Indeed, from the mid-1930s onward there was a general sense that the nation's interests were everywhere imperilled – from the Franco-German border through the Balkans to the Far East, from Poland to Tunis and Jibouti.

That said, Germany retained its place as the most probable and certainly the most dangerous of France's enemies. It was dangerous in three ways. First, and recalled as the French recalled it, the

Germans had attacked France in 1814 and 1815, again in 1870, again in 1914. Inflamed as they were now said to be with a hatred of the post-war Versailles settlement, how or why should one believe their momentary professions of peace? Second, since the Nazi takeover of power early in 1933, Germany had been committed to expansion in central Europe – as part of its claims to German-settled soil, notably in Poland, Austria and Czechoslovakia. But while it was true that Frenchmen would have preferred a German drive to the east than one to the west, it was also true that France was committed to the territorial integrity of those three states.[2] In short, any German decision to risk war in west or east, had the capacity to embroil the Third Republic in its second major war of the century.

Third, not only did Frenchmen commonly attribute to Germans a warlike disposition if not intention, they also conceded to Germany a superior war potential. That is to say, given Germany's larger labour force and industrial capacity, she was likely to triumph in any straight, bilateral war with France. Indeed, it was from this basic appreciation that successive post-war governments had constructed a network of allied or friendly states whose resources might be pooled in some form of coalition warfare against Germany. Clearly, what was not going to happen was an early, possibly pre-emptive French attack against Germany. More likely was an early German strike, launched with a view to eliminating the threat of an enemy coalition and with it a long war of attrition.[3] Accordingly, the French plan was to wait for the Germans to attack, thwart them, mobilize national and international resources against them, wear them down over a period of several years, and finally finish them off with a crushing offensive. But the entire notion of the long war hinged on one thing: denying the Germans a quick and early victory.

The key to doing this was again an alloy of diplomacy and strategy. As for the first, the French foreign ministry had tried to solicit suitable assurances of support for French security from the Belgians, Poles, Czechs, Rumanians and Yugoslavs. As we have seen earlier, not all of these treaties contained formal assurances of military support, but each at least implied that Germany would not be left alone to deal with France as she saw fit. Indeed, she might even be faced with a hostile front in the east. In the 1930s, confronted by the unsettling conduct and claims of Hitler, the foreign ministry sought to expand its collection of apparent friends. France and the USSR exchanged assurances of mutual assistance if either became the victim of German aggression. Italy and the United Kingdom were more elusive, with the former gradually drifting into the Nazi camp and the latter even more gradually, and belatedly, drifting into a de facto alliance with France. But in one sense, the biggest prize of all remained aloof. Despite French efforts to rally the United States and its vast economic and financial arsenal, the Roosevelt government refused to further irritate isolationist opinion at home by making too public a stand on issues abroad.

Such were the principal states which the foreign ministry sought to associate with French strategic planning, and sought to do so because of its understanding of the German problem.[4] That much is clear. But again the clarity is misleading, for the diplomatic problem was in reality never that simple. The fact is that all the options had to be explored, as they always do; choices had to be made, as they always do; and in the attendant debate over choices, there arose ambivalence, as it usually does.

Take the case of Belgium. Between 1920 and the spring of 1936 there had existed a Franco-Belgian military convention, one which provided for annual staff talks and for joint military planning. Central to French thinking from the start was the idea that their forces would join Belgian forces, *in Belgium*, and that together they would fend off any new German offensive in the west. The essence of the allied plan was as follows. Prior to, or on the point of, being attacked, Belgium would invite the French army to come to the rescue. The French would take up positions, alongside their Belgian comrades, in fortified defences prepared in advance by Belgian engineers. The merits of such a strategy were obvious, starting with the fact that France would confine German aggression to Belgian soil, well-removed from the industrially critical regions of Lille and Valenciennes. Moreover, the astronomical costs of fortifying the Franco-Belgian frontier could be avoided. Belgium, as an active ally, was therefore a considerable asset to French security. However, the truth was that this asset came with some riders.

If the Belgian defences had not been prepared, if agreement had not been reached on exact troop dispositions and locations, if the call for help were to come too late, the entire plan would be jeopardized. Failure in Belgium would mean that the German army could come pouring across the unfortified Franco-Belgian border, sweeping to the west and south, behind the big Maginot emplacements. Clearly, the entire strategic plan rested on close and confident relations between two allied governments. Technically, of course, not even the 1920 accord had made them allies; but as of 1936 that accord had been replaced by what everyone understood to be a Belgian declaration of neutrality. Thereafter, the dilemma faced by French military planners only intensified. The Belgians wanted nothing to do with French obligations in eastern Europe, or with the Franco-German great power rivalry. Furthermore, Belgium's eternal ethnic split between the Flemish and the French-speaking Walloon population meant that any public association with France carried its own domestic political liabilities. Indeed, there was always something paradoxical in Franco-Belgian relations. The closer they were, the more distant they became.[5]

All in all, therefore, there was more than a trace of ambiguity in French official perceptions of Belgium after 1936. To stand by the small kingdom, and to execute the forward defence plan within Belgium, certainly made sense – if the Germans chose that invasion route and if the Belgians did everything that was expected of them, and in enough time. To renounce the plan, however, and a neutral Belgium with it, also carried with it a certain logic. France could accelerate the programme of defensive works along the Belgian frontier – admittedly at great cost and with considerable technical difficulty – and so let the Belgians stew in their own juice. There were moments when the French high command were tempted to think along such lines, the more so when they could disconcert the British with the idea that France might not react to a German seizure of the Lowlands. By and large, however, French strategic planners clung to the strategy of the forward defence in Belgium, and French diplomats had to do what they could to keep relations between the two countries at their most cordial. As uncertain as they were about its prospects for success, and mindful of all that could go wrong, French officials regarded it as the most viable way of keeping the German army off French soil and keeping intact France's northern industries.[6] To borrow a phrase from today's language of ambivalence, when it came to Belgium the French exhibited a sense of guarded optimism.

For a very long time, the same was true of French appraisals of Italy. Even beyond the outbreak of war in September 1939.[7] The reasoning behind such appraisals varied, including those of a conservative character which sometimes evoked common Latin cultures and more often the praiseworthy efforts of Mussolini to stamp out communism. Neither, as it turns out, would have disturbed most of France's senior officers or diplomats. But they would have used, did use, arguments of another genre. Notably that of French security. The Italians' potential utility could be summarized as follows. Diplomatically, they could associate themselves with the security concerns of the Third Republic and represent those concerns through their own embassy in Berlin. As a fascist state, particularly after 1936 when relations had warmed between Mussolini and Hitler, Italy might coax and cajole Germany into some new European accommodation. Such, as has been suggested, was an aspiration of Pierre Laval. Conversely, firm warnings from the Italians against treaty revision by force would add appreciably to the vocabulary of deterrence. So it was that the Italians could be a positive force for peace in Europe, partly through their conciliatory offices and partly through their claims to military prowess.[8]

The latter claims were received with varying degrees of scepticism across Europe. However, no-one could deny the importance of Italy's strategic location relative to the continent and the Mediterranean world. Strategists in Paris had to consider the imperatives of defence along the Franco-Italian border, as well as Italy's potential to facilitate or impede rail and sea communications between France and central Europe. For instance, there was a time in 1935 when the French high command had explored in some detail the sending of supplies and military units across Italy to the Yugoslavs, Czechs and Rumanians, men and materiel intended to cement a military front on Germany's eastern approaches. Along similar lines, including the element of wishful thinking, the French high command flirted with the prospect of someday seeing Italian bombers fly missions over Germany. Finally, and more probable, authorities in Paris were mindful of the trouble Italy could cause along the maritime routes between North Africa and France. Indeed, operating either from their home ports or those acquired in the Balearics during the Spanish Civil War, the Italian navy could interrupt French troop transports to the metropole – troops whose presence in France was critical to the entire mobilization process.[9]

Thus phrased, the case for an Italian alliance was unequivocal. Doubts might have been expressed in the officers' mess about the combat quality of the Italian troops, and there was scepticism about both the quantitative and qualitative claims made by the Italians for their rearmament programme, but it would take few bombers or submarines to impede French naval traffic in the Mediterranean, and none at all to shut down the Italian rail lines to central Europe. And yet the doubts remained, and the debate continued. Once more, there were other perspectives on the desirability of Italy as ally. Domestically, any deal with fascist Italy had the potential for division, with the French left rhetorically adamant about Mussolini's betrayal and subsequent repression of socialism.[10] Diplomatically, the case for alliance had its blemishes, starting with the mercurial and unpredictable temperament of the Duce, carrying on through imperial rivalries such as the dispute over Tunis, and ending with sporadic but very public Italian claims to Corsica and Nice. These, when added to concerns that a Franco-Italian accord might alienate the United Kingdom, constituted a substantial argument for caution. Even strategically there was room for misgiving, quite apart from the risk factor associated with British reactions. Italy, some said, with its limited industrial infrastructure, inefficient agricultural production, and inadequate resource base, was going to be a liability to any ally. Better that it should constrain the Germans, by acting as a drain on goods and resources, than impede French efforts to rearm and refortify. In summary, therefore, the case in favour of Italy was not uncontested; and however much today's scholars may be converted to the arguments of one side or the other – like contemporary observers in the 1930s – the fact remains that all this was a matter of debate. And once more, in that debate, we find the element of legitimate uncertainty.

Should we expect any more or less when it comes to French appraisals of the alliances and accords with Poland and the three members of the Little Entente – Czechoslovakia, Rumania and Yugoslavia? Together, they had some potential for constraining Germany in central Europe. Together, they could employ their considerable divisional strengths and – in the case of the Czechs – their considerable field fortifications, to stop the Germans from carving them up one by one. Together, they could even put out enough offensive pressure in the east to harass a German attack on France in the west. Diplomatically, therefore, it was in France's interest to ensure this togetherness, to conclude some kind of mutual assistance pact between it and the tripartite Little Entente and, ideally, to include Poland in the mix. Simply posed, was it not better for France to have friendly and loyal states in central Europe who, in their togetherness, could constitute a second front against German aggression?

The answer is as obvious as the question is orchestrated. In fact, there was precious little togetherness either within or among these central European states. Rivals in ethnic diversity and pre-war competitors for Hapsburg concessions, they were bent on fashioning their own future and burying their collective past. The Poles and Rumanians were more obsessed with the Russian threat than the German, the Czechs, more with the Germans than the Russians, the Yugoslavs more with the Italians. Among them, the Czechs and Poles specialized in mutual animus, while the mortar of the Little Entente crumbled with the confirmed disappearance of the Hapsburg empire. Barring a miracle, there was very little chance that French diplomats or soldiers could fulfil the ambition of a united diplomatic and military block on Hitler's eastern flank.[11] Furthermore, the only way such an ambition could be realized was by France further tightening, perhaps even extending, her commitment to the security of these countries. Such, naturally, would be the price exacted by those who were being asked to tighten their commitment to French security. But in which direction would Hitler move first? Towards France? In which case the central states could be useful military assets. Towards the east? In which case those same states would be calling for rescue by France. Uncertain of the answer, the French preferred to stand pat. They did not, perhaps could not, strengthen their hold and interests in the east; but they did not abandon or renounce what they already had.[12] If not the most honourable way to behave, it certainly was in the finest traditions of self-serving diplomacy, and calculated ambiguity.[13]

Ongoing debate over Belgium, Italy and the central European 'allies' was matched, indeed surpassed, by that over the Soviet Union. Once more, the advocates of rapprochement and alliance had a strong case to present. Here was the colossus of eastern Europe, anti-fascist since its inception, as of 1935 the newest great power member of the League of Nations, and an unlimited reservoir of men and resources. Indeed, in its previous incarnation under the Czar, Russia had helped avert French defeat in the west by her heroic efforts on the eastern front. Now, by the mid 1930s, she had large air and armoured forces as well as great numerical strength in the infantry and artillery. Furthermore, as a neighbour of both Poland and Rumania, the USSR was in a position to lend direct assistance to any anti-German block in central Europe. Suddenly, with the insertion of Russia into the picture, the French vision of a grand coalition in the east took on a new allure. And it was precisely that vision, of a block that could either deter Hitler or defeat him, that prompted various French diplomats, soldiers and politicians to promote the Soviet connection.[14]

But they did not have the field to themselves. In fact, in military terms they only amounted to small pockets of resistance when compared to the battalions ranged against them.[15] Once more, the weaponry varied. Ideologists rehearsed all the sins of communism, and found every one in the record of the Soviet regime. To deal with Hitler by supping with the devil seemed a dubious and discreditable idea to men and women of conservative dispositions and ample fortunes.[16] More purely political considerations were added to the argument, notably the prediction that the fault lines between the French left and right would only be aggravated by a real alliance with Moscow. Diplomats who were inclined not to narrow the gap between France and the USSR drew upon another calculation. Given the strength of anti-Soviet animosities in England, would not a strengthened Franco-Russian accord have the unenviable result of distancing France from the United Kingdom? But it took a soldier to fashion the most compelling argument of all, precisely because it was a blend of ideological, political, diplomatic and strategic calculation.

Designed by one of the army's deputy chiefs of staff in late 1936, this argument went as follows. Fact: despite a surprising competence in certain areas, the Soviet military machine is in a state of disarray, incapable of fighting a major European war in the foreseeable future. Fact: Josef Stalin, like Lenin before him, is a splendid example of fanatic and opportunist, which is to say that Stalin will do anything to destroy capitalism – liberal or fascist. That includes befriending it, as the USSR has done by deals with Germany in 1922 and 1926, as it has done with France and Czechoslovakia in 1935. Prediction: despite assurances to defend the peace, and with it French security, Stalin will do whatever he can to provoke a war between the opposing forces of liberal and fascist capitalism – principally Britain and France versus Germany and Italy. Once the conflict is under-way, Russia will remain aloof until capitalism has dealt itself a mortal blow. Thereafter, the Red Army will pass triumphantly through Warsaw, Bucharest, Prague, Berlin, Brussels, Paris, Rome and London, eliminating the vestiges of resistance and installing communist regimes. In other words, the louder Stalin talks, the stronger his public utterances are against fascism, the more dangerous he is to the opponents of fascism and, especially, to the opponents of war.[17]

Who was right in this debate over the future? Once again, it is the question which is at fault. Only the simplifiers will insist on choosing between one set of arguments over the other, those who cannot lift more than one idea at a time. What we need to appreciate is the fact that both sets of arguments coexisted within French official circles, all the way through the 1930s, and that reasonable and prudent decision-makers knew that they could not be sure which forecasts would be borne out and which repudiated by events. In that sense, the same uncertainties applied to French readings of the USSR as they did to the appraisals of Belgium, Italy, Poland, and the countries of the Little Entente. Decisive and self-assured scholars will continue to fault them for vacillation and indecision. Those more impressed by the intricacies of circumstance and event will be more charitable.

Nor as yet have we exhausted the uncertainties which underlay French diplomatic ambiguity in the 1930s. Even from the perspective of potential friends and allies. As yet, nothing has been said of the two countries about which French officials came closest to consensus: the United Kingdom and the United States.

The United Kingdom was, without a trace of exaggeration, the key to the French vision of the war to come. The latter would begin with a German attack, quite possibly in the west, against France. When that attack failed, as it must, the Third Republic would slowly shift gears into a wartime economy, slowly take charge of an all-embracing industrial mobilization, and slowly accumulate a vast storehouse of resources for use in the second stage of the war, the offensive, victorious stage. For that to happen, the French navy would have to cut off Germany's vital imports, by means of a blockade conducted with the British navy. Conversely, significant quantities of vital imports to France would have to be carried in British bottoms, escorted by British naval vessels, from British production centres at home or from ports throughout the British empire. From coal and oil to aircraft engines and radar technology, British resources remained absolutely central to French calculations of how to win the next war.[18] Whatever might be said of the importance of Belgium, Italy and the others, this appraisal of Britain was in a category of its own.[19]

That does not mean, however, that reservations and contrary views were entirely absent. Even here there was ambiguity, although it was less ideological, political and strategic in nature than it was cultural. Great Power rivals since the days of early modern Europe, the French and British had only come together on rare occasions to fight a common enemy – once in the 1850s against Russia, and more recently in 1914 against Germany. And while victorious in both instances, their most recent 'victory' had led to a peace settlement with which neither was very happy and whose flaws each commonly credited to the machinations of the other. So it was that events unfolded from 1919, with the British only slowly coming to the view that the Anglo-French alliance would have to be reactivated if Germany got out of hand – but without being willing to say as much to the French – and the French developing a strategy for wartime which depended heavily on British participation – without exacting the requisite assurances from Whitehall. In such circumstances, it was easy enough for the British to suspect that they were being taken for granted, and that a less confident government in Paris might be more conciliatory towards Berlin and compliant towards London. In such circumstances, it was even easier for the French to suspect that the British were being deliberately obdurate and that they might even try to make their own deal with Hitler – as seemed to have been the case in June 1935 with the Anglo-German naval accord.[20] Such was the sense behind the expression 'la perfide Albion', not so much wicked England, as England ruthless in the pursuit of her national interests.

There is a hint here of something else that is cultural in nature and which also entered into French appreciations of the United States. The latter, too, was a reluctant but central player in the French approach to a long war, as befitted an industrial and financial giant. Certainly the French wanted to be able to count on the vast resources of the British and American empires, without whose assistance it was thought to be impossible to overpower Germany. But as in the case of their appraisals of Britain, French views of the United States also betrayed something of the dependant's resentment. There was a feeling that the great financial power of the 'anglo-saxons', while indispensable to another war effort, was a peacetime device manipulated to keep nations like France quiet and in their place. In other words, while Americans remained rigorously isolationist, determined to leave France and Europe to their fate, they were also determined to recover all of France's war debts before the Republic disappeared beneath a crest of German helmets. Understandably, given such a reading, French officials in Paris had very mixed feelings about America's contribution to the peace of Europe. On the one hand, the United States was a potential benefactor of unrivalled proportions for any French war effort. On the other hand, the American government seemed not to grasp the seriousness of the Nazi challenge to European peace, European democracy, even European civilization. Unmistakably, or so it seemed from Paris, the Americans exuded an irritating and dangerous mix of ignorance, naïveté, self-righteousness and financial self-interest.[21]

But, of course, the French appreciation of the problems at hand was anything but singular or uniform. Here, too, was a mix of certainty, probability and possibility, each categorized according to one's own prejudice and appreciation of paradox. Germany was the greatest threat to European peace, but not necessarily to the European social order. Despite the indigenous resource imbalance, Germany, the stronger of the two, had more to fear from a long war than France, the weaker of the two. In the interests of such a war, France would try to harness the resources of a fascist state, like Italy, with those of a communist regime in the Soviet Union, and add to the team countries which were as suspicious of Rome and Moscow as they were of Berlin. Strategically complex, diplomatically daunting, this was a crude formula thrown-up to cover as many contingencies as possible. No one appreciated its crudity more than the Quai d'Orsay where for a decade diplomats argued among themselves as to which 'ally' promised to be the most useful and the most reliable. Indeed, was there any ally as dependable as Germany was an enemy?

Repeatedly, throughout the decade, the answer from most soldiers, diplomats and statesmen was 'no'. Deprived of certainty on this score, and disillusioned by their inability to constrain Germany either through the international disarmament process or by means of the League of Nations Covenant, French governments realized that they had to concentrate on their own resources. Working from the premise of a surprise German attack, they laid down the plans and committed the funds for a formidable line of fortifications in eastern France, one which would protect the resource-rich provinces of Alsace and Lorraine. More than that, given its location, this line – soon to be named after war minister André Maginot – would further limit Germany's offensive options. Denied direct access to France's eastern departments, the German army would be forced to contemplate a drive either through neutral Switzerland or further to the north through Belgium. Unless, of course, desperation induced it to consider an attack through the rough and wooded terrain of the Ardennes forest between Luxembourg and southern Belgium. Since the latter possibility was deemed improbable, not to say foolhardy, French strategists concentrated their attention on the two remaining options.[22] A supplementary line of defences, concentrated around Belfort, would attend to a German move through Switzerland; and the Belgian avenue would be sealed off by means of French motorized columns rushing in to buttress Belgian defence forces along the rivers Meuse, Dyle or Escaut. Shut out on the Franco-Swiss border, on the Franco-German border, and the Belgian-German border, the Wehrmacht would have to accept all the risks associated with a long war: notably enemy naval blockade and a land war of accelerating attrition.[23]

Such was the outline, at least, of the French plan for victory, one which had to begin with a successful defence of French territory. It was not illogical, and it certainly was not impulsive.[24] Neither was it dependent on early allied assistance, even that of the Belgians. For it was always possible, if not desirable, for French forces to hold on their own frontier and so await a German army fresh from its victory over Belgium. In this respect, in the opening phase of the war, France could remain master of her own destiny, averting defeat if not securing victory.

That much is true, if incomplete. Compared to the imponderables which cloaked every diplomatic option, where friendships were less certain than enmities, the defence of French soil by French forces seemed a good deal more straightforward. Nevertheless, here too there was a succession of debates which further illustrate French doubts and uncertainties – doubts which afflict men of dubious character, or doubts which are the price paid by the sensible and reflective.

One of the most troublesome and enduring of these uncertainties arose from the natural tension between the strategies of a long war and a short war. That tension was expressed in a variety of ways. To begin with, it meant straddling both the fear of a surprise attack and the confidence with which one had to confront such an attack. In other words, too little confidence would undercut the chances of a successful defence; too much confidence would increase the danger by minimizing it. It proved a very fine line to walk for successive chiefs of staff in the 1930s. Early in the decade, General Maxime Weygand aroused government suspicions by too often sounding the alarm. Anxious to rearm France against a German threat as yet more potential than real, his principal card was that of stressing how a sudden attack might catch a still superior France sleeping. In part it was a device designed for future peril, and in part it worked. But it also gave rise to suspicions in some parliamentary quarters that the general was both a hawk and a liar. His successor, General Maurice Gamelin, faced a dilemma of another sort. Knowing the suspicions about Weygand's exaggerations, Gamelin replaced alarmism with self-assurance. But this was at a time, around 1936–7, when Germany was in a far stronger position to execute such an attack than she had been in 1933–4. Thus, whereas one general was criticized for magnifying the German threat, his successor was seen by some to be much too complacent – a criticism, of course, which peaked during his handling of the war in 1939–40.[25]

This was not easily resolvable, a judgement with which Gamelin would have been the first to concur. He could hardly forecast an early French defeat and thus the collapse of France's entire long war strategy, and yet he himself became increasingly concerned that members of the government were now impervious to the threat of a sudden German attack.[26] A related dilemma confronted him when it came to French allies. Since every effort had been made to secure their commitment to French security, he had little choice but to stick to the official scenario: France would first thwart the German attack and subsequently lead an allied coalition to victory. And if the attack first occurred in central Europe? It would hardly pay to state in advance that the French army would stay put, essentially ignoring Polish or Czech or Rumanian appeals for help. Rather, it made more sense to be ambiguous, if not outright misleading.

A second source of ambiguity in the French military response to Germany derived from the ongoing debate between the advocates of static defence and those of mobile defence. This is not the easiest of controversies to grasp in the wake of the famous armoured engagements of the Second World War. Today, even the vocabulary seems slanted, as words like 'static' do poorly against words like 'mobile'. But to understand the 1930s, one needs to fall back on the 1920s, not the 1940s.

Unlike the Germans, the French ended the First World War as victors, with more than a hundred infantry divisions intact, thousands of field guns, and a few thousand new tanks. Just as artillery pieces, fortified positions, and machineguns had staunched the flow of German troops towards Paris in 1914, in 1918 the same artillery units, together with the infantry, a newly mechanized cavalry, and a fledgling air force had ground the enemy down in one gathering strategic offensive. The Germans sued for peace in November, and by 1920 the demobilized French army had a surfeit of artillery weapons, tanks and airplanes. With hardly an enemy in sight. Even with the early forecasts of renewed German perfidy – as soon as the Boches had a chance to recover – this was no time to expect vast public expenditures on equipment for some future war. The best that could be expected, from the point of view of the military establishment, was that this used equipment could be integrated into the new plans for elaborate fortified zones in eastern France. In other words, while it seemed likely that the arguments for fixed fortifications would win the day in parliament – arguments which stressed the anticipated economies in French lives – it seemed just as likely that the French army would continue to refine its notions of mechanized and motorized warfare. If, for example, the future Maginot defences were to be fixed literally in concrete, the whole idea of the sweep into Belgium was predicated upon a mobile arm – one with enough speed and fuel range, enough firepower and armour protection to get to the Meuse defences and hold them.

But it is still 1920, or 1925, or 1930. The tank had been developed as an infantry support weapon, one which moved with the foot soldier, more or less at his pace. In short, it required no great capacity for speed, nor fuel range, and nothing much in communications equipment. Not until the infantry was carried by truck or half-track vehicles would the demands on its armoured attendant be changed appreciably. And in 1920, with the German army in disarray, or in 1925, with the Locarno spirit in the air, or in 1930, with all the talk of disarmament conventions, the political mood was not one which augured well for expensive mechanization programmes. Accordingly, French assessments of armoured vehicles were developed within an army which prided itself in comparatively immobile infantry and artillery regiments, and in superbly engineered, deep fortifications. Unsurprisingly, for a good decade the tank remained slow, overburdened with armour, endowed with a firepower better designed to handle opposing infantry than opposing tanks, and confined by fuel capacity to a limited operating radius. And for a good decade, there was little public debate over the wisdom of this doctrine, so well entrenched had it become and so sanctified by the Republic's greatest living heroes.

By the mid-1930s that debate was forced to become more public, and more animated. As fate would have it, it was Germany, France's most probable enemy, which was in the process of redefining the use of armour in warfare. In particular, and as reported by French intelligence, the Germans were experimenting with tank divisions, awarding to these units great latitude for operations that were largely independent of the infantry and artillery. These carried with them their own big guns, their own sappers and engineers, their own fuel and munitions, and as such were free to probe and penetrate enemy defences according to the judgment of their field commanders. French military officials, for the most part, thought this ill-advised and reckless to a fault. Their own field manoeuvres – with better armoured but slower moving tanks – had suggested that the Germans still had much to learn about the limitations of mechanized forces. After all, so they said in Paris, the Germans were relative newcomers to armoured units and would eventually have to take a page from France's book.[27]

Such conceits, it is true, made for some discomfort in some circles. Attempts to minimize, if not dismiss, German tests with panzer units, doubtless rang hollow in a few ears. Since Germany was the enemy most likely to launch a sudden attack, and since no-one could any longer deny the formidable firepower associated with tanks in concentration, there had to be some anxiety about whether the tank was better suited to freewheeling, slashing offensives, or to disciplined mobile defensive manoeuvres in conjunction with the infantry and the fortress artillery. To be wrong on this count, could mean disaster. Nor was it any longer possible to confine these uncertainties to confidential reports on French field trials or to intelligence reports on German experiments. In 1935 a young colonel by the name of De Gaulle, forced the debate into the open. Through published studies and private lobbying, this maverick officer upset the war ministry and high command by trumpeting the cause of armoured formations. Here, he said, was the wave of the future – an armoured, mobile cross between the big gun of the artillery and the machinegun regiments of the infantry. Free it from its tutelage to artillery and infantry, free it from the yoke of corps headquarters, and let it seek out and destroy a surprised enemy.[28]

So France did come to witness a debate over the best ways to employ this technology, out of which – it should be said with some emphasis – did come the army's three light-mechanized and three heavy armoured divisions. But the debate continued, as it did in Germany and Britain, and with it an enduring ambivalence. Those who were sold on the tank were nonetheless divided by the tension between the more autonomous concept of De Gaulle, and that of the coordinated, inter-arms concept favoured by the senior members of the general staff. Those more sceptical drew upon a variety of arguments to delay the tank's progress, ranging from the practical – the high cost and slow production time associated with a modern armoured vehicle – to the romantic – grease and petrol being poor replacements for fine leather and fresh hay.

Predictably, the subject of air power became yet another battle-ground between the confidence of traditionalists and the conviction of pioneers. And as usual, the debate both reflected and spawned uncertainties over the course to follow. The fact that the security of the nation might hinge on the outcome, did nothing to subdue the intensity of the debate or the depth of the misgivings. Here, too, there was ambivalence.

As in the case of the tank, there were instances of some very foolish things being said about the airplane, mainly by elderly infantry officers who had little faith in such modern contraptions. There was also an element of conflicting inter-service ambitions. Just as some were determined to keep the tank in the pocket of the infantry division, there were others who thought that the air units belonged there as well. Working from the officially endorsed premise that the infantry would remain the queen of the battlefield, in whose service the artillery and cavalry found their purpose, it was easy enough to see air and armoured units in the same light. No wonder, therefore, that eyebrows were raised when the air force was made an inde-pendent service in 1933, and made to understand that it should work with, rather than under, the army and navy. No wonder either, that the new arm attracted men whose vision of air power encouraged them to think of the land battle as subordinate to that in the air.

It was in the mid-1930s that the latter perspective found its fullest expression, in the arguments of the strategic bombing enthusiasts. Traditionally, since the mid-years of the last war, the air arm had flown reconnaissance and observation missions for the land army, and sometimes supported ground troops by machinegun fire and close support bombing. It was, after all, an arm of the land army. But an autonomous ministry and air staff seemed to justify a separate strategic role, just as the latter became part of the logic behind the new general staff. In brief, the idea was to send a large bombing force into the heart of enemy country early in a war, with a view to smashing that enemy's industrial infrastructure and demoralizing the civilian population. In the best of circumstances, such a bombing campaign might bring the enemy to its knees, before friendly ground forces had to sustain a single casualty. All being well, the air force could put both Germany, and the French army, in their place.

Naturally, the army took umbrage. The idea that wars could be fought and won solely through air power was absurd. So conceived, an air force built around long-range bombers would be of little use in that critical opening engagement when the French army was fighting for its life. Besides, it still remained unclear what the airplane could do against properly dug-in troops, or targets adequately defended by anti-aircraft guns. What was more, in its ambition to make air power the primary force in modern war, the French air force had done something particularly dubious. Intent on assuring itself of the strategic bombing mission, but mindful of army resistance, it had tried to develop a clandestine bomber. That is to say, rather than provoke further animosities by renouncing its reconnaissance, air defence and ground-support roles, the air force tried to develop a plane which could fulfil each of these missions – as well as that of strategic bombing. The result, so everyone had concluded by 1937, was a disappointment. The multiple-purpose machines could execute none of the individual missions as well as could specialized planes designed for specific roles.[29] And by then, by 1937, there was no longer any doubt that the German air force, the Luftwaffe, already had a fleet of bombers and fighters which far exceeded that of France in numbers and quality. What the airplane could do, against troops or civilians, how it should be used most effectively, were now questions of special import and urgency. Was it entirely clear, was there perfect accord, on how best to defend France?

All too familiar with the inherent tension between long and short war strategies, and seriously divided over the scale and employment of tanks and aircraft, the French engaged in one other defence-related debate. This differed from the preceding controversies, partly in the fact that this dispute was more one-sided and therefore less enduring, and partly in the fact that it had much more obvious political overtones. It was the issue of professional soldiers – long-service volunteers – versus citizen soldiers – short-service conscripts. Probably at the expense of his argument for armoured divisions, De Gaulle had argued that modern, high-tech weaponry like the tank was best maintained and employed by men who had been carefully trained for the job. Although the airplane was of less interest to him, the same argument could be made for the maintenance and operation of such sophisticated machines. In any event, the case was made first for much more intensive training and, second, for a much longer period of service than the current two-year period of conscript duty.

Made on such grounds, the argument provoked derision on others. It was not so much the training question that was sensitive, as it was the service question. Not for the first time, the Republic's leadership, military and civilian, rallied to the cause of the conscript soldier and against any significant increase in the numbers of career men. The latter, it was feared, would always identify more closely with the army than with the nation and its civilian population. Given the lingering suspicions that elements of the officer corps remained of uncertain loyalty to the Republic and to its democratic institutions, there were concerns that non-commissioned career soldiers might fall under the spell of suspected reactionaries much more easily than short-service conscripts who only wanted to get in and get out. And above all, the latter wanted no war, especially war that involved attacking someone else. Even if it were accepted that the training of the conscripts was bound to be less intensive than that of professionals, there was something to be said for ensuring that all of one's guns were held by citizen patriots.[30]

So the arguments went, ostensibly military-related arguments, but each of course being easily associated with competing political forces and interests. The case for the citizen soldier won the day or, more accurately put, was never seriously challenged – so deeply engrained was the connection between republican defence and an armed citizenry. Indeed, no voice was louder on its behalf than that of the army general staff, which felt that its job was difficult enough without anyone rekindling doubts about the army's loyalty to the Republic or its commitment to peace. Still, there were signs from time to time that the debate was never entirely dead – when internal reports sometimes cast doubts on the combat readiness of the conscript soldier, or when someone recalled that Hitler's expanding forces had been developed around the long-service army to which Germany had been confined in 1919.

Is it then, in the wake of such considerations, so difficult to fathom why French foreign policy seemed liable to the tug of competing currents, as suggested in Chapter 1, or why scholars have not been unanimous in their characterization of that policy, as argued in Chapter 2? More or less assured of their enemy, and of its intentions, French political and military *dirigeants* were far from unanimous when it came to military plans for averting defeat and diplomatic plans for ensuring victory through allied coalition. That should surprise no-one, and should not be regarded in any way as unique to France or the French. The fact is that the present can never be fathomed as confidently as we sometimes take the measure of the past. Ever mindful of their need for wartime allies, and familiar as they were with the assets associated with each potential ally – from the Belgians to the Americans – French statesmen never really knew upon whom they could count. Partly for that reason, they seemed willing to enlist anyone who would listen, unwilling to be too assertive or unequivocal. As for the defence of French security, should it come to that, they had trouble situating the danger of surprise attack within the forecast that such an attack would not succeed. The debate over the uses of armoured formations made them apprehensive, lest the official view be proven wrong; and that over air power led to as much anxiety as it did confident prophecy. The same was true for the debate over professional soldiers. It is easy, if untrue, to say that the French simply closed their minds to offensives, to armour, to air power, to career soldiers. It would be less easy, and even less true, to represent them in the opposite light: offensively-minded, entirely sold on tanks, aircraft and professional armies. The truth lies somewhere in between, between complacency and despondency, between doubt and certitude, between fear and confidence.

4 Consensus and Division: Politics and Ideology

The divisions which occurred over questions of diplomacy and strategic planning were not symptomatic of any exceptional fractiousness. If anything, they were part of a natural process of debate where the future was being pondered, where the stakes were high, in a country where dissent was still tolerated. But neither were they prompted solely by the obvious matters at hand, namely foreign policy and national defence. If the preceding discussion has identified some of the 'problems' confronting decision-makers in the 1930s, it has said next to nothing about the 'process'. It is this which takes us below the surfaces of diplomacy and defence, and affords a new look at the problems of peace and security, but from a different vantage-point. It is time, in other words, to say something about the institutions of decision-making in France of the 1930s, and something about that elite class of *dirigeants* to whom responsibility fell for attending to the national interest.

First, with respect to diplomacy, it may be worthwhile to outline the process by which policy emerges from debate. The latter is unlikely to be much in evidence at the primary, or embassy, level. The ambassador's job is to further, rather than impede, relations between France and the country to which he has been accredited; and it would be uncommon for him to brook overt opposition from any of his staff – councillors, secretaries or attachés – on how best to fulfil that mandate. In short, the view from the embassy is likely to be one in support of accommodation, entente or alliance – whether the country be Germany, Italy or Czechoslovakia. In fairness, however, it should be said that the ambassadors, too, often found themselves ambivalent about the best way to accomplish their task. In Berlin, and later in Rome, André François-Poncet occasionally wavered over how best to deal with Hitler and Mussolini, through soft words or strong, as did Léon Noel in Warsaw.[1]

By the late 1930s the reports from the European embassies were sent directly to the private *cabinet* of the foreign minister. The director of this office would then solicit commentary from: the head of the European desk, from the influential directorate for political and commercial affairs, and from the critically important secretary-general, Alexis Saint-Léger Léger.[2] The latter, the highest ranking member of the ministry's permanent civil service, is generally thought to have enjoyed unrivalled influence on a succession of ministers – an influence which goes part of the way to explaining why the British 'alliance' retained its pride of place and why those with Italy and Russia were left moribund. By contrast to the minister, any minister, Léger had become an institution within an institution. In 1938, he celebrated his 24th year as a career diplomat, and his 16th year at the Quai d'Orsay. Since becoming secretary-general in February 1933, he had witnessed the coming and going of six ministers, and twelve governments.

The minister, as one can discern even from this, was not in an enviable position. Given his predictable impermanence, he had nothing like the power he was supposed to have, especially when it came to his most senior officials. Given the party dynamics of cabinet government in France, where everything depended on coalition politics, his appointment might have come without any reference to previous experience or demonstrated aptitude. Given the French political tradition, which gave far more emphasis to domestic concerns and which meant that the cabinet 'plums' were the Interior, Finance, Justice and Public Works portfolios, his reward was a mixed blessing. If the accelerating sense of crisis in the 1930s gave to his office a somewhat heightened status, it also brought with it far more onerous and thorny responsibilities. All of this, the political impermanence, the relative inexperience, the mounting peril, made improbable any bold new personal initiatives. If decisiveness and audacity were all it took to dispel ambivalence, these were not the men nor the times. Not Laval, not Flandin, not Delbos nor Bonnet. Instead, they familiarized themselves rather than resolved the uncertainties over Russia, Italy, Germany, Poland; they familiarized their cabinet colleagues with the same arguments, on those occasions when foreign policy seems to have figured prominently on the cabinet's agenda;[3] and they did the same for parliament, on those infrequent occasions when international issues temporarily replaced those of domestic politics, economic recovery and social reform.

The foreign ministry's processes of information gathering and policy formulation were complemented by similar processes in the war, naval and air ministries. By the late 1930s it was common for France's principal embassies in Europe to have an attaché from at least two of the three services. These officers served as indirect advisers to the foreign ministry, through the device of the ambassador's reports to the Quai d'Orsay, and as direct advisers to whichever of the service ministries had been responsible for their appointment. In the case of the military attaché, he reported directly to the army staff's intelligence division, known as the *Deuxième Bureau*. From there, data and assessments were forwarded upward, through the chief of the army staff to General Gamelin, the chief of the general staff for national defence; and it was he who was expected to be the government's principal military adviser – specifically through the office of the minister for war and national defence.[4] Between 1936 and 1940 that minister was Edouard Daladier, a man whose exceptional tenure at national defence was further underscored by his coterminous premiership between 1938 and 1940. What this meant, in real terms, was that whenever the French cabinet met in 1938 or 1939, it had among its numbers a handful of quasi-experts. The air and naval ministers, through their respective *cabinets militaires*, chiefs of staff, intelligence bureaus and attachés, were fully cognizant of the strategic issues confronting their departments. The minister for war and national defence had been similarly apprised, through the same advising process within his ministry as well as through the services of the permanent secretariat for national defence and the interministerial council known as the *Conseil Supérieur de la Défense Nationale*.[5] The foreign minister, too, had every reason to be well acquainted with the nation's diplomatic and security concerns. Not only was he the beneficiary of the foreign policy data and advice generated through the embassies and the ministerial experts, but he was also privy to information that was exchanged, daily, between his officials and the army's intelligence service. There can be little doubt, therefore, that the Daladier government was amply informed of the diplomatic and strategic challenges posed by a rearming Germany, amply conversant with the foreign policy options confronting the Third Republic, and with the most fundamental issues of national defence.[6] The layers of ambivalence which we have tried to expose in previous chapters were not the deposits of ignorance. They were there because the readings of the knowledge base were disparate and contradictory. They were there because permanent officials in the foreign and defence ministries, and imper-manent cabinet ministers, could not agree on the best way to solve the German problem and all the others attendant to it.

The Legislature was no better, and pretty much for the same reasons. Despite periodic, and predictable, complaints that the government was always going behind the back of parliament and so corrupting the democratic process, there is little reason to believe that deputies and senators were kept ignorant of the overriding diplomatic and strategic issues of the day. And no reason to think that more frequent debate would have averted either the war or the defeat. It is true that parliament, traditionally and of its own accord, spent little time debating international issues, partly because the constitution had reserved a special foreign policy role to the Presi-dent of the Republic, and partly because it was domestic politics which were the key to re-election. It is also true that public discussion about the reliability of friendly or unfriendly states, or about the nation's current defence deficiencies, could be badly abused by the indiscreet and the ignorant. That said, the fact remains that there were cases of extended debate in the Chamber and Senate, where the premier or the foreign minister was called to account for the government's action, or inaction: Flandin addressed the German reoccupation of the Rhineland in 1936, as did Blum and Delbos the policy of non-intervention in Spain, Daladier and Bonnet the Czech crisis, Daladier the outbreak of war.[7] But far more important, from the point of view of keeping informed the elected representatives of the people, was the system of parliamentary *commissions*. It was here, in the Chamber's committees on foreign affairs or on finance, or the Senate's on national defence or the air force, that some 40 par-liamentarians per committee had frequent opportunity to familiarize themselves with international issues and rearmament costs, strategic planning and air defence.[8] Though sworn to keep secret much of the information provided by ministers and their professional advisers, these politicians were at liberty to keep party colleagues abreast of developments and to circulate less sensitive material through the party presses. Once again, their failure to agree on the answers should in no way sustain the plea that they were kept in a state of ignorance.

That failure is attributable to other causes, not the least of which were the intrinsic uncertainties which confounded predictions of where Hitler would take Germany, or Mussolini Italy, or Stalin

Russia or, for that matter, Joseph Beck Poland. But France's parliament had other problems, at the heart of which was a democratic process dependent on voting majorities in a country where no political party came close to commanding a majority in either house. In 1938–9 the Chamber of Deputies showed a roster of some 615 members, half of whose votes, theoretically, were needed to sustain the government of the day. Yet those 308 votes had to be solicited from a house in which at least 17 different political groupings flourished – the largest one of which had precisely half the required strength. To further complicate matters at the end of the 1930s, that particular block of votes was registered under the 'Groupe Socialiste' – deputies who were not at all comfortable with either the foreign or domestic policies of the incumbent Daladier government.[9]

Neither could that government expect much support from the 73 deputies sitting under the banner of the 'Groupe Communiste'; nor from the 186 deputies scattered between the 40 members of the centre-right 'Groupe de l'Alliance des Républicains de Gauche et des Radicaux Indépendants' and the 52 members of the conservative 'Groupe de la Fédération Républicaine de France'. Instead, Daladier had to rely mainly on a tenuous block of votes from the centre-left benches which, when voting as a block, could get close to an effective majority. That consideration, of course, does much to explain the composition of the cabinet which was called upon to address the Czech crisis in September 1938. With luck and prudence the Prime Minister could count on his own 'Groupe Républicain Radical et Radical-Socialiste' – particularly by distributing portfolios to those associated with the left-wing of the 'groupe' – people like Jean Zay (Education), Anatole de Monzie (Public Works), Charles Pomaret (Labour), Marc Rucart (Health), Guy La Chambre (Air) – those in its centre – like César Campinchi (Navy), Jules Julien (Post and Telegraph), and Fernand Gentin (Commerce) – as well as those on its right, people like Georges Bonnet (Foreign Affairs), Paul Marchandeau (Finance) and the three important senators: Camille Chautemps (Vice-Premier), Albert Sarraut (Interior) and Henri Queuille (Agriculture).[10] But at best there were only 117 votes among ministers and Radical backbenchers – which is why coalition politics were not only natural in France but *de rigueur*.

Raymond Patenôtre (National Economy) was recruited from the 'Groupe de l'Union Socialiste et Républicaine', a contingent of some 28 deputies who sat to the left of the Radicals. Louis de Chappedelaine was placed in charge of the Merchant Marine, partly because he had access to nearly 40 votes in the 'Groupe de la Gauche Démocratique et Radicale Indépendante'. Paul Reynaud was given the Justice portfolio, partly with an eye to the 42 votes clustered in the 'Alliance des Républicains de Gauche et des Radicaux Indépendants'. Further still to the right were the 14 deputies of the 'Groupe Démocrate Populaire' from whose ranks came the Veterans Affairs minister Auguste Champetier de Ribes; and from the 26 seats claimed by the 'Groupe des Indépendants Républicains' came Georges Mandel, Daladier's new minister of Colonies. Altogether, with luck and assiduous massaging, the best the Prime Minister could hope for was to keep in hand some 260 votes, to which he might add another 50 to 60 occasional votes from almost anywhere on the political spectrum – from the substantial communist block to the tiny right-wing cluster called the 'Indépendants d'Union Républicaine et Nationale'.[11]

This was not a context well suited to abrupt decision-making, even in the best of circumstances. International crises only aggravated the problem, for if such crises sometimes reinforced domestic solidarity, they could also magnify both the political and temperamental differences among cabinet ministers. The Czech crisis of September 1938 is a case in point. Although the government did weather the crisis, essentially by quietly abandoning the Czechs, it did so only after sustained debate. Foreign Minister Bonnet was the principal force behind this policy of peace with-or-without-honour. Himself on the right of the Radicals, he drew support from across the reaches of this peculiar, broad-based 'groupe' – from Chautemps and Marchandeau through to Pomaret and de Monzie.[12] His principal opponents were Mandel, Reynaud and Champetier de Ribes, none of whom was a member of the Radical block, all of whom were inclined to risk war now, with the Czechs, rather than risk it later, without them. And then there was the concentration of cabinet votes, all of it Radical though initially more inclined to Mandel than Bonnet: Daladier himself, Sarraut, Campinchi, La Chambre, Zay, Gentin, Queuille, Rucart, Julien, Chappedelaine, and Patenôtre.[13] Here was the heart of the centrist influence within the Radical group, men who listened to Mandel's case for resistance, as well as to appraisals from civil and military experts: England could not be counted on, neither could the Soviet Union or Poland; the army could do nothing to prevent the destruction of Czechoslovakia, or the air force the destruction of France.[14] All this, together with a divided cabinet and a fragile parliamentary base, led to a resolution which was closer to Bonnet than Mandel: insistence that France would honour her treaty obligations – in the event that Germany actually attacked Czechoslovakia – but would brow-beat the Czechs into the kinds of territorial concessions which would obviate the need for Hitler to attack.

Parliament, adjourned for its summer recess, played no direct role at all in the resolution of the September crisis. That is not to say, however, that the forces which could be counted on to animate its corridors and amphitheatre went on vacation as well. Not for a moment was the Daladier government left bereft of advice from the groups which had departed the Palais Bourbon. Not for a moment was the premier allowed to forget that his cabinet rested on a precarious coalition of disparate political forces. Indeed, there was daily evidence of the tensions, the suspicions, the hostilities which surged from both ideological shorelines. From the pages of *L'Humanité* and *Ce Soir* – with combined daily sales of some 600 000 copies – the communist party forecast the worst, unless the Soviet Union were recognized as a key player in the struggle against fascism. From the pages of *Le Journal* and *Le Matin* – with combined daily sales of 700 000 copies – one could extract evidence aplenty of communist machinations at home and abroad, as well as praise for the anti-Marxist policies employed in Rome and Berlin. And these two were only centrist papers by right-wing standards, not to be compared with the monarchist *L'Action française* or the weekly, profascist remonstrances of *Gringoire* and *Je suis partout*, and certainly not to be confused with the anti-Nazi proclamations in the new *L'Epoque* of Henri de Kérillis. Not surprisingly, there was much less certainty to be found across the broadly defined reaches of the centre itself – stretching from the socialist *Le Populaire* through the Radical *L'Oeuvre* to the more conservative *Le Temps* and the still more conservative *L'Echo de Paris*. Here, and presumably among their more than half-million readers, the questions all remained unanswered – whether fascism or communism was the greater evil, whether alliance with one was more perilous than the enmity of the other, whether peace was best assured through deterrence or conciliation, whether Czechoslovakia was really worth the price of another Franco-German war.[15] Ambivalent about everything except the stakes at play, the majority of Daladier's ministers were torn between the confident if contradictory forecasts of the left and right-wing press and their own reluctance to predict either the likelihood of confrontation with Germany or its probable outcome.

Parliament was back in session by 4 October. It was then that it was given a brief opportunity to hear the government's account of the Munich settlement and, in indirect fashion, to vote its support for what had happened. It was a moment when the country's relief was at its highest. France might have been discomfited by Hitler's brashness, even humiliated by the necessity of having to appease him, but the peace had been spared. That relief briefly papered over most of the internecine cracks, leaving only one or two conservative nationalists on the one margin and the communists on the other to condemn the backing-down to Berlin, the sellout of Prague and – so the communists feared – the future sellout of Moscow. However, the old rancours and suspicions were quick to resurface when the government tried to use the recent crisis to strengthen its executive powers. France, Daladier argued, urgently needed to redress the kinds of national defence deficiencies which had been exposed by the threat of war. The vote again went his way, but far more narrowly than that which had endorsed his handling of the crisis. This time, over 200 abstentions were added to the nearly 80 votes which had been assembled against Munich and against the bid for special powers.[16] In other words, almost half of the lower house, principally the communists, socialists and republican socialists, lacked confidence in the government's approach to foreign and defence policies. Clearly, their sense of what the Third Republic stood for, ideologically, was different from that of the centre-left vision entertained by the moderate majority among the governing Radical Socialists, and even more different from that promoted by either the conservative or the radical right.

Before undertaking an inquiry into these differences, however, it may be worth taking a moment to characterize the people whom I have called the *dirigeants*. For the fact is that, whatever the differences that divided them, there tended to be certain similarities that distinguished them – elected and unelected public servants – from the public at large. Members of the diplomatic, officer and parliamentary corps typically enjoyed levels of education that were far in excess of the national average. Most had finished off their secondary education with the coveted *baccalauréat*, and then proceeded to university faculties of law and medicine or to elite establishments like the *Ecole Normal Supérieure*, or the *Ecole Libre des*

Sciences Politiques or, in the case of civil as well as military engineers, the *Ecole Polytechnique*. Education such as this, of course, suggests at least three other characteristics which most of the *dirigeants* had in common. Few had immediate family roots in either the urban working class or the peasantry. Fewer still had any interest in leading proletarian lifestyles – whether or not they called themselves communists, socialists, radicals, or men of the left. But many had the aptitude and interest to engage in journalism, not only as readers of the nation's countless dailies, weeklies and monthlies, but as contributors, in some cases editors, even as publishers. Removed as they had been from the average condition – background, education, employment – these were men, especially those in politics, who knew something about animating as well as listening to the public debates which swirled back and forth from left to right.[17]

The French parliamentary Right in 1938–9 was inspired mainly by conservative republicanism, rather than by monarchism or fascism. Indeed, five of the nine groups which sat to the right of the Radicals in the Chamber had even incorporated into their name some formal reference to the Republic. In short, the vast majority of these deputies had long since reconciled themselves to the loss of the monarchy and to the corresponding installation of the Republic. What mattered now was no longer the form but the substance of this, France's third, Republic. Abroad, the obligation of the Republic was identical to that of the Bourbon monarchy or the Bonapartist empire – namely to assure the security of metropolitan and imperial borders and to advance the prestige and material interests of France in all domains. At home, it was to maintain public order in ways consistent with the customs and institutions of a participatory democracy; ensure that any state intervention in the economy was kept compatible with the interests of private property and capital; instil patriotism within its citizenry; and defend the cultural and religious traditions which generations of French elites had made the envy of the world. Emphases, of course, varied from group to group and from one member of parliament to another. Some were more obsessed with the threats posed by Marxism, or by the union movement, while others were confident that such perils could be contained if Frenchmen remained faithful to the Catholic Church. Some were preoccupied with the security threat posed by Germany, while others latched on to the idea that France's future lay not so much in Europe as in her empire. Whatever their particular anxiety or proposed solution, characteristically these were men who never again wanted to see the excesses of revolutionary change.[18]

That resolve was rooted not merely in 1793, 1830, 1848 or 1871. It had reappeared in 1936 and 1937, brought into full bloom by the menace of the Popular Front programme. The latter had been the brainchild of the French left – radicals, socialists, and communists – and was intended to be a counter-response to the threat of fascism at home and abroad and to the threat of the economic depression which had finally settled its full weight on France.[19] Brought to power in June 1936, in the form of Léon Blum's government, the Front first alarmed and then outraged the whole of France's political right – from the dominant conservative republicans right through to the monarchists whose time had passed, and the fascists whose time was nearing.[20]

Predictably, the Front's foreign policy was only an aggravation of its domestic offences. Conservatives, typically, were not upset by Foreign Minister Delbos' rather low-key attempts to consolidate France's ties with the countries of the Little Entente. It was fitting that France should cultivate a network of client states, here as elsewhere, and the more so if such 'allies' might someday be asked to prove their mettle in the defence of French security. More questionable was the government's apparent disdain for Italy, to whom many deputies and senators looked for help against Hitler. More outrageous were the furtive attempts to enter into staff talks with the Soviet Union, and the less than furtive promotion of Franco-Soviet cooperation by the outspoken Air minister, Pierre Cot. In other words, there was little this government was likely to do which politicians and journalists on the right were unlikely to condemn – including the failure to intervene in Spain on behalf of the Church and the nationalist cause of General Franco.

But the real battle was joined inside France, where labour disturbances through the summer of 1936 convinced many among the propertied classes that revolution was but hours away. Apart from its initiative in rearmament – through an ambitious programme generally supported by the parliamentary right – the government was pilloried by conservative spokesmen in parliament, press and public square. It had blundered into the economy and left chaos in its wake. Production costs had soared, they said, and productivity plummeted, thanks to the new 40-hour work week, the new regime of paid vacations, and the new proposals to nationalize a portion of the air and armament industries. Similarly, the government's decision to devalue the franc in August 1936 had the double effect of raising the costs of imported goods while diminishing French prestige in world money markets.[21]

There was no mistaking the levels to which fear and disgust had risen among conservative and very conservative circles. Although it now seems improbable that a moderate socialist like Blum could stir such pools of animus, the fact is that the ideological schism which had brought the Popular Front to power in 1936 remained deep and unbridgeable when that Front essentially dissolved in the spring of 1938. And it this which is part of the background to the Czech affair later that year, and the political calculations which Daladier had to make when forming a cabinet in April, holding it together through August and September, and soliciting the support of parliament in October.

By then, the fortunes of the Right were clearly improving, a trend signalled by Daladier's decision to put Paul Reynaud into the Finance ministry on 1 November and, almost simultaneously, to come down hard on the organizers of a would-be general strike. Certainly conservative witnesses were not blind to the fact that the prime minister who grudgingly had accommodated Hitler at Munich, now seemed more keen on keeping Stalin at bay and French workers under his thumb. Which is to say that by 1939 French conservatives were feeling less alienated from the Republic than had been the case two or three years earlier. This, of course, is less true of the radical Right, whose disgust with the Republic was carrying it closer and closer to an advocacy of fascism, German or Italian style, and whose popularity was waning accordingly.[22] But for the load-bearing ranks of parliamentary conservatism, the Republic had executed at least a partial return to its senses. The 40-hour week was being swept away in the rush to rearm, the state had reiterated the authority of the *patronat*, the franc was strengthening, and investors were bringing their money back from foreign refuges. What is more, conservative deputies and senators were mindful of the fact that in France, whatever its imperfections, there was still a free press, still freedom of religious conscience, still the rule of law. The Republic, in their eyes, may have done shameful things since its inception in 1870, may have flirted with Marxism and anti-clericalism, may have tried to raise the masses and level the elite. And for this it remained suspect. But it had done much to promote France's imperial interests, it had fought a victorious war against Germany, and it had avoided the worst excesses of Stalin's regime and Hitler's regime. No mass purges of suspected political opponents, no death camps. And for this it remained worthy. Between these two, the suspicion in which the Republic was still held, the worthiness which was now attributed to it, is to be found the ambivalence of the French Right.

The 224 deputies who sat to the right of the Radicals in 1938 were almost perfectly balanced by the 229 deputies on the Chamber's Left.[23] For them, the 73 Communists and 156 Socialists, the Republic meant something different from what it meant to the conservative Right. Not completely different, but different nonetheless. Certainly if the Right looked on the record of the Third Republic with suspicion, the same was true for their ideological opposites on the Left. If the Right could be thankful that the Republic had not realized the worst of their fears, the Left was disappointed that it had never realized the best of its promises. Indeed, from its inception in 1870–1, or so it was argued, it had stood with the army and the propertied classes against the protests and ambitions of the working class. It was this alliance which had been responsible for the bloody suppression of the Paris *communards*, and the judicial suppression of those who had survived the firing squads. It was the same alliance, that of capital and state force, which had slowed the pace of industrial and social reform in pre-1914 France, which had slowed the growth of public and private sector unions and, in a different sense, which had slowed the erosion of Catholic influence in the schools. Intent as it was on resisting Marxist impulses in France, and rooting out anarchism, this was a Republic which at times seemed too tolerant of anti-semitism, too soft on the anti-republicanism which was said to flourish in the war ministry and among the general staff. Simply put, and again in the argot of the Left, this was a bourgeois Republic which was far more committed to order than to change, to capital than labour, to tradition than innovation.

Recent history had confirmed the more ancient. Anxious to reestablish its imperium in Europe and abroad, France under the Republic had become embroiled in the war of 1914, and in its course had milked the venom of nationalism as effectively as had the German Kaiser. And in the postwar period it had used force against Arab nationalisms in the Levant and Africa, force against Lenin's fledgling regime in Russia, force against the new German Republic and its defiant coal miners.[24] More recently still, in 1934–5, centre-right governments in Paris had followed a predictable course abroad and at home. They had wooed Russia enough to isolate her from Germany, and then had stopped, a relationship neither curtailed nor consummated. They seemed far more keen on fascist Italy, at least until late in 1935 when it seemed that it was France which had been led astray as part of Mussolini's designs on Ethiopia; and that betrayal had been matched by the government's willingness to see the League of Nations collapse from embarrassment.[25] Domestically, the same conservative governments had refused to devalue the currency – of which their own backers had a great deal – and instead clung stubbornly to deflationary methods which reduced state expenditures and public service salaries while it raised interest rates, the value of the franc and the prices of French exports abroad.

For a time, about a year and a half, it seemed that this diagnosis had found considerable public endorsement. In 1936–7 the Popular Front governments of Blum and Camille Chautemps were given an opportunity to address France's foreign and domestic problems from a leftist perspective – one informed by the competing visions of Communists, Socialists and Radicals. That internal competition, of course, proved to be central to their short-lived collaboration, but so too did the resistance organized by conservatives in the public service, in the armed forces, in the business community, in parliament and the press. Blum was shaken by the intensity of the opposition, as well as by the animus to which that opposition had given rise within the ranks of his own followers. By the end of 1937 the old view of the Republic was reasserting itself, a selfish, grasping bourgeois creature which lashed out at the poor and then fled behind its monnied barricades.

1938 brought worse news. The Front was truly dead. Czechoslovakia was abandoned and staked out, as the communists saw it, as part of Hitler's route towards the Soviet Union. The Radical Paul Marchandeau was replaced as Finance minister by Paul Reynaud of the conservative (despite its name) 'Alliance des Républicains de Gauche', a replacement welcomed by the bankers and bosses. The government backed off many of the Popular Front's labour reforms, crushed the attempt at a general strike, and temporarily imprisoned some of the strike leaders. Throughout the country there was talk of the 'employers' revenge', the time when scores could be settled for the audacity, ignorance, and disrespect which the workers had shown towards their employers in 1936. And if the will to punish slowly diminished in the final months before the war – as the economy recovered, unemployment declined and profits soared – the resentment felt by the far Left in particular abated little. By its lights, the labour movement had buckled under pressure and allowed itself to be depoliticized, and in late August 1939 the Soviet Union had been driven by Anglo-French inertia into making its own pact with Hitler. Whether the mark of pure stupidity or capitalist machinations, the government's policy was condemned by French communists who energetically defended themselves against charges of Stalin's perfidy, and took the subsequent outlawing of their party as a badge of honour.

Numerically, of course, the Socialists were more than twice the strength of the Communists; and it was among them in particular that the Left's ambivalence towards the Republic is more evident. These men and women, most of them inspired in varying degrees by Marxism, had no illusions about the middle-class character of the Third Republic, and few disagreements about what that meant: slow to change, sensitive to the arguments of capital, half-deaf to the claims of the poor. Read by them, the Republic's history only confirmed what Daladier's policies in 1938–9 made transparent. But for all that, for all of its vices, the Republic was better than the Bourbons or the Bonapartes. It had slowly shoved aside monarchists and imperialists, it had proven itself capable of some social and educational reform, it had pulled France together to resist German militarism in 1914, and if it had conspired against the Popular Front it had also permitted its appearance. What is more, as a Republic, it had come nowhere near the excesses of Stalin's regime in Moscow, or that of Hitler in Berlin. No mass purges of suspected political opponents, no death camps. And for this it remained worthy. Between these two, the suspicion in which the Republic was still held, the worthiness which was now attributed to it, is to be found the ambivalence of the French Left.

Ambivalence was also visible on the current of the French Centre, if less clearly than on those of Left and Right. For one thing, the light was poor, obscured by the necessity of having to spot a group known as Radical Socialists out in the moderate mainstream. Indeed, they were the dominant centrist force, far ahead of the equally deceptive 'Union Socialiste et Républicaine' and the 'Gauche Indépendante'. As well, this centrist 'party' contained, however uneasily, its own collection of competing currents – ranging from those inspired by a quasi-socialism to those of a restrained but practised conservatism. The key to its surface cohesion lay in a lack of discipline, which is to say that it was not really a 'party' in the modern English sense of the word. Finally, there is the problem of seeing the Radicals in the midstream when they were outflanked – not on the left but the right – by some 80 moderate conservatives who called themselves 'Gauche Démocratique' and 'Alliance des Républicains de Gauche'. In short, the waters of this river are not easy to read, the more so when its Centre of 160 deputies – from the 'Union Socialiste et Républicaine' to the Radical Socialists – is overpowered by more than 200 deputies to the Right as well as to the Left.

Given the licence which has been taken on such matters, whether in vocabulary or logic, I will venture to characterize this Centre as 'liberal' – a word which does something to accommodate their own sense of being on the 'left' while disallowing any suggestion that they were either radical or socialist. And it is here, particularly among the 100 or more Radicals, that one can recapture that vision of the Third Republic which inspired the largest, non-socialist political 'groupe' within the Chamber and Senate.[26]

In the case of the Radicals, at least in the late 1930s, the record of the Republic was predominantly positive. By then, certainly, they had become a voice of the Establishment, attuned to the responsibilities and perquisites of government, and in this sense characteristically different from the loud accusations which were voiced from the left and the right. At one time, before the last war, they too had been associated with dissent, excoriating the regime for its clericalism, racism, militarism, imperialism, and financial conservatism. Now, it was they who were attacked by the socialist left for practising the very vices they once had condemned. The right, to be sure, saw things differently, accusing Radical governments of undermining the social foundations of France – through secular education, liberal immigration laws, anti-militarism, anti-imperialism and anti-capitalism. Thus defined, by critics who wanted no part of them and by their own volition, the Radicals assumed the mantle of the ruling 'party' and reassessed the Republic in that light.

Predictably, they heralded as virtues those which had been only grudgingly acknowledged by their critics on either flank. The Republic had proven itself open to reform, without being reckless. Since 1870 it had been responsible for improvements to the working and living conditions of urban and rural workers, without thoroughly alienating the ranks of property holders and investors. It had curtailed the influence of the Catholic clergy in education, and yet eventually had engineered accommodations with the Gallican Church and the Vatican. By fastening upon the altruistic, 'civilizing' role of great white powers, it had kept alive the idea and substance of the empire, just as it had embraced the traditional institutions of the army and the navy by marketing the idea of republican, democratic, citizen-soldiers. It had quashed the *communards* of 1871, the anarchists of the 1890s, the strikers of 1938, with a zeal that could only be applauded by French conservatives; but it had also defended itself against the unconstitutional challenges which had come from the disaffected right – from pre-war generals like Mac-Mahon and Boulanger, to the violent, street-brawling extremism of right-wing *ligues* in the 1930s. It was in fact a liberal Republic, and like all things liberal, it had earned much anger and some respect from a left, which saw it as too conservative, and from a right, which saw it as too radical.

That is not too say, however, that the Centre in general, or the Radicals in particular, were entirely satisfied with the Republic as it had come to be. Like sensible people anywhere, they had not yet confused this place with paradise. And in their discomfort with the way the Republic worked, in their misgivings about its defects, they shared with both the left and right a sense that all was not well. Proud of the Republic's adaptive capacities and attendant accomplishments, but made uneasy by these misgivings, centrist deputies were among those parliamentarians who could not entirely shake a sense of ambivalence towards the Third Republic. For them, the historical record had given rise to two sources of unease, one of which was constitutional in character, the other moral.

At the heart of the first was still more ambivalence. Coming as it did in the wake of the second Bonapartist experiment, the Third Republic was slowly moulded into a regime which would afford few chances for the abuse of executive power. What that meant, given the fact that its written constitution had been greatly influenced by monarchists intent on a Bourbon revival, was that precedence and practice would be used to constrain the powers of the President – and his appointed first minister – and amplify the authority of the elected Legislature.[27] From the 1880s onward, that was the trend, notwithstanding the energetic resolve of a President like Poincaré or a Premier like Clemenceau who, while often at cross-purposes, were resolved to resist the tyranny of parliament. But on balance the current was running against them. Time and time again, deputies who saw one peril in the existing government, and deputies who saw another, combined to repudiate the fragile coalition upon which the government depended and to send it packing. Ever fearful that power would be abused by the executive and used irresponsibly, parliament determined to withhold the power but to insist on accountability. What that meant was that every cabinet was kept on a very tight leash, subject at short notice to an *interpellation* during which deputies could not only pose questions to the minister but turn his response into an opportunity for a vote of non-confidence in the government.

This custom, of course, had at least two results. It explains why, for example, France knew 43 premiers between Clemenceau's government of 1917 and Pétain's Vichy regime of 1940, an average of more than two per year. It also says something about the derision with which executive authority was too often received not only in parliament, but in the press and in other branches of the public media. The predictable impermanence of the incumbent regime did nothing for its authority, and nothing to make more credible its efforts either to change or to preserve. Too often it was seen as a creature of parliament, stretched and twisted to accommodate too many differences. Too seldom was it understood that the very efforts to tie it to the will of the people's representatives ensured that unelected public servants would be left to formulate and execute national policy. Therefore, if France's famous ministerial instability bred a dangerous disdain for executive power among those least likely to exercise it, it also induced a certain despair and frustration on the part of those who would.

Related in a fashion to this matter of constitutional practice was the second source of misgiving, one which I have called moral. It is the matter of patronage, or worse, influence-peddling, or worse still, corruption. One could hardly enumerate the venial and mortal sins which have been gathered and then dropped at the feet of this fallen Republic, sins recorded by participants – left and right – and by observers – foreign and domestic. However unique this is to France, whatever its accuracy, and whatever the disarming ease with which a corrupt regime fits snugly into the defeat of 1940, there is certainly a widespread perception that the Third Republic ran on the oil of financial advantage. Before and after 1914 there were celebrated instances – from the Panama scandal in the 1890s to that of Stavisky in the 1930s – where some of the state's elected and unelected *dirigeants* seemed guilty of financial impropriety. Cabinet ministers could award lucrative contracts, deputies could find jobs for the undeserving, public servants could leak confidential financial information, newspaper editors could be influenced by favours here or there. And with all of this, there may well have arisen a sense of disgust among still honest men and women – in parliament, public service, press and public. This, together with the ephemeral nature of French cabinets, could have qualified the fidelity of some French citizens to the Republic, even those who supported and benefited from the policies of the Radical Socialists. Long castigated for its corrupt and seamy nature, by the right and left respectively, the Republic sometimes shook the confidence of centrists as well. And in those moments of doubt and uncertainty could be found expressions of further ambivalence.

The light cast by the preceding survey of political process and ideological context serves one purpose. It displays a little more of the problem at hand. Indeed, far from making it more soluble – as light metaphors usually imply – this inquiry has suggested that the ambivalence of interwar France has more corners and edges than was perceived at the outset. Beneath the uncertainties and indecision which plagued the conduct of foreign policy, beneath those which animated the debates over national defence, were those of a political and ideological character. How much decisiveness could one expect from governments which were unlikely to last a year, coalition governments which were always scrambling for their majority in a parliament determined to circumscribe their authority? Confronted by diplomatic advice to consolidate the alliance with Soviet Russia, and by equally authoritative advice to forge a bond with Fascist Italy, these governments of the 1930s hesitated. On the one hand, they could not predict the behaviour of Stalin or Mussolini, on the other, they could predict the divisiveness which a decision would cause within the cabinet, and the uproar which would be heard either from the benches on the left or from those on the right. How much decisiveness could one expect on some of the key issues of national defence? Because no-one wanted another war, there were parliamentarians who believed the key to peace rested on disarmament and

Franco-German accommodation, and parliamentarians who were convinced that rearmament was the answer. Some believed that the road to salvation was paved by professional soldiers, others that this was the road to damnation. There were parliamentary strategists on the right, and on the left, who argued that long-range bombing was the best insurance for peace, and others, on right and left, who dismissed aircraft as an empty shell or as a weapon too formidable to be developed by civilized people. Across the benches, from left to right, there were deputies who feared that war was more of a threat from the moment one accepted it as a possibility – and others who feared that it was at its most dangerous when that possibility was discounted.

And as these references to the political spectrum suggest, part of what underlay the debate over diplomatic choices and national defence priorities, was the ideological complexion of the respondents. Which Republic was one trying to defend, as perceived by what minority? The harlot regime savaged by the monarchist-inspired *Action Française*, the bankers' regime despised by the Communists, the liberal and progressive regime applauded by Radicals, the unimaginative but safe regime tolerated by moderate conservatives, the regime that had taken France to new glories during World War One, the regime that too often had been smeared with the brush of scandal? Little wonder that even the *dirigeants* did not agree on the answers to the nation's diplomatic and defence problems, for they did not agree on the problems.

5 Economic Prophecies and Counter-Prophecies

Economic calculation was yet another source of French ambivalence, that is to say the relationship between the country's productive resources and the demands placed upon them by the German problem. This calculation already has figured in our analysis, however implicitly, for in many respects it is at the foundation of the ideological debate. The political left, which characteristically associated themselves with the ordinary citizen, saw fascism as the primary evil of their time. Its emphasis upon nationalism and social discipline was antithetical to the interests of workers who needed international peace as a condition for improving their lot at home. Indeed, French socialists and communists subscribed to the view that fascism was nothing more than a particularly ugly form of capitalism. The political right, which characteristically attracted spokesmen from the possessing classes, saw fascism differently. Most, it would be fair to say, did not see it as an appropriate answer to their concerns; but in the anti-left protestations of the regimes in Berlin and Rome, they did see a commendable resistance to what they regarded as the primary evil of their time: socialism–communism. As for the political centre, and once more characteristically, its practitioners were people of modest fortunes whose concerns about Marxist-inspired property expropriations were at least partially offset by alarm over fascist incursions into civil liberties.

The preceding equations between levels of affluence and levels of conservatism are familiar enough, especially to those who attribute to them the constancy and precision of mathematics. I am not among them. Indeed, my reason for suggesting that politics are a front for economics is rather different. It seems unlikely to me that behind the diplomatic and strategic ambivalence, behind the political and ideological ambivalence, there is something hard and immutable, something that will at last explain how and why the French went to war in 1939. That is a pity, because there is something to be said for being sure of the truth. In this instance, however, what one finds in the economic currents is simply more uncertainty and with it, more ambivalence. As a way of illustrating this impression, I have chosen three substantial examples, all of which speak explicitly to economic calculation and implicitly to prevailing perceptions. The first addresses the bewilderment provoked in France by Nazi economic policy, the second, the debate over how best to prepare the economy for a military confrontation with Germany. The third raises the matter of an enemy of another kind – not fascism, not communism, but the pound sterling and the American dollar.

From the beginning, Nazi economic policy had generated much debate in France. To the business community and like-minded liberal economists, the intrusions of the state into the world of private commercial exchange were uncalled for. More bluntly, the Nazi government's Four Year Plan, its interference in price and wage policies, its meddling in import priorities, its attempts to organize capital, were as abhorrent as the same measures would have been under the yoke of socialism. By the end of 1936, however, two developments had tempered French criticisms of Berlin. First, the scourge of state intervention had arrived in France, embodied in the Popular Front government of Léon Blum. This, of course, did not make the German experiments any more palatable, only, by comparison, less threatening to French capital. Second, those experiments seemed to be working. By concentrating on rearmament and on an ambitious public works programme, the Nazi state seemed to have found a way to shake off the Depression. Unemployment had virtually disappeared, and with it the attendant costs of public support; revenues from direct and indirect taxes had increased with the rising rates of employment and consumer spending; domestic investment had risen accordingly, and with it the profit margins of many industries – electrical, mining, automobile, railway and chemical. Until 1938. It was then that conditions started to take on the shape of earlier prophecies from the west. And as they did, they erased any doubts about the wisdom of German policy, but magnified the doubts about its implications.[1]

Here is how the French witnessed it, and how they turned what they were seeing into a forecast of worse to come. The German economic bubble, they predicted, was about to pop. Inflated by reckless state spending on expensive imports and expensive construction projects, it would implode from the force of a worsening balance of trade and from a discredited currency. The prophecy was cast from the following. Rearmament had been a pillar of the economic revival. But rearmament had sharply increased the demand for high-grade iron ore, oil, rubber, aluminum, chrome, nickel and tungsten – none of which was available in Germany in anything like the quantities required. This demand, in combination with the priority awarded to national defence production, meant that expenditures on imports had soared while revenues from traditional export industries had slowly declined. By the middle of 1938 French observers had concluded that domestic investment was no longer expanding, and that money was in increasingly short supply – itself the product of a poor trade balance, and a gold reserve which was diminishing with relentless state expenditure. Long before the Munich crisis of September, the French ambassador in Berlin was reporting that Hitler's regime was already at the point of acute financial crisis. By the end of the year, word had it that directors of the German Reichsbank had warned Hitler of national bankruptcy.[2]

At first glance, one might well wonder why French diplomats, economists and financial analysts were concerned by the growing stresses on the German economy. Reason dictated that this was no way to prepare for a war, certainly not a long war for which huge quantities of a stable currency would be required. And in fact such expressions of the obvious were taken as assurances by wishful thinkers in both Paris and London. First of all, it made no sense to contemplate war with an already depleted treasury. Second, it was becoming clear that Nazi economic policies had soured in the mouths of many German producers and consumers. As for the former, profits were slumping at the same time as the regime interfered more in matters of labour allocation, raw material purchasing, even the deployment of a company's own financial reserves. As for the latter, consumers with improved purchasing power were finding it more and more difficult to find adequate quantities of beef and pork, eggs and butter – a condition which recalled the government's priority of industrial over agricultural production. That said, given the alarm in German financial circles, and the rumblings among both producers and consumers, there were grounds for hoping that the Nazis were on the way out. Reason would finally prevail, the regime would be unseated by some revolt of the military and civilian elite, and the path to economic self-destruction would be sealed off.

On reflection, however, the grounds for consternation seemed to be as firm as those for complacency. Indeed, by the reckoning of those most closely involved in diplomatic and military intelligence, much more firm. Once more, one can isolate two principal arguments for the unease which so many of these contemporary witnesses were experiencing. First, most of them, the ambassadors and the attachés, doubted that any domestic revolt against the regime was imminent.[3] The Führer himself was too popular, and the police too ubiquitous, for any organized resistance to have much success. Second, if the optimists could see economic reality forcing Hitler to moderate his ambitions, the pessimists feared that it would only make him desperate. Whereupon the pessimists themselves divided. The more sanguine detected in all this a clever ruse on Hitler's part. Stall the recovery by creating impossibly high demands for imported raw materials – in other words manufacture a crisis – and then allow the crisis to force Germany into another act of territorial expansion.[4] This could come against Poland, Rumania or the Ukraine, as it had against Austria and Czechoslovakia. It could also come in the west, against France and Britain, in a desperate attempt to overwhelm them before their own rearmament programmes had allowed them to close the gap with that of Germany.

Others saw a quality that went beyond mere deviousness. Far from working with an opponent of exceptional cunning, they feared that they were up against a madman. Literally, a man driven by internal forces towards some cataclysmic act of self-destruction. The sophisticated and discerning François-Poncet, French ambassador in Berlin between 1936 and October 1938, regarded the German Chancellor as a man beset by mad impulses, a totally intemperate man who valued only what he did not yet possess. Robert Coulondre, Poncet's successor, reached a very similar conclusion, referring to Hitler's hold on the German people as both diabolic and satanic. If the Führer were not clinically insane, he certainly was as dangerous and unreliable as a drunk who stumbled into neighbours' homes with a knife in his hand. And there was no sign that the drinking had diminished. In fact, both Coulondre and General Didelet, the military attaché, were afraid that Hitler was increasingly out of control, driven by some internal 'démon', perhaps the fear of imminent death.[5]

The problem, of course, was how to deal with him and his regime in 1938 or 1939 – without benefit of the smug if inconsistent diagnoses of Hitler's personality which have assailed us ever since the end of the last war. How to deal with someone who, wittingly, has painted himself into a corner? Compromise is as futile as intimidation in the glazed eyes of the deranged. It is this aspect which historians, steeped in the ways of reason, have for so long underestimated.[6] As if they feel similarly confident about the way in which our own contemporaries should cope with the challenges posed by suicide bombers. Too often, as Daladier and Chamberlain experienced at Munich, compromise is seen as a weakness, and evidence of further concessions to come. Subsequent threats are dismissed as the empty bravado of proven weak men. Ultimately, and out of a desire for peace, one either continues to give all that is demanded, or one takes up arms. In short, the rules are those of the madman.

So they seemed to have become by late 1938. French diplomats in Berlin were certain a financial crisis was at hand. The public debt was soaring, and with it the accompanying interest obligations.[7] Only two solutions presented themselves. Either the regime put the brakes on its rearmament programme, by so doing cutting the costs of its strategic imports and restoring some semblance of a trade balance, or the regime would try to solve its raw material requirements by further expansion in central Europe. In the event of the latter, France would have the option of acquiescing once again, or of taking a stand. But the price of acquiescence was mounting. How much of the central European resource base could Hitler be allowed to absorb before he had made Germany invincible, more than ready to wage the kind of long war in which France and Britain had seen their principal advantage? In fact, it was this consideration which we know played heavily upon Premier Daladier's mind in 1938, and which was central to his decision to go to war in August 1939.[8]

It was one thing to speculate on whether economics would moderate Hitler, or spur him on to more immoderate demands. It was another, something more fundamental, to wonder whether he intended to attack France for any reason. Were one certain that he did not, that some stock could be put in his professions of peace and his expressed interest in accommodation with the Third Republic, then France's economic system could be left to its own devices. The state could stay out of the nation's counting houses, the so-called 'free market' of liberal economic theory could be left to determine the nature and pace of production and profitability. The steel mills could concentrate on products better suited to the railway industry than artillery weapons. Shipbuilders might profit from contracts for merchant vessels instead of destroyers, automobile manufacturers more from car production than armoured vehicles. If, Germany was not intent on resorting to war. And of that no-one could be sure.

If war could not be discounted, whatever its folly, then everything hinged on the question of timing. How imminent was a German attack? Upon the answer to that, rested the determination of rearmament priorities and the urgency with which the economy had to be restructured from peace to wartime production. Since everything depended on a successful defence of the frontiers, there was no question but that the first priority would go to the fixed fortification programmes in the north and east, to the artillery, machineguns and anti-tank guns which provided those fortifications with firepower, and to the anti-aircraft batteries and fighter squadrons which would protect the land armies and the industrial centres. If the attack were deemed imminent, and the threat urgent, then production was the only thing that mattered – producing and delivering the vital armaments as quickly as possible. In fact, we need devote little time to this contingency of crisis production. It was never realized; and it was never realized because at no time in the 1930s were French authorities convinced that the Germans were about to attack. For all that has been written about the diplomatic crises of this decade, and about this fearful France, not once did the French intelligence services forecast an immediate German assault on France.[9]

Their prognosis of what was to come was situated somewhere between the suspicion of Germany's intentions and the conviction that the attack was not imminent. From an economic perspective, that meant that there was no sense in France acting precipitately, churning out one new gun after another. Why totally disrupt peacetime production for the sake of a suspicion, however credible? And why risk mass-producing weapons which could be rendered obsolete by the delay of a year or two in the enemy's attack? Instead, the adoption of a more realistic timeframe by the intended victim allowed for a more methodical approach to the problems of a wartime economy. In short, a longer range threat demanded a longer range solution than that of immediate armaments production. Only one admonition was relevant to both imminent and future menace: defend at all costs the frontier regions where were installed not only the French ground forces but some of the vital French industries. Ensure the inviolability of the national soil, by grinding down the

German offensive with withering defensive fire, and then roll out the giant economic batteries for the long war. Such was in summary form the French prescription for victory.

In fact, the prescription was a little more intricate. In sharp contrast to Nazi economics, which abused the Reichsmark and ran roughshod over the rules of international monetary behaviour, French policy started with the franc. Two conditions had become imperative by the late 1930s, first that the country possess a gold reserve large enough to keep the franc a premier international currency, second that the actual exchange value of the franc be set in relation to the American dollar and the British pound. As for the first condition, a healthy gold reserve meant that the franc could be used to purchase essential war materials anywhere in the world marketplace – unlike the Russian rouble and, increasingly, the German mark. Indeed, the high command had created a kind of mystique around a minimal holding of 50 billion francs – or some 3000 tons of gold – a figure, incidentally, below which the reserve had fallen in the autumn of 1938 when Daladier had met Hitler at Munich.[10] As for the second, it had become clear through painful experience that the franc could not afford to be overvalued with respect to the dollar and pound. Psychologically satisfying though this condition may have been, it worsened France's trade imbalance. French exports became too expensive and revenues dropped. Imports, on the other hand, became cheaper, with the result that increased volume ultimately led to increased expenditure. And if the trade imbalance continued for too long in the red, or became too acute, the value of the currency would be slowly undermined, gold reserve or no gold reserve. Ultimately, it was this consideration which prompted successive devaluations of the franc in 1926, 1928, 1936, 1937 and 1938.[11]

Both of these conditions were determined largely by state policy. Treasury reserves depended on the interplay between government revenues and government expenses. Currency valuation was a device which the state could use, sparingly, to regulate the performance of the national economy. But both impacted directly on the performance of private capital and, in turn, could be influenced by that performance. French industries that might be preparing to invest in plant retooling needed to know that their cost estimates were based on a stable franc – both for the sake of an expanded factory in France as well as for the purchase of imported machinetools.

Companies which depended on export markets also depended on a currency which did not overprice their products. That is why there was such a high potential for strife between the world of business and that of government, and why that strife had the potential to damage the economy. Inappropriate monetary policy – or what was judged so by private business – could mean the postponing of capital investment, cutbacks both in export production and in raw material imports, even the flight of capital to foreign markets and currencies. Indeed, every one of these responses was recorded in France in those turbulent years between 1936 and 1938, when private capital regarded itself at war with the governments of the Popular Front. That war is but one of many examples which testify to the incessant debate over monetary strategies and how they would relate to a future war – that with Germany.

Other doubts and divisions added to the halting character of France's economic preparations for war, notably over raw material stockpiling and capital investment in defence-related industries. With respect to the former, one need not look for long to uncover the irony implicit in the long war strategy. On her own, and confined to her own metropolitan resources, France was no better equipped to defeat Germany in a long war than a short one. The fact was that she had no manganese for high test steel, no rubber for aircraft or lorry tires, virtually no petroleum for land or air engines, or copper for the electrical industry. Her munitions industry was dependent on substantial imports of cotton, sulphur, pyrites, nickel and lead; and almost all of her industrial infrastructure was fuelled by coal – only two-thirds of which came from French mines. To make matters worse, three-quarters of the indigenous coal supply came from the regions closest to the German and Belgian borders, as did nearly the same proportion of the country's oil-refining capacity, and almost all of its iron ore and steel production.[12] Should the German army occupy these regions early in the war, as it had done in 1914, or should the Luftwaffe eliminate the mines and the factories, the long war strategy was likely to be in tatters.

But beneath the obvious there was a thick layer of obscurity – how much to buy, when to buy it, who should buy it, and finally for what should it be bought? Otherwise expressed, one could hardly expect metallurgical companies to invest in stockpiles of manganese and nickel when their largest customers were demanding steel for automobiles rather than for armoured vehicles. Clearly, it took the state to identify its defence priorities, issue contracts for prototype development, and provide some sort of modest production schedule, before private capital was going to commit much of its own resources. Until then, and deprived of a sense of imminent crisis, French industry was inclined to proceed with caution, mindful of the public opprobrium still associated with the manufacture and sale of armaments, mindful too that the state was as quick to alter the specifications of its orders as it was slow to pay its bills.[13]

Many of the same considerations were in play when it came to capital investment in industries which, some day, might be called upon to produce for the war effort. While some companies certainly did invest in the progressive modernization of their plants – notably the profitable steel industry at Saint-Etienne and the Paris-based Renault automobile company – and did aggressively develop new markets abroad, there were as many instances of excessive restraint.[14] Perhaps the most striking example was the machinetool industry, that is to say power-driven tools which were part of any modern company's productive process – machines like metal lathes and drill presses. In the mid-1930s the average age of French machinetools was 20 years, as opposed to seven in Germany and three in the United States. Even as late as 1939 the average age of these machines in the French metallurgical industries was 35 years. Just as telling was the fact that France had substantially fewer workers in the machinetool industry than had Switzerland. Deprived of capital investment, as well as of a substantial labour force, the industry could not satisfy even the modest demands of other French manufacturers. The latter were either obliged to go abroad for their requirements, or tolerate an average nine-month delay on the delivery date.

This is not the place for an intensive inquiry into the reasons behind this condition, especially when readers have at their disposal the indispensable work of M. Crémieux-Brilhac. However, since ambivalence is at the heart of the explanation, there is something to be said for summarizing its principal sources. The investment restraint demonstrated by many French companies clearly had something to do with severely reduced profit margins during the height of the Depression in the mid-1930s. Shareholders and management were in no mood to invest in an uncertain future. But there was more to it than that, especially when it came to the defence industries. While it is true that armament production was capable of yielding great profits under certain conditions, it is also true that arms producers faced an assortment of special taxes – including one from 1933 which was designed to claw back wartime profits in excess of 10 per cent. By 1935 they faced a special surcharge of 20 per cent on their current profits which, when added to the assortment of customary business taxes, brought the tax rate on profits to roughly 50 per cent. Furthermore, the government's own deflationary approach in the early years of the Depression meant that it was cutting expenditures rather than investing in research and development. Neither private firms nor the state-run arsenals could expect significant infusions of capital from that quarter. Not until the aggravating foreign situation coincided with the election of a more interventionist Popular Front regime in 1936.

And here was the most delicate point of all, and the one most central to French economic ambivalence. It was one thing for the state to husband its own financial reserves, to regulate currency value, even to assume an active, interventionist role in time of war. It was quite another for it to intrude into a peacetime economy, setting itself up in some instances as a competitor with big business, attempting to influence the investment priorities of such firms, and in one way or another also offending the politically important small business community by appearing to downplay its economic importance.[15] It was here that a collision of sorts occurred, between the obvious need to have a detailed blueprint for the industrial mobilization of the country in the event of war, and the prevailing wisdom of liberal economists who wanted to defer state intervention for as long as possible, including that of exchange controls on capital preparing to flee the country. In fact, it was not an especially violent collision, for neither the military nor the civilian *dirigeants*, and certainly not a majority of their political masters, were philosophically much in tune with state-driven economic centralization. Perhaps the most damaging aspect was the flight of capital between 1936 and 1938, one which was first a response and then a stimulus to Treasury borrowing from the Bank of France.[16] For the most part, however, there remained an uneasy acceptance of the existing system: closed bidding competition for state contracts and reliance upon private producers to pay their own costs of development and production. At base, it was the implicit consensus between the French state and French business which explains the ten-year parliamentary delay in approving an omnibus bill for organizing the economy in times of war. Very few deputies were anxious to award the government exceptional economic authority, whether such power might abuse the interests of capital, or whether it might further constrain the rights of labour.

All of the foregoing discussion, of course, is grounded in the perception of a mounting foreign peril. But a peril at mid-distance, not too far away to be discounted and to make irrelevant such considerations as stockpiling, not so proximate as to demand immediate and united action. So the question of timing is more than just symptomatic. It is central to the kind of response that is called for. When should the state start to cut into its financial reserves in the interests of stockpiling coal and petroleum, copper and nickel? When should it start pouring more of its funds into the research side of its own defence establishment, or start offering substantial financial incentives to companies prepared to invest in new technologies? When must it extend its authority over capital and labour, prodding car producers to make more tanks, steel producers to deliver products suitable for gun barrels, factory workers to upgrade their skills, miners to work longer days?

Hindsight, as always, has the answer; and in the light of what happened in 1940 that answer seems to have an even greater degree of authority. Clearly, the French state needed to have started much earlier than it did to ensure the refurbishing of the nation's infrastructure. But the problem with hindsight is that it is illuminated more by the present than the past. The issue of serial production, for example, seemed much less pressing in the mid-1930s than it appeared in August 1939 when war was a certainty. At the time war was declared, it was obvious that the French aircraft industry had come too late to the assembly-line kind of construction without which it could never hope to catch-up to German production. Everyone knew it, as everyone has known it ever since. But in a country still struggling with a depressed economy in 1936 – a country left uncertain by the friction between Hitler's actions and his professions of peace – prudence and practicality dictated another response. Confident that the attack was not imminent, confident too that the country's current defences could hold almost indefinitely, the government and the industry agreed on a mid-course. Modern prototypes would continue to be developed, in twos and threes, and those selected for adoption would be refined until that time when the international situation warranted a shift to serial production. In that way, wastage and obsolescence could be kept to a minimum. In all, it had a certain logic to it, more certainly than is acknowledged by those who will never be in doubt about Hitler's intentions or about the date of his attack on France.

There was a third cluster of doubts which worked in conjunction with those pertaining to Nazi economic nihilism and those pertaining to France's economic preparations for war. In its singular form, this was the concern about how France was to avoid being assigned a purely secondary and subservient role by international capitalism. More sharply put, alongside fears of a German military occupation of France, there were misgivings about an Anglo-Saxon financial occupation. These were hardly anxieties of the same magnitude, for in the political and diplomatic sense there was no more hesitation in identifying Britain and the United States as potential allies as there was in seeing Germany as the principal potential enemy. Still, the idea of being rendered subordinate by friends, was not appreciably more attractive than being suborned by enemies. And right from 1919, from the moment when the Americans had refused to associate French debts to America with German debts (reparations) to France, there had been sown many seeds for lingering resentment.[17]

In this respect, the interwar period had begun ominously, with France owing four billion dollars to the United States and three billion to the United Kingdom.[18] Although even in combination this was less than what the Germans had agreed to pay to France in reparations, the 1920s had been a decade of delayed, diminished and defaulted payments by Berlin. At the same time, of course, the French Republic had not been able to defer the heavy costs of reconstruction in northern France or the financial charges which it had assumed towards the support of French widows, orphans and disabled veterans. Moreover, the discharge of such responsibilities had been complicated by an early post-war recession and by a steady depreciation of a franc subject to both domestic and foreign speculation.[19]

By the early 1930s France's position had improved considerably, particularly with respect to the other western great powers. Germany, the United States and Great Britain were already struggling with the effects of the Depression: collapsed production, profits, and currencies. Indeed, both the pound and dollar had been devalued. By contrast, the franc was strengthening. Having itself been devalued in 1926 and stabilized, it was enjoying a period of exceptional acclaim and performance. Indeed, the gold stocks of the Bank of

France almost tripled between 1928 and 1933, and the franc had become the international currency of choice. But not for long. Depressed world markets soon demonstrated that in fact the franc was too strong relative to other currencies, and that France was falling into the throes of the global depression. What made matters worse was that French analysts were convinced that their own troubles had been induced by both over-production and a profligate use of credit in Britain and the United States.[20] French exports slumped, and with them the attendant revenues, subsequent production, profits and employment. As early as 1935, that is well before the advent of Popular Front governments, French capital was fleeing to refuges abroad where, in fact, other economies were beginning to experience an upturn.[21]

Besides, it was becoming more and more difficult for France to retain membership among the economic superpowers. By the early 1930s French banks certainly had assumed heavy financial commitments in Rumania, Yugoslavia and Czechoslovakia − substantially more than those of Britain − and France's direct investments in Polish industries were greater than any other foreign country. However, there were very tight limits on the volume of agricultural goods which the French economy could afford to import from central Europe − limits which created new opportunities for Germany to strengthen its economic relations with the region.[22] And the basic fact remained that 40 million Frenchmen belonged in the second division of world economic competition. Measured by value in gold francs, French exports in 1939 were down by 26 per cent over where they had been in 1912; and the commercial deficit between imports and exports had come close to doubling over the same period. At no time in the 1930s did the nation's industrial production recover to the peak it had reached in 1929, a constraint which partly reflected the fact that nearly three-quarters of the workforce were still located in small firms of less than five hundred employees.[23] In fact, there were still as many peasant producers as there were urban workers, a figure suggestive of the 50:50 urban–rural split that had just been reached in 1931, suggestive too of the fact that only in the 1930s were half the population being introduced to homes with electricity and running water.[24] As for the population overall, the old concerns about the still declining birth-rate and an ageing citizenry continued to alarm army recruiters, tax collectors, commercial agents and domestic producers.[25] Indicators such as these, together with the war debts still owing to the Americans and French dependence on Anglo-American oil supplies, the characteristically outdated industrial plant and the decline in industrial production, the rise in wholesale and retail prices and the restrained nature of domestic investment, all suggest that France was waging a losing battle with 'lès Anglo-Saxons.' Indeed, following the 12 per cent devaluation of May 1938, and the effective pegging of the franc to the British pound, a new word entered the French lexicon – the 'franc-sterling'.[26] Anglo-American raw materials and markets, production methods and technologies, transport facilities and capital, to say nothing of the English language, represented a challenge of another nature to a France already beset by the German menace.

Given the sea of uncertainties which this chapter set out to explore, it may be worthwhile to review what it has found, and what it has not. Principal among the findings – or, more truthfully, the arguments – is the absence of certainty. Better put, it is the presence of so many conflicting certainties. Together, they made for much ambivalence in money markets and investment circles, in France as well as elsewhere. Much of the debate derived from the discord over how best to address that acute worldwide economic failure which was called the Depression, a debate which featured prophecies and counter-prophecies from advocates and opponents of state intervention or *dirigisme*. Part of it, too, arose from differences over the degree to which France had to bow to *force majeure*, most observers concluding that the country had to align itself with the superior wealth of the Anglo-Saxons, especially given the German peril, but with some observers continuing to have visions of a European counter-block founded on Franco-German cooperation.[27] But again the majority of French witnesses, those who remembered and those who only had been told of the last war, were most preoccupied by the threats to national security as represented by Hitler's Germany. Would his economic engine run out of fuel, and if so would that induce restraint or some desperate act of expansion? How long did he have to make up his mind, and where would he go if he settled on audacity? With what urgency should France try to close the gap between her armaments production and that of Germany or, in light of a still faltering economy and lack of confidence in the franc, try to complete the appeasement of Germany?[28] And at what point should the state run the risk of further upsetting private business by conscripting its capital, plant and labour force for full-scale economic warfare?

It is a luxury not to have to answer any of these questions – which makes it all the more surprising that so many historians have chosen to rough it. For my part, mindful of the remarkable rearmament successes that *were* recorded between 1938 and 1940, it is enough to uncover the host of uncertainties which certainly delayed those successes, and to appreciate why no prophecy before the summer of 1939 was fully convincing – whether it was made by military intelligence or financial attachés, by cabinet ministers or journalists, by investment bankers, steel manufacturers, or currency traders. That much seems clear, the very unclarity of the situation. But no more so for the French than for the British, the Belgians, the Poles or the Yugoslavs. That is why it would be quite wrong, if supremely easy, to read into this diagnosis some kind of uniquely French malady. The President of the German Reichsbank did not know what Hitler would do, neither did the British Foreign Office, nor the White House in Washington; and none, it should be said, has escaped the censure of scholars who have looked at them rather than the French. No one knew, probably including Hitler himself, and therefore choices without guarantees had to be made, as they always do in the present. The sooner we start treating the past like the present, and our predecessors like ourselves, the better.

6 Alarm and Assurance: Public Moods and Perceptions

Public opinion was very much like elite opinion, full of shades and textures. Indeed, the French public was no more united, no more visionary, no more decisive than those who professed to represent them, speak for them, and protect their material interests. How or why could it have been otherwise? The debates within the National Assembly reflected and reinforced the country's diverse ideological complexion. The uncertainties expressed by the generals and diplomats, by cabinet ministers and financial analysts, were echoed time and time again in public media like the newspaper and commercial press, radio broadcasts and cinematic productions, public exhibitions and commemorations, even some early opinion polls. None provides evidence strong enough to dispel doubt about the national 'state of mind'. On the contrary, they combine to compel it, to make it clear that the men and women of France were still at sixes and sevens, more unsure than sure whether the future held peace or war, economic recovery or further collapse, social reconciliation or renewed tension.

There was no mistaking the sense of apprehension and peril that had settled over the country, some of it new, some of it lingering. By 1938–9 the German menace and the attendant threat of war was everywhere intrusive. Those who spoke and wrote of it were no longer dismissed as left-wing provocateurs, accused of exaggerating the danger for their own selfish ends. Indeed, the power of the Luftwaffe alone, was now great enough to lighten the burden of French alarmists. But German squadrons and divisions were not the whole of it. There were still misgivings about France's moral readiness, some of which stemmed from old conservative judgments on godless republicanism, some from left-wing views on state and private capitalism, some from a social scientific despondency over France's feeble birthrate and powerful class antagonisms, some from a humanistic sense that French culture was being overrun by foreign influences. Any of these, singular or in combination, could have been enough to deepen the alienation from a Republic which seemed short on money, guns and imagination, long on political bickering, cabinet instability, and executive dithering.

But that is not the whole story, only the version which prepares us best for the collapse to come. Amid all the talk of war, there remained a hard core of people whose faith in peace could not be shaken. Whether it was a faith fashioned in the face of evidence, or a conclusion based on the rational calculation of war costs, it remained to the end a beacon for those who still believed, and for those who only hoped. There was also, among the uncertainties, yet another perception, this one government-sponsored. War certainly would constitute failure of a sort, but it did not mean certain defeat. The foreign peril would revive national unity, while the allied strategy for economic warfare would slowly diminish Germany's capacity to make war. France would triumph, a prophecy which drew new force from the unmistakable signs of national recovery in 1939. Capital was returning, unemployment was all but eliminated, rearmament was on a marked upswing, and Premier Daladier was arguably the most popular man in France.

The first current, that which ran closer to the banks of pessimism, had even a troubled surface appearance. Here were the eddies suggestive of deeper turbulence below, those which I have earlier summed up with the word 'moral'. It is not the most satisfying of words for this context, but it serves well enough as a generic replacement for more toxic words like 'decadence'. By it, I mean only to imply that some French citizens in the late 1930s were convinced, or almost convinced, that the Third Republic had for-feited its moral authority both in the eyes of its own citizens as well as in those of the international community. The evidence on which some of these charges were based was as enduring as it was inconsistent. Traditional conservatives like the monarchists of *Action Française* had never forgiven the Republic for being a Republic. The truly radical republican left had never forgiven it for being too conservative. The latter lamented a state which had made its peace with capital and Church, the former complained of its failure to have done so. United in their distrust, the two poles had nothing more in common, lest it be the passion and the presumed sincerity of their otherwise antithetical indictments. However, the fact remains that these were eddies inspired by minorities, even tiny minorities when it came to people who by 1939 or 1940 would really have put Daladier's Republic on the same moral footing as that of the dictatorship of Adolf Hitler.

More serious than these rather hackneyed charges and counter-charges – including those which attributed to the other responsibility for class antagonism in France – were those which questioned the Republic's ability to resist more fundamental challenges. One of these was the threat posed by foreign cultural influences in France, a threat most frequently perceived and articulated by conservative guardians of the national culture. Not by coincidence, for it was right-wing intellectuals, in alliance with the Church, who had led the quest for a renewed moral order, one which questioned the modern cult of individualism and reaffirmed the primacy of God, Catholi-cism, community values, family unity, orderliness and personal discipline.[1] In this case, what distressed them was what one writer called 'xenophilia'. Foreign art, he said, had reduced the French to servile adoration – no matter what the form or its provenance. Russian music, Viennese opera, American films, Mexican dance, German architecture, Czech painting, it did not matter as long as it was foreign. And there was more. There was discerned in much of this a preoccupation with subjects that were foreign, language that was foreign, and customs that were said to be to be foreign: including alcoholism, drug-taking, pornography, homosexuality and, above all, bad taste.

Some of the outrage was addressed to Americans, their money and their marketing being central to what Georges Duhamel called *America, the Menace* and what Arnaud Dandieu called *Le Cancer américain*. Some of it had an anti-semitic cast, cut and coloured to exploit apprehensions about the flood of foreign Jews from eastern Europe. More of it, from the peace settlement on, was expressly Germanophobic, as French newspapers, books and cinema played upon the blond beast, and as some classroom teachers clung to the wartime practice of referring to Germans as 'swine'. By the late 1930s spy literature had soared to new heights of popularity, highlighted by Marc Chadourne's *Dieu créa d'abord Lilith*, the story of the apprehended German spy Lydia Oswald, and by Charles Robert-Dumas whose invented hero, Captain Benoit of the French intelligence service, was the nemesis of German espionage agents. For its part, the French cinema knew a good thing when it saw it, including the featuring of German-born spies and paymasters and the recalling of specific acts of German barbarism against French women and children.[2]

Another, and in some ways even deeper, challenge to France's domestic tranquillity was the menace of depopulation. Here again was an old apprehension that continued to breathe life from the incessant publicity which it received from the press and cinema. While explanations for the phenomenon varied, there was little debate about the condition. France's population growth was inferior to that of Germany, Britain and Italy. Indeed, it had been so for most of the 19th century, a condition so acute that by 1890 nearly two-thirds of her *départements* seemed to have fallen below the minimum rate for population replacement. Death was almost as common as birth, even before war returned in 1914 and started consuming hundreds of thousands of prospective fathers and mothers. But particularly the fathers, young men of less than 30 years whose collective deaths erased nearly a third of that national age group. Such carnage left legacies of other kinds. By 1936 national birth figures had slumped below the death figures. Adding to the alarm was the fact that France's interwar growth rate – at 7 per cent – was only half that of the German and Italian. In fact, by 1940, the number of French males between the ages of 20 and 34 was well under half of the German total – a chilling statistic for those in charge of military conscription. And a chilling theme for the interwar cinema industry which, for 20 years, persistently wedded a preoccupation with the German barbarian to an equally strong fascination for the orphaned child and blood-drenched cadavers.[3]

What this meant, or was said to mean, was that France was showing signs of being a spent force, a nation lacking the will to renew itself, a citizenry too caught up on material acquisition to be deflected by raising families. Add this to the suspicion that here was a country auctioning itself to foreign bidders, a country obsessed by class antagonism and only lukewarm about the republican regime, and one has read part of the current flowing in the direction of pessimism. But still the upper waters, not the depths. It is in the latter that one discerns the outline of what France feared most between the wars, something that ran below the more specific concerns about German birth rates, or German art, or German ideas, and the specific memories of the last German invasion. That something was the dark shape of war. Compared to this, at least for the vast majority of French citizens, the concerns about birthrate, the concerns about cultural defence, the concerns about constitution, Church, capitalism or communism were the stuff of academics and politicians. It was war they feared, and war they wanted to avoid, some at almost any cost.

It can be called pacifism, as long as the word will stretch from those who wanted to avoid a new war for as long as possible, to those who refused to countenance the possibility of war. The emphases differed, but not so the inspiration. That, they had in common. And it was the last War.[4] In this country of 40 million inhabitants, as many as eight million had served with the colours between 1914 and 1918. Of those, a million and half had been killed, another three million wounded: nearly five million casualties, most of whom had parents and grandparents, wives and sweethearts, brothers, sisters, children, loved ones who had discovered in their grief what war was like. Altogether, the direct and indirect casualties, it has been estimated that one out of every six French citizens in 1938 had personal links to the Kaiser's war.[5] Had they all been left to age and to heal, had the spectre of war disappeared for a few more generations, doubtless their hurt would have been forgotten in some new call to arms. But the madness had returned long before millions of bereaved had made their own peace with what had happened, which is why 16 million of them were said to have supported an international pacifist organization known as the *Rassemblement uni pour la paix*.[6] For them, ordinary fathers and mothers, that was what 'Munich' was all about, not justice for the Czechs, not resistance to fascism, not the calculation of opposing military strengths.

There were, of course, others who could never forget the last war, many of them better organized and more vocal than widows, orphans or parents. These were the veterans, over five million of whom were alive in 1938, representing almost 40 per cent of the entire male population. And a million and a half of them were still eligible for recall to service in one of the second reserve divisions. Of the five million total, two-thirds were formally registered in one of the many veterans' associations, virtually all of which had one thing in common: the determination to avert a future bloodbath. Membership included commissioned officers and ordinary soldiers, peasant farmers and city bankers, communists and conservatives, young and elderly, the full range of male society. But of all the things that separated them, glorification of war was not among them.[7] When, in November 1938, they joined in the 20th commemoration of the armistice, they saw to it that memories were not confined to the parade on the Champs Elysées. Teams of relay runners ran as far as 300 kilometres out of Paris, carrying torches to the men who lay buried in the massive military cemeteries of Compiègne, Amiens, Châlons-sur-Marne, Notre-Dame-de-Lorette, and Douamont.[8]

When the runners returned from the countryside, they left not only the dead but the living. In fact, half of France's population remained on or very near the land, part of a lifestyle still determined by season and village, much of it still innocent of electric lights, modern plumbing, or telephones. Yet what they knew, they knew with a sureness that would have been the envy of a professor at the Sorbonne. They knew war. They knew that at least half of the country's war dead had come from villages like their own, few of which had since failed to erect an imposing public monument to the fallen. They knew, too, that the local teachers, so many of them eager patriots before the last war were now among the chastened and the doubtful.[9] And whether briefed by a communist paper like *La Terre*, a socialist paper like *La volonté paysanne*, or a rightist newspaper like *Le paysan de France*, they knew that there was no way that France should ever again go to war to protect anything which lay an inch outside her frontiers. At least until 1939, the last year of peace, it seems clear that the French peasantry was 'overwhelmingly pacifist'.[10]

Reflecting the truth of peasants, veterans, and mothers, and recasting it for greater eloquence and larger markets, was a good portion of France's creative community. The process had started with the guns – eye-witness accounts by Barbusse (*Le Feu*) of 1916 and Duhamel (*La vie des martyrs*) of 1917 – and carried on long after they had been silenced: from *Les croix de bois* (1919) by Roland Dorgelès to Louis-Ferdinand Céline's *Voyage au bout de la nuit* (1932). None glorified war. Each stressed the destruction and the suffering, the macabre and the bizarre. To be sure, there had been exceptions, Montherlant, Drieu la Rochelle, Barrès; but certainly most of the 150 war-addressed titles which appeared between 1918 and 1929 were not out to salvage war's reputation. Nor were those that were part of the new literary flow in the 1930s, written just as recollections of the past were giving way to apprehensions about the future. Perhaps that is what accounted for the tone of desperate men – Jean Gionno urging the peasantry to refuse military call-up, Jean Guéhenno justifying desertion, Gabriel Chevalier defining military heroism as fourth-fifths fear.[11] On stage there were similar themes, ranging from the early anti-war productions of Georges Bourdon, Henri Bataille and Charles Méré to the most famous and most hopeful of them all, Jean Giraudoux's *La guerre de Troie n'aura pas lieu* of 1935.[12]

Film was another medium where the message was the same. By the early 1920s there was a movie theatre for every 9 000 inhabitants, and by 1938 the annual toll of movie goers had exceeded the 200 million mark. And here, in the dark, they were given plenty of opportunity to see for themselves the destructive power of modern military machines, and to witness what happens to a man when he shoulders a gun: more widows and orphans, more barbarism and abuse of power. The most famous by far was the French film version of Remarque's pacifist novel *A l'ouest rien de nouveau*, released in 1930 to popular acclaim in France, and to a ban against its distribution in Germany. But there were others, including Abel Gance's *J'Accuse* (1919), a work which reduced the horror of war down to the rape of a single French woman by a German soldier, Jean Choux's *Paix sur le Rhin* (1938) which was interpreted by many as counsel for appeasing Germany, Marcel Carné's *Quai des brumes* and Jean Renoir's *La règle du jeu*, both of which were later fingered as 'defeatist' by the Vichy regime, symptomatic of the country's prewar malaise.[13]

All in all, therefore, it is inconceivable that any French man or women, of adult competence, had not been touched in some way by the experience of war past. Take the dead and multiply them by the bereaved family members. Take the surviving veterans, the wounded and the whole, and multiply them by the readers of novels, the theatre-goers, the film buffs. Take the recent graduates and multiply them by teachers who had seen the downside of patriotism. Take all those who had converted to causes like internationalism and pacifism, in a desperate hope that these were antidotes to war. Take those who wanted no more causes of any kind, whose beliefs had not survived the last war and who now only wished to be left in peace. Take them all, by their millions, and you will never again mistake their genuine abhorrence of war, never again condemn their irresolution before the menace that was Hitler.

For the remarkable fact was that they were not resolved on peace at any price. Almost two decades of painful reminiscences, of graphic depictions of military carnage by word and image, of national tomb-making, had failed to stamp out the will to resist foreign domination. The Chamber of Deputies had overwhelmingly endorsed the government's handling of the Munich crisis, by nearly 90 per cent. The French public, according to an early opinion poll, was more divided: 57 per cent in favour, 37 per cent critical. 70 per cent of the respondents in October 1938 believed that Britain and France had to resist all future demands from Berlin; and by December the same number were convinced that France should not try to buy German goodwill by means of colonial concessions. This is not to say that the French were looking for a fight, much less a new war, but it does suggest, again, that theirs was a river of more than one current.

At this point, one hardly wishes to be told to forget the preceding depiction of popular moods in interwar France; ignore what was written and staged, disregard the grief and the fear, while we try another read of the French pulse. As far as I know, that depiction is not far off the mark. It has invented nothing, nor even exaggerated. In that sense, it has tried to be truthful. But it is not the truth, not as it stands, not given the misrepresentations which it will surely encourage. Had pacifism touched the lives of most interwar French citizens? Yes. Had it committed them to the preservation of peace *almost* at any price? Yes. Had it taken them to a point where most would have done anything to avoid war? No. Had it deafened them to all appeals for armed resistance against foreign invaders? No.

Thus expressed, there remained from one war to the next an opening for its return – which was precisely what the small group of absolute pacifists feared the most. Indeed, among all observers, it was they who were most conscious of the nation's latent willingness to take up arms in defence of its interests. The committed pacifists thought it folly, but they never under-estimated the vulnerability of their fellow citizens to appeals for some new *grande levée* against the Boches. Committed to international reconciliation, they condemned the heavy expenditures that had gone into naval rearmament throughout the 1920s, and the still heavier bills that were chalked up by air rearmament from the mid-thirties on. Committed to Franco-German entente, they were unhappy with the exceptionally high costs of the Maginot fortifications, and the attendant, ever-escalating demands for more artillery weapons, more machineguns, more tanks and anti-tank weapons. Of all observers, French and foreign, contemporary and historical, these were the men and women who knew that the old ways of solving problems had not been shelved, understood that Frenchmen would still rally to their flag, and that mothers would still resign themselves to war.

One of the reasons why we have been so forcibly struck by the interwar proscription against war is that it had the field more or less to itself. After the Marne and the Somme, it would have seemed an obscenity to celebrate the old images of military glory. It was easier and more truthful to write of the mud and re-enact the dying. After Verdun, patriotism meant something far more sober, as did war itself. To be sure, there was a market for war literature; people and therefore publishers were interested in it. But the millions of surviving veterans were not going to be lied to, and the bereaved only wanted some sign that their sacrifice had meaning. For all of them, apart from the pain, there had to be acknowledgement of a soldier's contribution to the war that was to end all war, and a recognition that he had done his duty.

This word 'duty' struck terror in the hearts of the no-holds-barred pacifists, for once activated, it encouraged men to say and do dangerous things. From their vantage point, the clock started ticking in late 1938, after the Munich concessions, as soon as it was obvious that the Sudetenland was *not* Hitler's last territorial claim in Europe, that one demand would follow another until there was nothing left to give him. It was the grudging acceptance of this truth that started the defections from the pacifist organizations, and the corresponding *ralliement* to the French state and the cause of national defence. By 1939 a country which had set its heart against war for almost 20 years now set its mind to the possibility.

That shift in attitude was not wholly natural or by chance, any more than pacifist sentiment had grown exclusively from the masses, without nurturing from the dramatists, the novelists and the film-makers. In the case of the shift towards national resistance, various agencies of government played prominent roles, particularly in such fields as rearmament, propaganda and foreign policy.

Central to all was the exceptional post-Munich economic recovery, a condition without which military production would have faltered along with efforts to convince the public that Germany was still beatable. The explanation for this recovery is complex and, there-fore, contentious. Some historians would credit it to the foundations laid by the left-inclined Popular Front governments of 1936–7, while others attribute it to the tearing-out of those foundations and their replacement with rules more favourable to private capital.[14] Predictably, this is a divide fashioned from ideology as well as economics, one which will continue to draw spectators for years to come. For our purposes, however, it is sufficient to say that those spectators are at least agreed on the accomplishment.

The index of industrial production jumped from 83 in October 1938 to 100 in June 1939, the first time it had recovered to that level since 1928. Metallurgical production increased by 41 per cent, and construction was up by 36 per cent. Unemployment almost disappeared, dropping by roughly 10 per cent in the same period; consumer price increases slowly levelled off to near zero, and the country went from an average work week of just under 40 hours to one of nearly 42 hours. For its part, capital responded to the assurances of a government which promised not only better terms, but a rearmament effort which could bring the country to war readiness. Having fled France for foreign havens, between 1936 and 1938, much of it now returned for investment opportunities at home. The gold reserves of the Bank of France quite suddenly inflated from some 50 billion francs – the minimal figure settled on by a high command anticipating a long war – to over 90 billion. In all, given the labour movement's lingering suspicions about the ties between state and capital, capital's uneasiness about those between state and labour, and the state's uncertainty about the compliance of either, what happened between 1938 and 1940 did indeed have something of the 'miraculous' about it.[15]

Certainly the fortunes of the rearmament industries brightened very considerably as they went from an 8 per cent share of industrial production in 1938 to 14 per cent in the eight months prior to the outbreak of war. Measured in 'constant money', the country was already spending more on national defence than it had on the eve of the 1914 war, and a higher percentage of the national income. By now over a third of the state's global expenditures was going to national defence – as compared to less than a quarter in 1936 – and most of that, in turn, to new fighting machines like tanks and aircraft.[16] Within the space of two and a half years, between January 1937 and September 1939, the numbers of modern French tanks increased from 162 to 2254; 25mm anti-tank guns from 1800 to 2668; 75mm anti-aircraft guns from 140 to 392; 105mm artillery guns from 0 to 132. In September 1938 the air industry had produced a grand total of 39 modern aircraft. By August 1939, 11 months later, that total had risen to 285.[17] No one said it was enough, and anyone in the know realized that the French performance was still far behind that of Germany – reckoned by monthly production figures or first line strength in modern aircraft. But at the same time, no-one who read the newspapers, in any language, could have been oblivious to the signs of France's economic and military recovery. And no-one believed that this recovery was far removed from a spirit of resistance or, indeed, from a deliberate state strategy to inspire that spirit.

Two themes dominated this patriotic revival in 1938–9, the Empire and the Anglo-French entente. Both were obvious and familiar, given the roles they had played in overcoming the German war machine of 20 years earlier. And both were central to the long war strategy upon which the French high command had staked its fortunes. That strategy demanded enough men to defend the Rhine against an enemy with a larger population – as well as a significantly larger proportion of young men – and enough material resources to finally overcome what was at base a more industrially powerful enemy. In these respects, the Empire was a very considerable asset – provisioner of colonial troops from Africa and Asia, and an important supplier of metropolitan needs in rubber, phosphates, nickel, lead and, if necessary, high-grade iron ore. The same was true for the redeveloping alliance with the United Kingdom, a country whose own resources – indigenous, imperial and commonwealth – were reckoned to be critical to the defence of France and the Lowlands. Like the French Empire, this alliance was capable in time of contributing many army divisions and aircraft squadrons to the defence of France, just as it was expected to be an important provider of war-critical imports – like oil, coal, rubber, tin, manganese – and of the merchant vessels in which such commodities would be carried to France.[18]

Little wonder, therefore, that in the months following the Munich conference – at which Daladier's glum appearance had advertised French impotence in central Europe – there should have been an unmistakable crescendo in French attentiveness to things imperial and British. To be sure, it was in no sense an entirely new sound, as is evidenced by the strong imperial theme that had long since been incorporated into many interwar school textbooks. But it increased in volume and frequency – in the pages of popular weeklies like *Marianne*, in radio broadcasts beamed from Paris to an estimated five million domestic receivers, or in those from the new government-run stations in Tunis, Tangier, Tenerife, Dakar and Saigon.[19] On a more spectacular note, there was the pageantry associated with two highly publicized events of 1939, one addressed to the past, the other to the present and future. The former was the 150th anniversary of the French Revolution, a national celebration which seized every opportunity either to parade colonial troops from Morocco or Senegal, or to transform old Anglo-French rivalries into a new commitment to a common cause. The latter was the state visit of President Albert Lebrun to England, where he was hosted by Their Majesties, King George VI and Queen Elizabeth, another occasion when no effort was spared to link monarchy and republic, king and president, lion and cock.[20]

Nowhere, however, were the imperial and entente themes more in evidence than in the cinema. Again, this simple chord had been played before, notably by the official film service of the French army; but now, in 1938–9, both state and private film-makers proved eager to tap a gathering public enthusiasm for all manner of things colonial and British. There was, for example, the prize-winning *Légion d'honneur* of 1938 and *La grande inconnue* of 1939, both of which stressed the imperial theme, both of which were launched at gala premières attended by cabinet ministers and members of the diplomatic corps. There was Marcel L'Herbier's feature-length film, 'Entente Cordiale', different in that its theme was the Franco-British connection, similar in that it too was premièred in the presence of Georges Bonnet and the British ambassador, Sir Eric Phipps. Finally, still by way of example, there were the many shorter news productions that emerged from French companies like Pathé-Journal or from French subsidiaries of American firms, like Paramount Actualités. It was companies like these that produced the news 'shorts' which usually preceded a feature-length film – like the 13-minute coverage of Daladier's celebrated trip to Corsica, Tunisia and Algeria in December 1938.[21]

Within all of this cinematic creation, there was almost always some kind of hyphen between empire and entente. Sometimes it was military potential, an emphasis often provided by the 'shorts' and documentaries addressed to the combined resources of the mighty French and British empires. Sometimes it was military readiness, in films like the 1938 feature-length production *Sommes-nous défendu?* which played upon the firepower of the Maginot Line, or the Pathé-Journal 'shorts' which offered reassuring footage on the power of the British navy, the effectiveness of the newest anti-aircraft batteries or of the unruffled confidence of General Gamelin. Sometimes, indeed often, it was merely the German menace, 15-or 90-minute reminders that it was the Hun, again, who was disturbing the tranquility of Europe. It was the Hun who made orphans, who murdered women and took hostages, and who stood condemned in such films as *Marthe Richard, Soeurs d'armes* and *Les otages*.[22]

On the diplomatic stage there were other signs of French impatience with German behaviour. Not all of them, for Georges Bonnet was still the foreign minister, and was still bent on doing whatever was necessary in order to avoid another war. To that end, it was he who had negotiated a new accord with Germany in December 1938, one which was as full of rhetorical good will as it was devoid of substance and sincerity. Certainly it did nothing to raise Hitler's appraisal of France or retard German rearmament, nothing to retard French rearmament or weaken their new-found resolve. And Bonnet's wishful thinking aside, it did not mean that France intended to leave central and eastern Europe to its fate.[23]

For Bonnet, Munich and the sellout of the Czechs had been a precedent as well as a benefaction. For his premier, Edouard Daladier, it had been a humiliation, and a turning-point. If Hitler kept on taking, Daladier had said to his son, as doubtless he would, 'we will be at war within a year'.[24] Not over the Slovaks, whose rump and undefendable state was quietly absorbed by the German army in mid-March 1939, but over the Poles or the Rumanians. As for the former, his government publicly reaffirmed its commitments under the Franco-Polish alliance, despite its many misgivings about the sanity of Polish foreign policy; and it was quick to underline those commitments by associating itself with the British guarantee of Polish security which had followed Hitler's action against Slovakia in mid-March. As for Rumania, the Daladier government had undertaken a series of related initiatives. In the immediate wake of Munich, it had stepped up its commercial and investment interests in Rumania, Yugoslavia and Bulgaria, as part of a strategy to thwart German economic penetration of the Balkans. In March–April 1939 it had led the way in fashioning an Anglo-French guarantee of Rumanian security; and early that summer it completed a month's-long negotiation for a mutual assistance pact with Turkey, a state which was seen as a potential buttress to the Balkan countries and which, accordingly, now figured prominently in the 'second front' strategy of the French high command.[25]

New energies were also in evidence elsewhere, notably in connection with the Russians and Italians. The disappearance of the Czechs in October 1938 had been one more sign to Stalin that the western powers were encouraging Hitler to expand eastward. The disappearance of the Slovaks in March 1939 was confirmation to the western powers that Hitler was out of control and that only the threat of a two-front war would restrain him. With that in mind, the Chamberlain and Daladier governments finally set out to conclude a genuine military alliance with the Soviet Union. That process proved to be long, frustrating and unfruitful, impeded as it was by two decades of mutual distrust. It ended on 23 August, the moment it was known that Stalin had opted for an accord with Hitler instead. But until then, through the spring and summer of 1939, it was the French government, and the French delegation, that had taken much of the initiative, repeatedly urging compromise on the British, on the Russians and on the Poles.[26] Here, at least, was a subject on which Daladier and Bonnet were agreed. Bring back an accord, they had said, whatever the cost. Certainly no-one had confused their sense of urgency with the cautious torpor displayed by Whitehall.

If the Daladier government succeeded in setting aside, if not discarding, its reservations about the Soviets, at least until late August, it never managed quite as much when it came to the Italians. Here, the ambivalence never disappeared, nor the debate which expressed it. The problem was not with Bonnet. He was out to avert war. If a Franco-Italian alliance could accomplish that, he would do it. If French economic, even territorial, concessions would help, he was prepared to close no door. Daladier is a far more complicated case. Publicly, his position was much stronger, and in that sense more consistent with the renewed national purpose that accompanied economic revival, rearmament, and the heightened propaganda effort. By means of personal visits to North Africa, firm statements to parliament, and speeches on state-sponsored radio broadcasts, the Prime Minister lifted the national morale with his dismissal of Italian claims to French territory. Privately, he was more open to the idea of some kind of accommodation than his public utterances would have allowed; and he remained so as late as September 1939. Whether this suggests the indecisiveness which some have detected within his character, or rather a persistence in trying to rob Hitler of an Italian ally, is a subject for debate.[27] Either way, one finds in the Prime Minister the personification of a nation which had the strength to accept war, but the wisdom to regret it.

The economic recovery and attendant military revival of 1938–9 were thus accompanied by intensified efforts to revitalize public morale with sanguine appreciations of France's empire, the developing alliance with Britain, and a more assertive foreign policy. That much is clear. What is less so is whether those efforts necessarily were what explains the apparent change in the national mood. But the change was there, and in some key constituencies. Take for example the Catholic newspaper *La Croix*, one which had been divided like so much of France over the best way to deal with Hitler – until 1939 when the tone of its editorials and columns perceptibly hardened against further concessions to Berlin. The same configuration can be traced among the veterans in 1939, as more and more of them concluded that they had been duped by Hitler's professions of friendship. The pattern was similar among the peasantry who, having clung to a war-taught pacifism, were now fed-up with German threats and German lies. Overwhelmingly pacifist for most of the interwar period, they now rallied to the flag of national resistance.[28] The opinion polls confirmed the trend, as the percentage of respondents who had come to accept the possibility of another war nearly doubled between April and July 1939. Accordingly, and despite their admitted deficiencies, these early polls testify to the presence of an 'irreducible' core of frustrated citizens – over a third of the respondents – who already had resigned themselves to a new call to arms. As in 1914, so in 1939, the prevailing sentiment was 'il faut en finir'.[29]

So it was that government and people went to war, in the first week of September, agreed at last that there was little more to do, more or less united in their resignation.[30] There was no eagerness, no jubilation, but almost no refusal to answer the call-up notices, and certainly no premonition of the disaster that lay ahead. Daladier promised victory through the device of the alliance with the United Kingdom, but when he asked parliament for supplementary funds to prosecute the war, he still spoke mainly of France's desire for peace. The public mood was similarly confident, and solemn, qualities that were highlighted by the calm acceptance which observers noticed everywhere. The British embassy, for example, reported to London that all of the military and civil defence measures had been carried out 'efficiently and calmly in a spirit of quiet determination'. For his part, Ambassador William Bullitt privately informed President Roosevelt of the mood in France:

> The whole mobilization was carried out in absolute quiet. The men left in silence. There were no bands, no songs. There were no shouts of 'On to Berlin' and 'Down with Hitler' to match the shouts of 'On to Berlin' and 'Down with the Kaiser!' as in 1914. There was no hysterical weeping of mothers, and sisters and children. The self-control and quiet courage has been so far beyond the usual standard of the human race that it has had a dream quality.[31]

Journalists saw the same thing. The *Washington Post* reported 'an amazing impression of calm', while Janet Flanner told readers of *The New Yorker* that Paris had faced up to the coming of war, 'completely calm':

> There are no flags, flowers, or shrill shouts of 'Vive la patrie!' as there were in 1914. Among the men departing now for the possible front, the morale is excellent but curiously mental. What the men say is intelligent, not emotional. 'If it's got to come, let's stop living in this grotesque suspense and get it over with once and for all. . . . Few Frenchmen are thrilled to go forth to die on the Somme as usual – this time for Danzig. Yet all the French seem united in understanding that this war . . . is about the theory of living and its eventual practice.[32]

P.J. Philip, the Paris-based correspondent for the *New York Times*, was similarly impressed by the national mood, one part resignation, one part resolution:

> [T]here were no cheering crowds, no enthusiasm, no passionate battle spirit. On the other hand, there was implicit obedience. There were no more than a few muttered curses of protest, no grumbling . . . no disobedience. . . . The evacuation of Paris . . . has been carried out methodically and calmly. . . . [T]here was none of the panic and hurry evident here during the Sudetenland crisis of last September. Everything has been different this year. The mobilization of the French Army, step by step, was conducted with the greatest order and calm. . . . Among the men, from whatever part of the country they arrived, one found the same silent, grave resolution. 'We have got to put an end to this Hitler nonsense . . . .'[33]

Maurice English, correspondent for the *Chicago Tribune*, had taken the same reading. There was, he said, 'no sign of desperation, only 'order . . . discipline [and] clockwork' precision. Even the children were disciplined, over 30 000 of them evacuated from Paris, some of them as young as three, saying tearful goodbyes to their parents, before being carried off to the countryside by bus and train. Two days of turmoil, a total of 48 trains, the little ones upset and confused, the older ones doing their best to put on a brave face.[34]

Portraits such as these, at least as they are invoked here, are not intended to imply unanimity. Given the thrust of the previous chapters – addressed, without exception, to opposing certainties – it would seem ill-advised to argue now that all Frenchmen were suddenly agreed. Not all of the differences which had characterized the national debate for 20 years had been consumed in the low fires of mobilization. There were still men and women on the radical right and left who were not fully reconciled with the regime. No doubt there were many in the labour movement who still resented the government's recent clampdown on the unions, and employers who were apprehensive of the state intrusions which were escalating with economic mobilization. Not all pacifists had been recruited to the war effort, and not all peasants. Some regretted the loss of Soviet assistance, and condemned the government, others the loss of Italy, and condemned the government. But for the moment, in early September 1939, there was a much higher level of national consensus than there had been for 20 years. Some of it was due to the government's strenuous efforts after Munich. Most of it, of course, was due to Hitler, whose threats and broken promises had slowly reset the fracture between those who for so long had argued for deterrence and those who had counter-argued for conciliation. Now, they were both too late, and in war they found common disappointment.

7 Lingering Doubts and Certain Defeat

France went to war on 3 September 1939, her ultimatum to Berlin having expired without a sign that Hitler had considered stopping the attack on Poland. In that sense, again, it was he who had made the decision for war. In another sense, however, this was more than a decision by default. As early as 24 August the Daladier cabinet had resolved on war in the event that Germany actually attacked the Polish state. The reasoning behind that resolution was in part psychological, in large part strategic. For one, their patience and their credulity were exhausted. They had watched Hitler opt for rearmament over disarmament, reintroduce conscription, unveil the air force, recover the Rhineland, seize Austria, swallow the Czechs and Slovaks, and then prepare for the conquest of Poland. They had watched and done nothing, intent as they were on avoiding a new bloodbath, even when it had meant – as it had with the Czechs – the abandonment of an ally. Now it was time to call a halt, out of pride, or honour, or self-respect. And also out of self-interest.

The fact was that the strategy of a long war could not tolerate further territorial aggrandizement on the part of Germany. That strategy was based on the calculation that Germany's indigenous resources for war would fall short of those that could be marshalled by France, Britain, their respective empires and allies. But allow Hitler to seize at will the natural resources of Poland, Rumania, Hungary, Bulgaria and Yugoslavia, and some new thinking would be called for. Let him gain control of Swedish iron ore, and negotiate the provision of other vital imports from Russia, and all bets would be off. Alexis Léger, now thoroughly estranged from his minister, Georges Bonnet, sadly concluded that it was now or never. Edouard Daladier, equally disgruntled with Bonnet, shared the same view. If left unchecked, Hitler's empire would become unstoppable. It was this point which the Prime Minister stressed in his radio broadcast of 25 August, an address in which he reaffirmed France's commitments to Poland and Rumania – on the grounds of honour and of self-interest. Give Hitler a free hand in the east, he said, and France is certain to be attacked with resources greater than those which we face today.[1]

As befitted a country that had no plans for an early offensive, and had not for over a decade, France rallied around the theme of self-defence. This was not a war against fascism, not even one to topple Hitler or Mussolini. It was a war of survival, one in which the Polish campaign would serve as prelude to the final onslaught against France, and eventually Britain. It was, perhaps, this difference in the degree of urgency which does something to explain the apparent difference in national response. For in the early months of the war, as long as Neville Chamberlain remained Prime Minister, elements of the British public begged Downing Street to get them out of the war immediately. By mid-September, just under 20 per cent of these correspondents were of such a mind; by early October, the proportion had risen to three-quarters. As might be expected, the grounds for such appeals varied, including those which denounced the war as a capitalist, even Jewish conspiracy. More common, however, were those which recalled Germany's 'humiliation' in 1919, and the subsequent, shabby treatment which she had been accorded by countries like France. Indeed, there seemed to have been many who still thought that France was the underlying problem. Chamberlain himself, still hopeful that Hitler would be overthrown in a coup led by 'good' Germans, ventured to say that the one remaining cloud on the horizon would be France.[2]

By then, two months into the war, there were very few in France who still believed in 'good' Germans. For them, Ambassador Phipps reported, Germans had been bent on conquest since the days of Frederick the Great. Now, simply put, it was time to confront them once again, to turn back their attack, eventually to overwhelm them, and finally to impose a peace which would subdue them forever. Such, Daladier said, was France's principal war aim.[3] In the interim, the task at hand was to prepare the nation materially and psychologically for the ordeal ahead. On the surface, the current of resistance had all but taken over the river of French opinion. Apart from the military front, where the emphasis was entirely on defensive preparations and waiting, everywhere else there were signs of an intensified national activity – within the government itself, within the spheres of economic mobilization and propaganda. Whatever else one might say of them, however qualified the success of their efforts, this was not a people who were smug about the invincibility of the Maginot Line, or so supine as to resign themselves to defeat.

On 14 September, ten days into the war, Premier Daladier announced a small reshuffle of his cabinet. Now that the Rubicon had been crossed, there was to be an Armaments ministry, and a ministry of Blockade. The dissolution of the ministry for National Economy meant that most of its functions were shifted to Paul Reynaud at Finance, a development which was seen to strengthen the hand of an outspoken critic of the policy which had led to Munich. Georges Bonnet, that resolute appeaser, had been sent over to Justice, leaving the Foreign Ministry to none other than Daladier himself: the Premier, the national defence minister, and now the foreign minister. For assistance in fulfilling these punitive responsibilities, the Premier also announced the creation of two Under Secretaries of State: one for the National Defence ministry, where he installed Hippolyte Ducos, a fellow Radical, teacher and distinguished war veteran; and another for the Quai d'Orsay, where he installed Champetier de Ribes, one of the ministers who had offered to resign over Munich. Another, Georges Mandel, remained at Colonies, where he continued to be in the vanguard of efforts to stop Hitler.[4]

Adding to the impression of a stronger and more tough-minded regime was a series of inter-related developments. One of them was Edouard Daladier's exceptional position – leader of the government, chief diplomatic spokesman, and coordinating officer for the preparations of army, navy and air force. Another was the steady erosion of parliamentary influence, and the attendant increase in the use of executive decree law. That trend had been evident before the end of 1938, in the rush to remedy the weaknesses exposed by the Munich crisis. By the outbreak of the war, it was well entrenched. Legislators had less and less to do, indeed, they were not even in session from early September until the end of November. And in the interim, the government continued to get things done by decree law – including those which imposed press censorship, interned enemy aliens and outlawed the Communist party. Even the new ministries, Armaments and Blockade, were created by this device. Little wonder, therefore, that when Hitler had finished off the Poles in early October and offered to open negotiations with the western powers, Daladier turned him down, on his own initiative, without benefit of either parliamentary or cabinet discussion. And little wonder that this man who is often seen as being too weak and indecisive, is sometimes criticized for being too authoritarian.[5]

There were some who were equally critical of the government's handling of economic mobilization – owners and employers who did not like interference by decree law, unions and workers who resented the increased controls and the diminished representation. But for all the criticism, there was a sense that something was happening, that the national leadership – whatever its perceived faults – was determined to accelerate defence production. There was plenty of evidence: the programme to buy American aircraft engines and to invest in that industry; the various missions exchanged with Britain for the purpose of discussing the sharing of economic, financial, military and technological resources; the widescale recruitment of women workers for offices and factories; the addition of more light mechanized divisions and the constitution of the first armoured divisions; the steady acceleration of aircraft production. With respect to the latter, that industry had quadrupled its workforce between the autumn of 1938 and June 1940, by which time it had a quarter of a million men and women producing close to 300 planes a month.[6] Short, as they still were, of skilled labour and machinetools, impeded as they were by ministerial turf wars and bureaucratic palsy, these were the people, and this was their government, which accomplished what Crémieux-Brilhac has called a 'gigantic' industrial effort between September 1939 and June 1940.[7]

No such claim has yet been made of the government's efforts in wartime propaganda. Compared to the practised, money-rich ministry of Dr Goebbels in Germany, the French counterpart was an orphan of sorts. Upon its creation in July 1939 it had been given Commissariat – rather than Ministerial – status, a fancy headquarters in the imposing Hotel Continental, the promise of a budget before long, and a director whose commitment to Franco-German reconciliation was almost as well known as his literary talents. His name was Jean Giraudoux, and before long he had enlisted the skills as well as the reputations of other dramatists, novelists, artists, musicians, and scholars. Someone said that Giraudoux had assembled all the pieces for a Rolls Royce; but clearly it was going to take time before the thing was running smoothly, smooth enough to handle the daily press conferences for domestic and foreign newspapers, the press censorship, the publication service, the photographic and cinema service, the translation service, the radio broadcasts. In fact, there proved too much to do, in too little time, all of it under an artist's aptitude for administration and an artist's inclination to tell the truth. Therein lay the Commissariat's strength and its weakness. It was less gifted than perhaps it should have been when it came to mass propaganda and the need to reduce the complex to the simple, but it attracted international attention – and respect – because of the men and women of letters who spoke on its behalf and who always associated France with civilization, democracy, and beauty: Julien Cain and René Huyghe, of the National Library and the Louvre; Gaston Rageot, president of the Société des Gens de Lettres; Paul Hazard and Emile Coornaert of the Collège de France; Henri Torrès from law; Christian Pineau from cinema; Jules Laroche from the diplomatic corps; Philippe Hériat winner of the Prix Goncourt; André Maurois of the Académie Française; Eve Curie, writer and now spokesperson for women's issues within the Commissariat.[8]

That said, the Commissariat was appreciably less successful at home than it was among educated Francophiles abroad, the rearmament efforts fell short of bringing France to military equality with Germany by the spring of 1940, and the Daladier cabinet was neither as united nor as vigorous as the preceding remarks may have suggested. Once more, we are faced with the task of balancing one set of partial truths with another. Before doing so, it is worth underscoring my intention to this point. And it has been a simple one – merely to say in another way, with other data, that the French war effort was no tautology. France was no more confident of victory than of defeat. And in that perennial uncertainty there was found enough reason and enough fear to mobilize the nation for a long war of attrition.

Still, there is no denying that there were plenty of mistakes, misreadings, and miscalculations, more than enough to fill the baskets of those who collect reasons for the collapse of 1940. The propaganda effort was too late in coming, and is said to have had two flaws. It did not target Nazi ideology as the real danger to peace. Second, by dissolving the French Communist party and, subsequently, by launching a propaganda campaign against Russia's attack on Finland, it managed to blur the nation's focus on the one imminent danger.[9] The economic mobilization and the attendant rearmament effort have also drawn much criticism. Despite projections of wartime needs, the country's industries were still critically short of modern machinetools. Despite projections, provision had not been made to replace quickly enough the 100 000 tons of German coke which French industry had consumed every month. But more striking by far was the collision between economic and military mobilization. Within two months, five million men had been called up for military service – leaving behind them the mine and the steel foundry, the drill-press and the blowtorch, the wheelhouse and the locomotive. Not surprisingly, industrial production suddenly slumped to 60 per cent of what it had been in July. Tank production at the Renault factory which produced the new B1 *bis* dropped from twelve units per month in August to nine in November. In fact, apart from its aviation subsidiaries, the whole Renault operation lost over half of its workforce to military call-up. Somewhere, amid the plans and the figures, there had been a signal failure of communications within this would-be nation at arms.

Experiences like these were embarrassing at best, demoralizing at worst. And this in a nation where morale had to be a fragile thing. The decision for war had been taken with no enthusiasm, the product solely of a desire to stop Hitler before Germany became invincible. But to keep that desire uppermost in the popular mind, and to prevent it from being replaced by a desire to stop the war itself, there had to be initiatives on a scale beyond those taken by government and high command. Propaganda was part of it. It had to be more domestically and mass oriented, and it had to be more passionate in its exhortations against the Hun and against the evil that was National Socialism. But there are times when words require action, and here too the will to resist was sorely tested by a military strategy which put all of its emphasis on patience and preparation.

No question but that the campaign opened timidly, when it came to direct military engagement with the enemy. Its mind completely focused on defensive measures against the German army and air force, the French high command replied to Hitler's attack on Poland with an early, tentative offensive. For less than a week a force of ten divisions and a few tank battalions slowly advanced into the Saarland for some ten kilometres beyond the German frontier. By 12 September, with the Poles nearly overrun, the forward progress stopped, and the order was given for a slow retirement back to French soil and French fortifications.[11] The truth was that it had been a 'phoney' offensive, and an appropriate beginning for the nine months of war that lay ahead.

Wedded as they were to the strategy of the long war, the key to which was averting an early collapse, the government and high command weighed every possible implication of premature offensive action – particularly in the west. In short, there were to be no new attempts to penetrate the German defences, no aerial raids against German industries, no mining of German rivers. The Italians were of less concern, but the arguments for trying to knock Mussolini out of the war seemed less persuasive than those which argued the dangers of attacking Italy – which had shown little disposition to do anything – and thereby creating an opening for Germany. More attractive was the chimera of a second front somewhere in eastern Europe. But months of discussions, with and without their British counterparts, produced neither agreement nor much concrete action. The old idea of an expeditionary force through Salonika proved unworkable. So did that of cutting off supplies of Rumanian oil to Germany by sabotaging the Ploesti oil fields; and that of sending a force to support the Finns against the Russians; and that of closing the sea lanes between Germany and the vital Swedish iron ore.

There were reasons for these failures, and no cryptic inventory should be allowed either to obscure them or to leave the impression that it came down purely to a matter of will. Not the least of these were the complexities associated with an allied command structure that was only months old. But what concerns us here is the relationship between this period of prolonged military inactivity and the state of mind of French soldiers and civilians. Here, too, there had been a retreat. Having steeled themselves for the worst, determined to get it over with, having rejoined their regiments with almost no complaint, the soldiers occupied themselves with either training or waiting. Both were boring, and irritating, the more one thought of family and workmates. True, there was soccer, even gardening, to reduce the boredom, mulled wine at night to ward off the cold, trench newspapers like the *Anticockroach* or *Laughing Outloud*, all of which were used to convey the confidence and imperturbability of France's soldiers. But underneath, the text read differently. Underneath, there was a growing uncertainty of purpose, and a growing sense that there really was no war after all – the very hope to which so many had clung for so long. And to this fertile ground came more seeds of doubt, including that which questioned whether

Hitler was really still interested in trying to conquer France – having absorbed Poland in October, and most of Denmark and Norway by May 1940. Still another was that which raised questions about the urgency of the crisis. Even if Hitler intended to strike, how much could he do against these huge Maginot defences, against over a hundred French and British divisions, with tanks and aircraft numbering well into the thousands?

How one characterizes this mood is a matter of interpretation. Is it the complacency which some have detected, or rather a confidence born of desperation? Throughout the whole of this phoney war period, General Gamelin exuded neither one nor the other. He was far too intelligent to under-estimate the German war machine, but sufficiently self-confident not to feel despair. In September, or November, or March, his gameplan was still intact, most of it studied and restudied for the better part of a decade. The Germans would not attack through Alsace–Lorraine, because of the Maginot emplacements; they would not attack slightly to the north, because of the terrain and cover of the Ardennes forest; and they would not attack to the south, through Switzerland, because of the French defences around Belfort. If they were coming, they would come from the north, through Holland or central Belgium; and it was there that they would meet a powerful French army, one sufficiently motorized and mechanized to be able to respond to the direction of the German attack: towards Namur on the Meuse, between it and Louvain on the Dyle, or towards Antwerp from the Breda region in Holland. Whatever the German plan, on the first signal of the Wehrmacht's intentions French and British divisions would push deep into Belgium, using the Ardennes sector as their hinge with the heavy fortifications to the south.

On 10 May 1940 that attack began, more or less where Gamelin had expected it, across southern Holland and northern Belgium – and with what seemed more like a diversionary attack from the Ardennes forest, much further to the south, towards a gap between the Belgian town of Namur and the French town of Sedan. Predictably, the appointed Anglo-French divisions raced northward, some as far as Breda, most to set up their defences along the Dyle, particularly around Gembloux. And there it was that they managed to hold back the German tide, until the 15th, when they were ordered to disengage. By then a greater danger had arisen further to the south, in fact between Namur and Sedan, one which threatened to cut off the allied armies in Belgium from the major part of the French army. By then the Germans had crossed the Meuse and were starting a sweep northward, led by seven panzer divisions and squadrons of Stuka dive-bombers.

The Reynaud government scrambled to respond. Having become Prime Minister in March 1940, Paul Reynaud had chosen to keep Daladier at National Defence and Gamelin as commander-in-chief of the allied forces. In fact, both had been political decisions, particularly in the case of Gamelin, in whom Reynaud had long since lost confidence. Indeed, the one bright spot on the disastrous horizon of mid-May 1940 was the opportunity finally to dump General Gamelin and replace him with the older but apparently more vital Maxime Weygand.[12] But General Weygand's presence in the Levant had meant that he could not assume command until 19 May, a delay which had left the Germans several days to further confound an enemy which no longer knew its commander. By the time Weygand was in place, and had started to implement the outline of Gamelin's final battleplan, it was too late to catch the panzer armies in a north–south pincer movement between what was left of General Billotte's divisions around Arras-Cambrai and those of General Touchon's Sixth Army to the south. Thereafter, for the next three weeks it was purely a matter of trying to contain the German advance southward – principally along the line linking Amiens, Péronne, Laon, Neufchâtel and the Ardennes Canal – and of evacuating from Dunkirk the stranded British and French forces in the north. But it took no seer to know where the momentum lay. On 5 June the Germans began their breakthrough towards Paris, and less than three weeks later the new Pétain government had sued for peace.

There must be a thousand books which in some way address the fall of France in 1940.[13] I have read a few of them, an admission which is less damaging if one keeps in mind the principal purpose of this work. That was to explain the origins of France's engagement in the Second World War. But given the rapidity with which the military campaign fell apart, that primary problem is forever associated with a secondary one. What is the connection between the wartime collapse and the degree and nature of the pre-war preparation? It is to that question that the following analysis addresses itself.

In the most particular sense, France collapsed because of the breakthrough at Sedan, because her armies could not recover in time to confine the damage and then to exact a heavy toll for the risks assumed by the German high command. But the reasons behind that reason are surely more complex. There is no doubt that these included the efficiency of German staff planning, the initiative of their field commanders, and the underlying audacity which explains the risk they ran of trapping the cream of their forces between two powerful enemy armies. That said, the plan they devised only in the spring of 1940, was aided and abetted by French assumptions and attendant plans, some of which were old, some new. General Gamelin expected the attack across central or northern Belgium – not through the Ardennes, because of the terrain, not through the Saar, because of the Maginot guns, not through Switzerland, because of the Belfort and Rhine defences. He was three-quarters right. They did not come across the Franco-German border, or the Franco-Swiss border. They did come across north-central Belgium, but their *schwerpunkt* was delivered from the south, below Namur, across southern Belgium and the Ardennes terrain which the French thought so ill-suited to rapid movement. And so the attackers had the benefit of surprise.

They also enjoyed the benefits which came with their concentration of superior firepower. Globally, army for army, the divisional strengths were roughly comparable. The German total, including strategic reserves, was approximately 136 divisions, the French approximately 93 divisions. The 10 British divisions, 10 Dutch and 22 Belgian thus brought the allied total to within one division of the German total. Furthermore, the number of allied tanks – approaching 4000 in all – was actually slightly superior to the German total. But where it really counted on 10 to 15 May, principally on the sector south of Namur, the Germans had assembled over 40 divisions, including three motorized infantry and seven armoured divisions. Against them stood, at best, France's First Army Group of 22 divisions, including three motorized and two light mechanized.

At worst, and in truth, that powerful German force was even more strongly advantaged, because the best-equipped, most mobile, and most northerly third of the French First Army Group was assigned to advance into Belgium and occupy the Dyle defences north of Namur. But the main German attack force was poised to strike in a sector south of Namur, a sector which had limited and incomplete field defences, and which was held by the eight divisions of the French Ninth Army and the seven divisions of the French Second Army. Furthermore, against the German Army Group A, with its seven powerful armoured divisions, these two French Armies could only muster one motorized infantry and three cavalry divisions. More precisely still, the German attack was concentrated on the seven divisions of the Second Army, two of which were second-line divisions manned by older troops. Entrusted with the defence of a long, 50 mile front extending from Sedan, these troops, with their older equipment, would prove no match for the firepower of an enemy who had materialized from a direction long considered improbable.

Finally, the combination of surprise and superior firepower drew further advantage from the material and psychological support rendered by the Luftwaffe. Here, the Germans enjoyed a superiority of at least two to one over the allied air forces, as well as better ground defences against allied bombers and reconnaissance aircraft. The implications of this imbalance quickly mushroomed once the attack was underway. On the one hand, allied air units were called upon to fly mission after mission from Holland to Luxembourg, keeping track of an enemy which seemed everywhere, trying to interrupt its communication lines and impede its advance, as well as flying cover for the Anglo-French forces which were advancing in a north-easterly direction into Belgium. On the other, German units were less concerned with slowing that advance northwards than they were with providing their own westward bound troops with air cover and with frustrating French attempts to move reinforcements to the crumbling Ardennes sector. Thus, having seized the offensive initiative and selected its primary target, the German high command was able to concentrate its armour and air power more effectively than the allies who were obliged to disperse their resources until the attacker's intent was fully clear. By then, by 15 May, the Meuse had been crossed, the panzer divisions embarked on their race northwest, and the reputation of the screaming Stuka dive-bomber made forever.

So France fell because of this critical breakthrough; and the breakthrough in turn is explained by a crushing local superiority in armoured and aerial firepower, and the attendant speed with which the German forces were able to sweep away the advance defence forces, cross the Meuse, breakout to the plains, and wreak havoc on the allies whose best forces were now having to fight their way back from advance positions in Belgium. That said, the inquiry must widen with the ensuing question. Why then did the French and allied armies fail to contain the breakthrough and subsequently extinguish it with powerful counter-offensives? In short, why did the loss of an opening battle lead so precipitately to the loss of the war? It is at this level that one may detect certain connections between this dramatic military event and a number of the interwar debates discussed earlier.

For instance, the whole of French grand strategy between the wars had been predicated on the belief that any future military victory over Germany was dependent on the assistance of allies. At the very least it meant active cooperation from Belgium and Britain, possibly from Holland and, preferably, from the United States. Ideally, it meant such an alliance in the west, supplemented by a second front in east-central Europe, one that envisaged various combinations of Polish, Czech, Rumanian and Yugoslav forces, abetted in various ways by the Italians, Russians and Turks. But in the spring of 1940 most of the promise had disappeared. The United States had remained neutral, the Rumanians, Yugoslavs and Turks had found various formulae to become essentially neutral, the Italians had opted for Hitler and, in their own way, so had the Russians. The Czechs were gone, the Poles too, and with them any hopes for an early eastern front.

That left the Belgians, Dutch, British and French, united by now in their determination to resist German aggression in the west, but not on a great deal more. Most telling, from the point of view of what happened in mid-May, was Belgium's insistence on maintaining all the outward signs of neutrality, a policy which neither fooled nor deterred Hitler but badly frustrated Anglo-French efforts to coordinate defensive plans in the Lowlands. It was this, for example, which explains why some of the British and French forces advancing into Belgium on 10–11 May had to install themselves in positions still not fortified by Belgian engineers. More serious was the Belgian decision to surrender on 28 May, only 18 days after the opening attack, although ten days after the Dutch. Thus, before the end of May, less than three weeks into the war, the French found themselves without the Dutch, without the Belgians, and without a good part of the British Expeditionary Force, key elements of which had been either destroyed or evacuated from Dunkirk. In that sense, and for that reason, it may be said that the allied collapse is at least one part of the explanation for the French failure to contain the German breakthrough.

There is another sense in which this was truly an allied collapse, not a peculiarly French one. Central to the failure to contain the German breakthrough was the inability of the defenders to gauge, accurately enough, the speed with which the attacker was moving. Repeatedly, through the second half of May and the first half of June, they anticipated attacks which would develop much more slowly than they did – partly because the allies still believed that a well-organized defence would undo an offence, especially if the armoured vanguard got ahead of its supporting infantry and artillery, and partly because they believed that rapidly unfolding offensives were vulnerable to communication and logistical breakdowns and to deadly counter-offensives. Reassembled, these arguments go part of the way to explaining why the allied armies – with their light superiority in the actual number of tanks – were well behind the Wehrmacht in concentrating this firepower into actual armoured divisions. Characteristically, in other words, the respective allied armies were more circumspect about the potential of such divisions, and more mindful of their vulnerability to anti-tank guns and counter-attacking armour.

It was not a matter of ignorance, in the neutral sense of the word. French intelligence, for example, had remained very much on top of German tank theory and field experiments. They had the figures on tank production, and the specifications for armour thickness, weaponry, speed performance and fuel capacity. But such knowledge, shared among the allies, did not necessarily mean understanding.[15] Secure in other things they knew – that tanks counterattacking with infantry and artillery were likely to be more effective than tanks attacking without them, that tanks were limited by terrain and fuel supplies – they were inclined to magnify the problems facing the German commanders. Once the attack began on 10 May it was too late for them to upgrade their expectations of how fast a panzer division, supported from the air, could really travel in open country. Thus, they tended to calculate fuel needs by the gallon instead of the ton, time by the day instead of the hour, distance by the mile instead of the tens of miles. In this sense, particularly, the collapse really was the product of a failure of intellect – a judgment which applies to a collective allied failure, rather than to an exclusively French one, and which is offered without forgetting either the numerical superiority of the allied tanks in 1940 or the technical superiority of some of their latest models.[16]

Since 1940 it has taken little effort to see the intellectual shortcomings within this persistent confidence in the superiority of French armoured doctrine. And it will take little more to detect the connections between that confidence and the broader assumptions of French grand strategy. It was to be a war of years, not of weeks, a war which was to commence by rejecting a German attack with modern defensive technology: concrete fortifications, land mines, artillery, machineguns, anti-tank guns and anti-tank obstacles; some motorized infantry divisions; small armoured units widely distributed throughout the regular infantry divisions; a few larger armoured units assembled in cavalry, light-mechanized and, eventually, heavy armoured divisions. Air power, too, in the first instance, would be assigned an equally defensive role, providing air cover for the troops and for presumed strategic targets like industrial and transportation centres. Essentially the sole objective in this first stage of the war was to avert defeat, employing modern firepower within a primarily defensive context, even for the counter-attacking role assigned to the larger armoured units.

Rephrased, the French army was not contemplating any kind of early, deep-penetration, offensive. Apart from the limited requirements of the few divisions assigned to advance into Belgium – should the latter call for help in sufficient time – there was little in the defensive plan which absolutely demanded a high level of mobility on the part of the artillery and infantry. Their job was to hold and overpower, not to bob and weave. Eventually, to be sure, their role would change with the passage of time and with the transition to the offensive stage of the war. And in the interim, the fully mobilized war economies of France and her allies would be churning out the self-propelled field guns, the armoured cars and lorries, the motorized fuel and munitions services, the tanks and aircraft, all of which would take the fight deeper and deeper into Germany. In no sense, or at any time, did the French high command as a collectivity renounce mobility on the battlefield or the instruments of war which would assure it. But it would be fair to detect a link between their anticipation of a long war and their confidence that the current mix of static and mobile defence would be good enough to get them through the initial stage of the war.

So it is one senses that the calibration of ideas is more important than that of the guns, that there is a more fundamental problem below the surface shortages, below the faulty radio equipment, the delayed orders, the premature withdrawal, the unarmed fortifications. At bottom, there remained the familiar tension between confidence and apprehension, with the latter going far towards explaining how much was done in the name of the Republic's defence, and with the former doing the same for the shortcomings and oversights which have preoccupied us ever since 1940. It had not been easy to convince a nation which, by the mid-1930s, had invested so heavily in the Maginot emplacements, that it was in mortal peril if it did not plough even more money into new weapons and new machines. It had not been easy to find the exact balance between promoting a confidence in the country's defensive capacities, and promoting an apprehension great enough to combat complacency. General Gamelin had sat on this rail since 1935, shifting his weight between the alternate claims that France was in danger and that France had nothing to fear. The only thing that made it comfortable, for him, and for his principal seat-mate, Edouard Daladier, was the belief that the war would be long and that time would allow them to remedy their most serious deficiencies – and with the most modern equipment available. Neither, in short, could afford to believe that they had run out of time, and that a real-enough German danger was on the point of becoming invincible. It was this inability, understandable as it was, that had to qualify the sense of urgency with which the entire rearmament effort was conducted between 1936 and 1940.

In the face of such cherished assumptions, one can only imagine the impact which the German breakthrough must have had on morale, even by the end of May. By then every French officer knew three things. First, their men, like themselves, were part of a population which had resisted the prospect of a new war for as long as it could. Second, many of those men had used the phoney war period to become bored, resentful and perplexed. Especially the latter, for either there was a danger which had to be eradicated, or there was not, in which case everyone could go home. The sitting and waiting had done them no good, affording them plenty of opportunity to ridicule the silliness of it all and, at the same time, to read or listen to German propagandists who fed on their doubts. Third, these soldiers were now being asked in May–June 1940 to

recover the determined mood of the mobilization period, to re-en-
gage an enemy of now demonstrable efficiency, in the interests of
their commander's all but discredited war plan. By early June, with
the Germans secure in northern France, the Republic's capacity for
a long war had plummeted in the wake of German seizures or
German bombing. Three-quarters of French steel production had
been shut down, half of the gun powder plants, nearly half of the
bomb manufacturing capacity.[17] More simply put, a scenario that
has been refined for over a decade could not be totally rewritten, and
rewritten again, over a few crisis weeks, without some loss of
credibility and conviction – an observation for those who are
tempted to magnify the ease with which the Reynaud government
might have continued the war from North Africa .

This is not to say for a moment that the French, or their allies,
were instantly demoralized or that they refused to fight. In fact, the
authoritative voice of M. Crémieux-Brilhac has likened the tenacity
shown by French troops on the Somme and Aisne in late May–early
June with the spirit of the Marne in 1914. And if death and injury
count in such calculations, it should be known that over 100 000
French soldiers gave their lives in the course of those six weeks of
warfare, and that another 250 000 were wounded. It should be
known that the 1600 French and English planes that were lost by the
time of the armistice had helped in the destruction of some 1400
German planes. It should be known that some of the German panzer
units, for all their vaunted power, had lost up to half of their tanks
to enemy fire.[18] Any suggestion that there had been no resistance is
therefore a calumny. Just as it would be an exaggeration to say that
all units had fought well to the end. Some were quick to collapse
under the blistering firepower assembled by the Germans, surrende-
ring after only limited resistance or withdrawing in disorder. In fact,
it has been said that there were really 'two armies' within the French
army of 1940, one of which was resolute, the other more quickly
demoralized. It had to do with their level of training, the age of the
troops, the state of their weaponry, their defensive location, the
quality of their leadership, and several handfuls of other variables.
But the point is that the overall record of the French army and air
force was mixed, and better than is often acknowledged in more
facile attempts to make the defeat intelligible.

A similar rectification seems in order for the civilian regimes of
Edouard Daladier and Paul Reynaud. And for the same reason.

Somehow, through some haphazard but persistent process of allusion and innuendo, we have become accustomed to the notion that these defeated leaders had it coming to them, that they were architects of their own misfortune, and that the real flaw was in their character. No doubt there is some truth in it, as there always is – except among hero worshippers. But there is another side, one that had linked the *Munichois* and the *anti-Munichois*, the *mous* and the *durs*, the appeasers and the hardliners, from the time the guns had been silenced in 1918. And that link became totally exposed in June 1940, when the Reynaud government in particular had to ask itself about the price of further resistance. To be frank, had to ask itself how many more young men it was going to commit to a collapsed allied cause, against an enemy which had badly outclassed its opponents for the best part of a month – and which, on 11 June, had been further encouraged by the opening of an Italian offensive against France.

To this day, some will be offended by the question, seeing it as some subtle apology for the armistice and the ensuing excesses of Vichy France. Such is hardly my intent. Rather it is to correct an impression. Just as the resistance displayed by the armed forces was more considerable than is often allowed, so there is something about the civilian leaders which warrants a second look. Implicit, always, in the criticism of the Daladier and Reynaud administrations is their gutlessness. In a word, they folded, when they should have stayed in the game. Whatever it is called – will-power, resolution, courage – it failed the Bonnets, the Daladiers and the Reynauds; and in their failure France fell.[19]

But Georges Bonnet was a decorated war hero, a recipient of the *croix de guerre*. So was Edouard Daladier. So were Paul Reynaud and Henri Queuille, both of whom had been commended for bravery during their service with the medical corps during World War One. So was Guy La Chambre. So was the twice-wounded Jean Giraudoux, and the twice-wounded Yvon Delbos, who had returned to the cabinet when Jean Zay had resigned in order to join his regiment. César Campinchi was a Verdun veteran, wounded and decorated, whose brother and three cousins had been killed in the war. René Besse was another *grand mutilé*, having lost a hand in the previous war. The war wounds of Champetier de Ribes had been recognized in his promotion to Chevalier in the Legion of Honour, an honour similarly conferred on Albert Lebrun, President of the Republic, for his service in the artillery corps. Albert Rivière, at Veterans Affairs in 1940, was another wounded war veteran. So was Georges Pernot, Daladier's minister for the Blockade. Hippolyte Ducos, at National Defence, was a decorated war veteran. Laurent-Eynac, the Air minister, was an air force veteran, whose service record carried several citations for valour. Alphonse Rio, at the Merchant Marine, was a veteran naval officer; Albert Sarraut had been an infantry company commander; Camille Chautemps, long time deputy premier, had been a volunteer in 1914.

So did they fold in 1938, and fold in 1940, despite those records? Or because of them? Anyone who heard Edouard Daladier's speech to parliament in early September 1939, at the outbreak of hostilities, was struck by his reluctance even to use the word 'war', and by his insistence on clinging to 'peace'. Three months later he took obvious satisfaction from the fact that the armed forces had so far suffered fewer than 2000 deaths, compared to the 450 000 deaths which had been recorded by December 1914.[20] Georges Pernot, appearing before the Chamber's foreign affairs commission in November 1939 as minister of the Blockade, managed to put it more poignantly. I am a father, he said, with three sons already in service and two more about to join their regiments. 'I have the feeling that in conducting the economic war I am protecting the lives of my children, and those of others'.[21]

Men in their fifties and sixties, for the most part, many of them fathers of families, these were people who had to endure two agonies which – happily – are beyond the experience of most readers. Their youth had been interrupted and traumatized by one war; and then in middle-age they had been called upon to jeopardize the youth of their sons and daughters. That is why, as I see it, the decision to go to war had been more courageous than is often credited. And perhaps that is also why the decision to end it was taken, because this was no war of economic attrition, because the numbers of dead had soared from a few thousand to a hundred thousand in the space of six weeks. It is here that the memories and mood of the French leaders accorded very closely to those of the French public. Torn by the decision to return to war, and torn by the decision to leave it, this government and people remained true to the ambivalence which had characterized their behaviour since the armistice of 1918.

In the end we are left with an old impression, that of two Frances. It is a familiar enough theme, even a little worn by repeated efforts to distinguish between rich and poor, urban and rural, agricultural and industrial, left and right, secular and religious, common and elite and – too often, implicitly – good and bad. But is this a country divided, or multiplied, by two? The former is the more familiar; and it has the benefit of straight lines and simplicity. The latter is more complex, incorporating rather than separating. Thus this single France is neither aggressive nor passive, but both; neither complacent nor apprehensive, but both; and more or less at the same time. This ambivalence is not easy to grasp, and even harder to express, but it is at the very heart of the French condition between the wars.

Conclusion

Books, like undergraduate essays, do require a few concluding remarks. It is not simply a matter of convention, for the convention has its reasons. First, it is a way of separating the analyst from the data which he or she has chosen for analysis. In this case, the data have been used to describe and explain how and why France entered the Second World War, and how and why her military campaign ended so badly. But the book is independent of that collapse, and cannot simply end with it. Rather, a conclusion affords an opportunity to remind both author and reader that we have, at best, no more than an interpretation. Also, it affords authors a moment to recall whatever points they consider the most salient and instructive, while offering readers the same moment to judge whether the author's conclusions are consistent with the author's evidence, and whether the inquiry seems to have been fair-minded.

Early in this volume I admitted that mine was not a new mind, that I already had impressions of interwar France, and that I was inclined to sympathize with the plight in which it found itself. I should be surprised if that sympathy did not at times betray itself in the ensuing chapters. Indeed, some may find it too intrusive, and for that reason suspect my judgment. To them I would make two replies. My intent throughout was never to deny or even minimize the indecisiveness of French society between the wars, but to portray it and explain it with reference to conflicting certainties. It was the latter which gave rise to the ambivalence, and it was the ambivalence that occasioned the indecisiveness. Additionally, one of the reasons why this seems an approach of some merit is my long-term discomfort with the most common alternative − namely that of the judicial inquiry into which historians strut with armfuls of indictments. Mainly to make the perplexing more readily intelligible. Our subjects are not defendants; they cannot now speak for themselves even if they were; and we are not in the trial business. I have tried to keep that in mind, however much such counsel may arouse suspicions of special pleading.

The trick, it seems to me, is to neither inculpate nor exonerate. It is to explain. I have said earlier that interwar France was at sixes and sevens, and now offer a reminder of my reasoning. Diplomatically, the government knew that it required allies if it hoped to win another war against Germany. But such a simple formula belied its inherent complexities. Understandably, no country wanted to be used by France, for French purposes. Each demanded reciprocal commitments from Paris, and each expected more of French policy – either to be more firm towards Germany, or more conciliatory. Such contradictory pressures, combined with those from French domestic politics, made it exceptionally difficult for the Foreign ministry to come up with really bold initiatives in the 1930s. The National Defence ministry faced similar conundrums. Fully committed to the strategy of a long war, during which the superior resources of France and her allies could be marshalled against Germany, the government and high command had to be alive to the chaos which might be induced by an enemy bent on a short war. And it was stakes such as these which added intensity to the ongoing debates between the partisans of fixed and mobile defence, and between those of citizen and professional armies.

Politically, the executive branch of government had to operate within constraints of another order. Well before the 1930s, the Legislature had resolved to defend with full vigour its parliamentary authority against any accretion of executive privilege. That resolve, combined with a multiple 'party' system that precluded any group from approaching a majority, meant two things. First, every cabinet was a coalition cabinet. Second, every cabinet was as fragile as the momentary truces worked out in the Legislature. And of course those truces, and their founderings, were in part a reflection of ideological affiliation and disaffiliation. The many groups to the right of the political centre were not going to tolerate state incursions into private business or closer ties with the Soviet Union. The many groups to the left of the political centre were not going to support deflationary economic policies against those of modest or lowly fortune, or closer ties with Fascist Italy. Together, this combination of political and ideological constraints further underscored the difficulty of knowing with certainty what to do.

Economic analysts only compounded the uncertainties. So much depended on what Hitler was doing to the German economy, and how long it could sustain the Nazi regime's manhandling. Collapse might lead to a more subdued and conciliatory profile, if Hitler were not mad or if he were overthrown by moderates. Or it might provoke desperate and acquisitive measures against another of Germany's neighbours. And on the answer to that question rested the nature and timing of the French counter-response. Should emphasis continue to be placed on the development of infrastructure for the long war that might be in the offing? Or should all hands be put immediately to work on emergency measures for war production? Less pressing, but troublesome all the same, was the partly related, partly discrete issue of Anglo-Saxon economic and cultural influence in a country already feeling threatened by the Germans.

Finally, there was one overriding uncertainty in the social psychology of interwar France. The greatest single menace was war, from the time the guns had been silenced in 1918. How best to prevent its return? By refusing to countenance it in any shape or form, against any enemy, at any time? Or by accepting it as a possibility, and making the necessary diplomatic, economic and military arrangements to confront an enemy with certain defeat? The most committed pacifists apart, the French reluctantly subscribed to the latter notion, not so much as to prepare for war as to avert it. When that failed, as ultimately it did in September 1939, the doubts slowly resurfaced and finally triumphed in the following summer. To the relief of many French men and women, and to the despair and resentment of others. There was no way that this could be called anything but a defeat; and out of that has come generations of critics intent on finding who or what was to blame.

I am not among them, or at least I have had tempered any inclination to criticize the French of the inter-war period. While I share with others many misgivings about trying to make Adolf Hitler the sole cause of the Second World War in Europe – as if no-one else mattered or had any share in the responsibility – I have also tired of the attempts to concentrate on the faults and miscalculations of his victims. Here, my objections are again on two counts. First, but least, all of the prescriptions for what the French government should have done between the wars have been made up with only one condition in mind. They should have allied with Stalin, and over-ridden the self-serving objections of French conservatives. Or they should have recruited Mussolini, and ignored the specious complaints from the left. They should have used more muscle and stronger words with the Weimar Republic, as well as with Nazi

Germany. Or they should have been more conciliatory, less menac-
ing, to both regimes. All of these formulae remain truths to someone,
just as they were in the 1920s and 1930s; and the unanimous verdicts
of single authors should not be allowed to disguise that fact. Second,
whatever its scandals, its instances of corruption and venality, its
political turbulence, the Third Republic never approached the Third
Reich on anyone's scale of 'decadence'. Ask Hitler's opponents in
parliament and press, ask the ethnic minorities, ask the Christian
community, and ask the Jews. It is time to stop flogging that old
notion of Sartre's priest, namely that France had it coming, that
defeat at the hands of the Nazis was the mark of a lost and morally
disoriented people.

It is time, but it will not be easy. There is something reassuring
about pursuing the guilty few, or attributing blame to an entire
society gone wrong. Either constitutes an answer, and is thus a
benefaction to anyone intent on finding a single reason for the
collapse of 1940. But understanding is another matter. I have offered
a more complex explanation, one that does not rely on conspirators
and traitors, or moral drift and disintegration. Rather it relies on a
belief that the foreign policy with which a country confronts the
prospect of war is itself the product of many calculations: strategic,
ideological, economic, cultural and psychological. And it has placed
much emphasis upon the way people – collectively and individually
– remember their past. That is at the root of this complexity, for the
fact is that people do not remember the same past. Out of that,
comes the dissent, then the discord, as alternate truths collide and
compete for the attention of reflective people who have yet to make
up their mind.

Ultimately, when one takes away the conveniences of traitors and
degenerates, this is the single greatest charge against the Republic's
leaders. And their greatest defence. They could not make up their
minds about how best to deal with the German problem, the
Depression, the challenges contained in modern military technology,
the ideological threats of communism and fascism, the economic and
social menace of Anglo-Saxon currency and culture, the intellectual
and moral spectre of another war. I do not dispute that charge, or
at least would quickly concede that they found it very difficult to
decide. But it would take someone more confident than me to say
precisely when, and how, these leaders should have decided, when
and how they should have acted. And in my own personal indecision

I find some little incentive to defend these soldiers and civilians from the derision of those who never doubt.

Ambivalence, I would argue, is the prerogative of all thoughtful men and women who are not convinced that the arguments on one side of a debate are always more compelling than those on the other. It is the dilemma of reasonable people who rely on evidence and argument, who are no-one's true believers, and who live in societies where debate is not silenced by men with guns. It is also, I believe, at the heart of the human condition. Forty million French men and women, by my telling, were not convinced that they could handle the German challenge. Or convinced that they could not. Characteristically, they were neither complacent nor despondent, but hovered between the two, drawn one way by the assurances of optimists, drawn the other by the premonitions of pessimists. This strikes me as entirely unexceptional, the responses of sensible people, even reminiscent of the qualified, guarded optimism with which we ourselves survived the Cold War period, and with which we are adjusting to its sequel.

Expressed in more recognizable form, the ambivalence of interwar France reminds me of the difficulty which all of us have in drawing the line between moderation and excess. The concept is easy enough. It is the measurement that is a problem. This woman, we say, is armed with self-assurance, that one crippled with conceit. This man is industrious, that one a workaholic. Parents want children to be neat, but not compulsive, good-natured but not flippant. The problem is that people are not digitally programmed. We, like the people of interwar France, transmit and receive from a broad band of frequencies, and so like them we experience confidence and apprehension within moments of each other, hope and despair, anger and compassion. It is what we are, sufficiently inconsistent to take it for granted. We accept it within ourselves, among ourselves. Surely we could do the same for our predecessors.

Notes

1. FRANCE AMBIVALENT, 1919–40

1. Jean-Paul Sartre, *Iron in the Soul* (Harmondsworth: Penguin, 1967) 246; Marc Bloch, *Strange Defeat. A Statement of Evidence Written in 1940* (New York: Norton, 1968) 132; Jean Dutourd, *The Taxis of the Marne* (1957) as found in Samuel M. Osgood (ed.) *The Fall of France, 1940* (Boston: Heath, 1972) 109.

2. Jean-Jacques Becker, *1914: Comment les Français sont entrés dans la guerre* (Paris: FNSP, 1977) 574; *Sunday Times*, 27 August 1939; Wladimir d'Ormesson in *Le Figaro*, 30 June 1939; Jacques Maritain, *France, My Country* (1941), as quoted in Samuel M. Osgood (ed.) *The Fall of France, 1940*, 122.

3. Maurice Vaïsse, 'Le pacifisme français dans les années trente', *Relations Internationales*, no. 53 (Autumn 1988) 51.

4. Geneviève Colin and Jean-Jacques Becker, 'Les écrivains, la guerre de 1914 et l'opinion publique', *Relations Internationales*, no. 24 (Winter 1980) 425–42; also Stéphane Audoin-Rouzeau, ' "Bourrage de crâne" et Information en France en 1914–1918', in J.J. Becker et al (ed.) *Les sociétées européennes* (Paris: Université de Nanterre, 1990) 163–74; and Jean-François Sirinelli, 'Les intellectuels français et la guerre', in *Les sociétées européennes* 145–61.

5. Georges Soutou, 'La France et l'Allemagne en 1919', in J.-M. Valentin, J. Bariéty, A. Guth (eds) *La France et l'Allemagne entre les deux guerres mondiales* (Nancy: Presses Universitaires de Nancy, 1987) 9–20.

6. See *Journal Officiel* (J.O.) Chamber Debates, 2–3 September 1919, 4099–114, 4124–9; 18 September, 4422–3; also Young *Power and Pleasure. Louis Barthou and the Third French Republic* (Montreal: McGill–Queen's University Press, 1991) 155–60.

7. Pierre Miquel, *La paix de Versailles et l'opinion publique française* (Paris: Flammarion, 1972) 563.

8. André Martel, 'La doctrine française de contre-offensive à l'épreuve de la deuxième guerre mondiale', *Relations Internationales*, no. 35 (Autumn 1983) 356.

9. See Norman Ingram, *The Politics of Dissent. Pacifism in France, 1919–1939* (Oxford: Clarendon Press, 1991); also Antoine Prost, 'Les anciens combattants français et l'Allemagne, 1933–1938', in *La France et l'Allemagne, 1932–1936* (Paris: Editions du CNRS, 1980) 131–48.

10. See Vincent J. Pitts, *France and the German Problem. Politics and Economics in the Locarno Period, 1924–1929* (New York: Garland, 1987) 327; also Sally Marks, *The Illusion of Peace. International Relations in Europe, 1918–1933* (London: Macmillan, 1976) 48–53; and 'The Misery of Victory: France's Struggle for the Versailles Treaty', *Historical Papers* (Canadian Historical Association, 1986) 126.

11. Edward D. Keeton, *Briand's Locarno Policy. French Economics, Politics, and Diplomacy, 1925–1929* (New York: Garland, 1987).

12. See Walter A. McDougall, *France's Rhineland Diplomacy, 1914–1924. The Last Bid for a Balance of Power in Europe* (Princeton, NJ: Princeton University Press, 1978) 9.

13. Jonathan Helmreich, 'The Negotiation of the Franco-Belgian Military Accord of 1920', *French Historical Studies*, iii, no. 3 (Spring 1964) 360–78.

14. Piotr S. Wandycz, *The Twilight of French Eastern Alliances 1926–1936. French–Cze-choslovak–Polish Relations from Locarno to the Remilitarization of the Rhineland* (Princeton, NJ: Princeton University Press, 1988) 3–16.

15. See Judith M. Hughes, *To the Maginot Line. The Politics of French Military Preparation in the 1920s* (Cambridge, Mass.: Harvard University Press, 1971) 192–93; Jeffery A. Gunsburg, *Divided and Conquered. The French High Command and the Defeat of the West, 1940* (Westport, Conn.: Greenwood Press, 1979) 11–12; and his original dissertation 'Vaincre ou Mourir: The French High Command and the Defeat of France, 1919–May 1940' (Durham: Duke University Press, 1974) 24–7; Henry Dutailly, *Les problèmes de l'armée de terre française, 1935–1939* (Paris: Imprimerie nationale, 1980) 91–114.

16. Vivian Rowe, *The Great Wall of France* (London: Putnam, 1959) 63.

17. For a useful survey of French strategy, see Robert A. Doughty, 'The French Armed Forces, 1918–1940,' in Allan R. Millett and Williamson Murray (eds) *Military Effectiveness*, vol. 2 (Boston: Allen and Unwin, 1988) 53.

18. For a summary of this internal tension, see Maurice Vaïsse, *Sécurité d'Abord. La politique française en matière de désarmement, 9 décembre 1930–17 avril 1934* (Paris: Pedone, 1981) 597–615.

19. See Young, 'The Making of a Foreign Minister: Louis Barthou (1862–1934)', in Michael G. Fry (ed.) *Power, Personalities and Policies: Essays in Honour of Donald Cameron Watt* (London: Cass, 1992) 83–106.

20. As Geoffrey Warner argued in an important early work, Laval was also inclined to minimize the complexities of international affairs and by so doing to exaggerate his grasp of them. See *Pierre Laval and the Eclipse of France* (London: Eyre and Spottiswoode, 1968).

21. For the most recent account of this event, from a French perspective, see Stephen A. Schuker, 'France and the Remilitarization of the Rhineland, 1936', *French Historical Studies*, xiv, no. 3 (Spring 1986) 299–338.

22. See Gordon Dutter, 'Doing Business with the Nazis: French Economic Relations with Germany under the Popular Front', *Journal of Modern History*, vol. lxiii, no. 2 (June 1991) 296–326; 'Doing Business with the Fascists: French Economic Relations with Italy under the Popular Front', *French History*, iv, no. 2 (June 1990) 174–98.

23. For the relationship of economics and foreign policy, see René Girault, 'The Impact of the Economic Situation on the Foreign Policy of France, 1936–1939', in W.J. Mommsen and L. Kettenacker (eds) *The Fascist Challenge and the Policy of Appeasement*, (London: Allen and Unwin, 1983) 202–26; and Gilbert Ziebura, 'Determinants of French Foreign Policy after 1932: On the Relationship of National and Foreign Policy and International Politics and Economics', in Fred Eidlin (ed.) *Constitutional Democracy. Essays in Comparative Politics* (Boulder: Westview Press, 1983) 449–69.

24. A drift for which Blum and Delbos have been held largely responsible, see William I. Shorrock, *From Ally to Enemy. The Enigma of Fascist Italy in French Diplomacy, 1920–1940* (Kent, Ohio: Kent State University Press, 1988), 291–293.

25. John C. Cairns, 'Planning for *la guerre des masses*: Constraints and Contradictions in France before 1940' in H.R. Borowski (ed.) *Military Planning in the Twentieth Century*, (Washington, DC: United States Air Force, 1986) 51; and Robert Frank(enstein), 'The Decline of France and French Appeasement Policies, 1936–1939', in W. Mommsen and L. Kettenacker (eds) *The Fascist Challenge and the Policy of Appeasement* (London: Allen and Unwin, 1983) 237.

26. See Patrice Buffotot, 'The French High Command and the Franco–Soviet Alliance, 1933–1939', *Journal of Strategic Studies*, v, no. 4 (December 1982) 546–59; Maurice Vaïsse, 'Les militaires français et l'alliance franco-soviétique au cours des années 1930', in *Forces armées et systèmes d'alliances* (Paris: Cahiers de la Fondation pour les Etudes de Défense Nationale, 1984) 689–703; Michael J. Carley, 'End of the "Low,

Dishonest Decade": Failure of the Anglo-French Soviet Alliance in 1939', *Europe-Asia Studies*, xlv, no. 2 (1993) 303–41.

27. See Nicole Jordan, 'Léon Blum and Czechoslovakia, 1936–1938', *French History*, v, no. 1 (March 1991) 48–73.

28. See Robert Frank(enstein), *Le prix du réarmement français, 1935–1939* (Paris: Publications de la Sorbonne, 1982); also Jean Doise and Maurice Vaïsse, *Diplomatie et outil militaire, 1871–1969* (Paris: Imprimerie nationale, 1987) 321–5.

29. Elisabeth Du Réau, 'Enjeux stratégiques et redéploiement diplomatique français: novembre 1938, septembre 1939', *Relations Internationales*, no. 35 (Autumn 1983) 327.

30. See Frédéric Seager, 'Les buts de guerre alliés devant l'opinion (1939–1940)', *Revue d'Histoire Moderne et Contemporaine*, xxxii (October–December 1985) 617–38.

31. See Paul Stafford, 'The French Government and the Danzig Crisis: The Italian Dimension', *International History Review*, vi, no. 1 (February 1984) 48–87.

32. Guy Rossi-Landi, *La drôle de guerre. La vie politique en France 2 septembre 1939–10 mai 1940* (Paris: Colin, 1971) 17.

33. Alfred Sauvy, *De Paul Reynaud à Charles De Gaulle* (Paris: Casterman, 1972) 97.

34. Sartre, *Iron in the Soul*, 245.

35. J.B. Duroselle, *L'Abîme, 1939–1945* (Paris: Imprimerie nationale, 1982) 25.

36. Rossi-Landi, *La drôle de guerre*, 171.

37. See Martin S. Alexander, 'Maurice Gamelin and the Defeat of France, 1939–1940', in Brian Bond (ed.) *Fallen Stars. Eleven Studies of Twentieth Century Military Disasters* (London: Brassey's, 1991) 107–140.

38. See Serge Berstein, *La France des années 30* (Paris: Colin, 1988) 169.

39. Jean-Paul Sartre, *Nausea*. Translated by Lloyd Alexander. (New York: New Directions Paperback, 1964) 13.

2. AMBIVALENCE REVISITED: HISTORY AND HISTORIANS

1. Assemblée Nationale. Session de 1947. No. 2344. *Rapport fait au nom de la commission chargée d'enquêter sur les événements survenus en France de 1933 à 1945*, 2 vols; Annexes (Dépositions). Témoignages et documents recueillis par la commission d'enquête parlementaire, 9 vols. (Paris: Presses Universitaires de France, 1947).

2. Marc Bloch, *Strange Defeat* (New York: Norton, 1968).

3. Sartre, *Iron in the Soul* (Harmondsworth: Penguin, 1967) 245–6.

4. See Young, 'Partial Recall: Political Memoirs and Biography from the Third French Republic', in George Egerton (ed.) *Political Memoir: Essays on the Politics of Memory* (London: Cass, 1994) 62–75.

5. See Georges Castellan, 'Wehrmacht vue de la France, septembre 1939, *Revue historique de l'armée*, no. 2 (1949) 35–49; *Le réarmement clandestin du Reich, 1930–1935* (Paris: Plon, 1954).

6. In particular, see Pierre Renouvin's two volumes on *Les crises du XXe siècle* (Paris: Hachette, 1957–8) in his own series *Histoire des relations internationales*; Maurice Baumont's two volumes on *La faillite de la paix* (Paris: Presses Universitaires de France, 1951); J.B. Duroselle, *Histoire diplomatique de 1919 à nos jours* (Paris: Dalloz, 1953).

7. The original work was published in two volumes, under the title *Les crises du XXe siècle*. The translated second volume is entitled *World War II and its Origins. International Relations, 1929–1945* (New York: Harper and Row, 1969). See particularly pp. 343–55. See Halperin's own essay on 'Pierre Renouvin' in S. William Halperin (ed.) *Essays in Modern European Historiography* (Chicago: University of Chicago Press, 1970) 243–65.

8. Maurice Baumont, *La faillite de la paix (1918–1939)*, 894–5; see also his *Les origines de la deuxième guerre mondiale* (Paris: Payot, 1969).

9. J.-B. Duroselle, *Histoire diplomatique de 1919 à nos jours* (Paris: Dalloz, 1966) 174–5. The original edition appeared in 1953.

10. Philip C.F. Bankwitz, *Maxime Weygand and Civil–Military Relations in Modern France* (Cambridge: Harvard University Press, 1967); John McVickar Haight Jr, *American Aid to France, 1938–1940* (New York: Atheneum, 1970).

11. See the unpublished doctoral dissertations of Fred Greene, 'French Military Leadership and Security Against Germany, 1919–1940' (Yale University, 1950); Alvin D. Coox, 'French Military Doctrine, 1919–1939: Concepts of Ground and Aerial Warfare' (Harvard University, 1953); Donald J. Harvey 'French Concepts of Military Strategy, 1919–1939' (Columbia University, 1953).

12. See Judith M. Hughes, *To the Maginot Line. The Politics of French Military Preparation in the 1920s* (Cambridge, Mass.: Harvard University Press, 1971); Robert W. Krauskopf, 'French Air Power Policy, 1919–1939' (Georgetown University, 1965); Jeffrey J. Clarke, 'Military Technology in Republican France: The Evolution of the French Armored Force, 1917–1940' (Duke University, 1969).

13. Hughes, *To The Maginot Line*, 261.

14. André Géraud (Pertinax), *The Gravediggers of France* (New York: Doubleday, 1944); Pierre Cot, *The Triumph of Treason* (New York: Ziff Davis, 1944).

15. This collection is now complete. Published over the space of 20 years, the *Documents Diplomatiques Français*, are organized in two Series. The first, in 13 volumes, covers the period 1932–5. The second, in 19 volumes, covers the period 1936–9.

16. Alistair Horne, *To Lose a Battle: France 1940* (London: Macmillan, 1969) 515–17; William L. Shirer, *The Collapse of the Third Republic* (London: Heinemann, 1970) xiii; Guy Chapman, *Why France Collapsed* (London: Cassell, 1968).

17. See John C. Cairns, 'The Fall of France, 1940: Thoughts on a National Defeat', *Annual Report of the Canadian Historical Association* (Ottawa, 1957) 55–70; 'Along the Road Back to France 1940', *American Historical Review*, lxiv, no. 3 (April 1959) 583–605; 'Some Recent Historians and the "Strange Defeat" of 1940', *Journal of Modern History*, 46, no. 1 (March 1974) 60–85.

18. John C. Cairns, 'A Nation of Shopkeepers in Search of a Suitable France, 1919–1940', *American Historical Review*, 79, no. 3, (June 1974) 710–43.

19. Anthony P. Adamthwaite, 'French Foreign Policy, April 1938–September 1939, with Special Reference to the Policy of M. Georges Bonnet' (University of Leeds, 1966); Robert J. Young, 'Strategy and Diplomacy in France: Some Aspects of the Military Factor in the Formulation of French Foreign Policy, 1934–1939' (University of London, 1969).

20. See Robert J. Young (ed.) *French Foreign Policy, 1918–1945. A Guide to Research and Research Materials* (Wilmington: Scholarly Resources, 1991) 43–5, 215–18. For a measure of the increase in documentation now available for research in France, one could compare the contents of this volume with those of the original 1981 edition.

21. For example, see their contributions to *Les relations franco-britanniques de 1935 à 1939* (Paris: CNRS, 1975) as well as the closing report presented in the same volume by Professor Renouvin.

22. See, for example, René Girault, 'Léon Blum, la dévaluation de 1936 et la conduite de la politique extérieure de la France', *Relations Internationales*, 13 (1978) 91–109; Jean Bouvier, 'Contrôle des changes et politique économique extérieure de la S.F.I.O. en 1936', *Relations Internationales*, 13 (1978) 111–15; Robert Frank(enstein), 'Le financement français de la guerre et les accords avec les Britanniques (1939–1940)' in *Français et Britanniques dans la drôle de guerre. Colloque Anglo–Français, 1975* (Paris: CNRS, 1979) 461–89.

23. J.-B. Duroselle, 'L'influence de la politique intérieure sur la politique extérieure de la France. L'exemple de 1938 et 1939' in *Les relations franco-britanniques, 1935–1939* (Paris: CNRS, 1975) 225–42; 'Les milieux gouvernementaux en face du

problème allemand en 1936', in *La France et l'Allemagne, 1932–1936* (Paris: CNRS, 1980) 373–96.

24. See Antoine Prost, 'Les anciens combattants français et l'Allemagne (1933–1938)' 131–48; J. Droz, 'Le parti socialiste français devant la montée du nazisme', 173–90; J. Bruhat, 'Le parti communiste français face à l'hitlérisme de 1933 à 1936' 191–212; Henri Michel, 'Conclusion' 397–403, all in *La France et l'Allemagne, 1932–1936* (Paris: Editions du CNRS, 1980); James O. Safford, 'French Attitudes Toward Impending War, 1935–1939' (Cornell University, 1976).

25. Vincent J. Pitts, *France and the German Problem. Politics and Economics in the Locarno Period, 1924–1929* (New York: Garland, 1987) 333; Edward D. Keeton, *Briand's Locarno Policy. French Economics, Politics, and Diplomacy, 1925–1929* (New York: Garland, 1987).

26. Stephen A. Schuker, *The End of French Predominance in Europe: The Financial Crisis of 1924 and the Adoption of the Dawes Plan* (Chapel Hill: North Carolina University Press, 1976; reissued 1988); Sally Marks, *The Illusion of Peace. International Relations in Europe, 1918–1933* (London: Macmillan, 1976); Walter A. McDougall, *France's Rhineland Diplomacy, 1914–1924. The Last Bid for a Balance of Power in Europe* (Princeton, NJ: Princeton University Press, 1978); Marc Trachtenberg, *Reparation in World Politics: France and European Economic Diplomacy, 1916–1923* (New York: Columbia University Press, 1980).

27. Anthony P. Adamthwaite, *France and the Coming of the Second World War* (London: Cass, 1977); Robert J. Young, *In Command of France. French Foreign Policy and Military Planning, 1933–1940* (Cambridge: Harvard University Press, 1978); Jeffery A. Gunsburg, *Divided and Conquered. The French High Command and the Defeat of the West, 1940* (Westport, Conn.: Greenwood Press, 1979).

28. J.-B. Duroselle, *La Décadence, 1932–1939* (Paris: Imprimerie nationale, 1979).

29. J.-B. Duroselle, *La France et les Français, 1914–1920* (Paris: Editions Richelieu, 1972).

30. See Jacques Néré, *The Foreign Policy of France from 1914 to 1945* (London: Kegan Paul, 1975) 261; Jean-Pierre Azéma, *De Munich à la Libération, 1938–1944* (Paris: Seuil, 1979) 29; Foreword by Henri Michel, to Gunsburg's *Divided and Conquered*, xv–xvii.

31. René Girault, 'Les décideurs français et la puissance française en 1938–1939', Girault and R. Frank (eds) in *La Puissance en Europe, 1938–1940* (Paris: Publications de la Sorbonne, 1984) 39; 'L'imaginaire et l'histoire des relations internationales', *Relations Internationales*, no. 33 (Spring 1983) 7.

32. Marc Tractenberg, *Reparation in World Politics*, ix.

33. Dan Silverman, *Reconstructing Europe after the Great War* (Cambridge: Harvard University Press, 1982) v.

34. Eleanor M. Gates, *End of the Affair. The Collapse of the Anglo-French Alliance, 1939–1940* (Berkeley: University of California Press, 1981) 10; Nicholas Rostow, *Anglo-French Relations, 1934–1936* (London: Macmillan, 1984) 246–7.

35. Robert Allan Doughty, 'The French Armed Forces, 1918–1940' in Allan R. Millert and Williamson Murray (eds) *Military Effectiveness*, vol. 2 (Boston: Allen and Unwin, 1988) 66; *The Seeds of Disaster. The Development of French Army Doctrine, 1919–1939* (Hamden, Conn.: Archon Books, 1985) 188.

36. See Henry Dutailly, *Les problèmes de l'Armée de Terre Française (1935–1939)* (Paris: Imprimerie nationale, 1980); and his review of Duroselle and Young in *Revue Historique des Armées* no. 4 (1979) 243–5.

37. Maurice Vaïsse, *Sécurité d'abord. La politique française en matière de désarmement, 9 décembre 1930– 17 avril 1934* (Paris: Pedone, 1981).

38. Robert Frank(enstein), *Le prix du réarmement français, 1935–1939* (Paris: Publications de la Sorbonne, 1982).

39. See Maurice Vaïsse, 'Le pacifisme français dans les années trente', *Relations Internationales*, 51. See also Christine Sellin, 'L'Image de la puissance française à travers

les manuels scolaires', *Relations Internationales* (Spring 1983) 103–111; and Elisabeth Du Réau, 'Enjeux stratégiques', *Relations Internationales* (Autumn 1983) 319–35.

40. Gilbert Ziebura, 'Determinants of French Foreign Policy' in F. Eidlin (ed.) *Constitutional Democracy. Essays in Comparative Politics* (Boulder: Westview Press, 1983) 449–69.

41. Serge Berstein, *La France des années 30* (Paris: Colin, 1988) 80, 169.

42. Piotr Wandycz, *The Twilight of French Eastern Alliances 1926–1936. French–Czechoslovak–Polish Relations from Locarno to the Remilitarization of the Rhineland* (Princeton, NJ: Princeton University Press, 1988), 478.

43. Nicole Jordan, 'Maurice Gamelin, Italy and the Eastern Alliances', *Journal of Strategic Studies*, xiv, no. 4 (December 1991) 428–41. See also her book *The Popular Front and Central Europe: The Dilemmas of French Impotence, 1918–1940* (Cambridge: Cambridge University Press, 1992).

44. Michael J. Carley, 'End of the "Low, Dishonest Decade: Failure of the Anglo-French Soviet Alliance in 1939" ', *Europe–Asia Studies*, xiv, no. 2 (1993) 303–41; and 'Prelude to Defeat: Franco–Soviet Relations, 1920–1939', *Historical Reflections/Réflexions Historiques* (forthcoming).

45. Anthony Adamthwaite, *Grandeur and Misery. France's Bid for Power in Europe 1914–1940* (London: Edward Arnold, 1995) 231.

46. William I. Shorrock, *From Ally to Enemy. The Enigma of Fascist Italy in French Diplomacy* (Kent, Ohio: Kent State University Press, 1988) 290–2; John C. Cairns, 'Planning for *la guerre des masses*' in H.R. Borowski (ed.) *Military Planning in the Twentieth Century* (Washington, DC: United States Air Force, 1986) 51.

47. John E. Dreifort, *Myopic Grandeur. The Ambivalence of French Foreign Policy towards the Far East, 1919–1945* (Kent, Ohio: Kent State University Press, 1991).

48. Robert A. Doughty, *The Breaking Point. Sedan and the Fall of France, 1940* (New York: Archon Books, 1990) 329.

49. Martin S. Alexander, 'Did the Deuxième Bureau Work? The Role of Intelligence in French Defence Policy and Strategy, 1919–1939', *Intelligence and National Security*, vi, no. 2 (April 1991) 125; 'Maurice Gamelin and the Defeat of France, 1939–1940' in B. Bond (ed.) *Fallen Stars. Eleven Studies of Twentieth Century Military Disasters* (London: Brassey's, 1991) 128. See also his recent book *The Republic in Danger. General Maurice Gamelin and the Politics of French Defence, 1933–1940* (Cambridge: Cambridge University Press, 1992).

50. See William D. Irvine, 'Domestic Politics and the Fall of France in 1940', *Historical Reflections/Réflexions Historiques* (forthcoming); Jean-Louis Crémieux-Brilhac, *Les Français de l'An 40* vol. 1, *La guerre oui ou non?*, vol. 2, *Ouvriers et soldats* (Paris: Gallimard, 1990).

51. Philip Bankwitz, 'Comment', *Journal of Strategic Studies*, xiv, no. 4 (December 1991) 442–5.

52. See Paul Stafford, 'The French Government and the Danzig Crisis', *International History Review*, vi, no. 1 (February 1984) 85. See also Anthony Adamthwaite, 'France and the Coming of War', in W. Mommsen and L. Kettenacker (eds) *The Fascist Challenge and the Policy of Appeasement* (London: Allen and Unwin, 1983) 246–56.

3. ACCORD AND DISCORD: DIPLOMACY AND NATIONAL DEFENCE IN THE 1930s

1. For French responses to Japan, see John E. Dreifort, *Myopic Grandeur: The Ambivalence of French Foreign Policy Toward the Far East, 1919–1945* (Kent, Ohio: Kent State University Press, 1991). For their perceptions of Italian ambitions, see William Shorrock, *From Ally to Enemy. The Enigma of Fascist Italy in French Diplomacy* (Kent, Ohio:

Kent State University Press, 1988), and George W. Baer, *The Coming of the Italian-Ethiopian War* (Cambridge: Harvard University Press, 1967) and *Test Case: Italy, Ethiopia and the League of Nations* (Stanford: Hoover Institution Press, 1976).

2. Poland and Czechoslovakia by separate treaties, Austria by virtue of France's subscription to the treaty of Saint-Germain and the League of Nations Covenant.

3. Michael Geyer stresses that neither the French, nor the Germans, believed they could win a war 'decisively'. General Ludwig Beck, one of the German army's most senior officers, 'saw no escape from an all-European war which the Germans could not win'. See 'The Crisis of Military Leadership in the 1930s', *Journal of Strategic Studies*, xiv, no. 4 (December 1991) 456.

4. This is what Jacques Néré meant when he said that France had to do what was 'necessary and unattainable. ' In order to avoid German hegemony, France had to preserve the Versailles system, a goal which was unattainable 'without the active cooperation of the three allies who had won the war'. See *The Foreign Policy of France from 1914 to 1945* (London: Kegan Paul, 1975) 261.

5. One of the most succinct and recent treatments of Franco-Belgian relations in the 1930s is to be found in the seventh chapter of Martin S. Alexander, *The Republic in Danger. General Maurice Gamelin and the Politics of French Defence, 1933–1940* (Cambridge: Cambridge University Press, 1992) 172–209. See also Brian Bond, *France and Belgium, 1939–1940* (London: Davis-Poynter, 1975).

6. General Gamelin, for one, was a firm believer in this forward defence, arguing that monies not expended on fortifying the frontier with Belgium should be put towards the development of new weapons, including armour, and improved training. See Martin S. Alexander, 'In Lieu of Alliance: The French General Staff's Secret Cooperation with Neutral Belgium, 1936–1940', *Journal of Strategic Studies*, xiv, no. 4 (December 1991) 471.

7. See Chapter 1, p. 32.

8. For evidence of the longevity of these hopes, and their currency in both the Bonnet and Daladier camps, see Paul Stafford, 'The French Government and the Danzig Crisis: The Italian Dimension', *International History Review*, vi, no. 1 (February 1984) 48–87.

9. See Young, 'Soldiers and Diplomats: The French Embassy and Franco-Italian Relations, 1935–1936', *Journal of Strategic Studies*, 7, no. 1 (1984) 74–91; and 'French Military Intelligence and the Franco-Italian Alliance, 1933–1939', *Historical Journal*, 28 (1985) 143–68. More recently, and in a more critical vein, we have Nicole Jordan's 'Maurice Gamelin, Italy and the Eastern Alliances', *Journal of Strategic Studies*, xiv, no. 4 (December 1991) 428–41.

10. William Shorrock, for example, places much responsibility for the impasse in Franco-Italian relations on the ideological posturing of the Popular Front governments in 1936–7. See his *From Ally To Enemy*.

11. Once again, the most recent and best account of French military and diplomatic efforts to fashion an allied block in central Europe is to be found in the eighth chapter of Martin S. Alexander, *The Republic in Danger*, 210–35.

12. See Elisabeth Du Réau, 'Enjeux stratégiques et redéploiement diplomatique français: novembre 1938, septembre 1939,' *Relations Internationales*, no. 35 (Autumn 1983) 328. For a recent work which strongly reiterates the Popular Front's determination to hold on to eastern Europe, see Nicole Jordan, *The Popular Front and Central Europe: The Dilemmas of French Impotence, 1918–1940* (Cambridge: Cambridge University Press, 1992).

13. Nicole Jordan evokes the 'eddy of conflicting emotion' which troubled even Léon Blum in 1938. Blum, long a supporter of the alliance with Czechoslovakia, was embarrassed by the sense of relief he felt over Munich. René Massigli, a senior official in the foreign ministry and another supporter of the Czechs, confronted the same crisis

with a similar 'ambivalence'. See Jordan, 'Léon Blum and Czechoslovakia, 1936–1938', *French History*, vi, no. 1 (March 1991) 71; and Georges Soutou, 'La Perception de la puissance française par René Massigli', *Relations Internationales*, no. 33 (Spring 1983) 18.

14. For conflicting French military appraisals of the USSR see Patrice Buffotot, 'The French High Command and the Franco-Soviet Alliance, 1933–1939', *Journal of Strategic Studies* (1982) 546–59; and Maurice Vaïsse, 'Les militaires français et l'alliance franco-soviétique au cours des années 1930', *Forces armées et systèmes d'alliance* (Paris: Cahiers de la Fondation pour les Etudes de Défense Nationale, 1984) 689–703; and 'La perception de la puissance soviétique par les militaires français en 1938', *Revue Historique des Armées* (1983–84) 19–25.

15. For a useful survey of this debate, and on recent literature, see the extended review article by Michael J. Carley, 'Down a Blind-Alley: Anglo-Franco-Soviet Relations, 1920–1939', *Canadian Journal of History*, xxix (April 1994) 147–72.

16. For the intense resistance of the Bank of France and senior echelons in the Finance ministry, see Michael J. Carley, 'Five Kopeks for Five Kopecks: Franco-Soviet Trade Negotiations 1928–1939', *Cahiers du monde russe et soviétique*, xxxiii, no. 1 (Jan.–March 1992) 23–58.

17. The published text of this report by General Victor Schweisguth can be found in *Documents Diplomatiques Français*, series 2, vol. 3, no. 343, 510–14. The immediate context in which the report appeared, including a far more positive report from 1935 – for which his predecessor was reprimanded – may be found in Young, *In Command of France. French Foreign Policy and Military Planning, 1933–1940* (Cambridge: Harvard University Press, 1978) 145–49.

18. See Young, *In Command of France*, 22.

19. As Anthony Adamthwaite puts it, 'France could not contemplate war against Germany without an assurance of British support'. See his 'France and the Coming of War' in Mommsen and Kettenacker (eds.) *The Fascist Challenge and the Policy of Appeasement* (London: Allen and Unwin, 1983) 252. For that reason, the search for such support became the 'leitmotiv de tout l'"*establishment*" français'. See Jean Doise and Maurice Vaïsse, *Diplomatie et Outil Militaire, 1871–1969* (Paris: Imprimerie nationale, 1987) 297.

20. Brian McKercher has recently lent credence to this suspicion. Munich was possible because the British were prepared to compromise on an issue which did not threaten their vital interests. But in March 1939, when the European balance seemed to be at stake, they led the charge, 'dragging the French along'. See ' "Our Most Dangerous Enemy": Great Britain Pre-eminent in the 1930s', *International History Review*, xiii, no. 4 (November 1991) 754.

21. See Henry Blumenthal's, *Illusion and Reality in Franco-American Diplomacy, 1914–1945* (Baton Rouge: Louisiana State University Press, 1986).

22. Speaking of the Ardennes, Bradford Lee acknowledges that 'this was the best place to risk being thin'. The Allies nearly made the same mistake in 1944 when they were caught by another 'surprise' German offensive through the same region. See 'Strategy, Arms and the Collapse of France, 1930–1940', in R.T.B. Langhorne (ed.) *Diplomacy and Intelligence during the Second World War: Essays in Honour of F.H. Hinsley* (Cambridge: Cambridge University Press, 1985) 45.

23. See Henry Dutailly, *Les problèmes de l'armée de terre française, 1935–1939* (Paris: Imprimerie nationale, 1980) 25–70.

24. Colonel Doughty describes the French system as 'supremely logical' and 'the product of a long and careful process in which virtually every course of action was identified and analyzed. ' See 'The French Armed Forces, 1918–1940', in Allan R. Millet and Williamson Murray (eds) *Military Effectiveness*, vol. 2 (Boston: Allen and Unwin, 1988) 65.

25. In fact, according to our argument, neither charge was entirely just. Weygand's alarm and Gamelin's complacency were calculated public responses, which is to say that Weygand in 1934 was more confident in private and Gamelin, in 1939, more alarmed, than either wished to admit. It is this which explains why the high command is seen to 'oscillate' between fear and confidence and why Gamelin is seen as someone who 'souffle le chaud et le froid'. Cf. Doise and Vaïsse, *Diplomatie et Outil Militaire*, 316.

26. Martin S. Alexander, *Republic in Danger*, 75, 138.

27. See Young, 'French Military Intelligence and Nazi Germany, 1938–1939', in Ernest May (ed.) *Knowing One's Enemies: Intelligence Assessment Before the Two World Wars* (Princeton: Princeton University Press, 1984) 303.

28. See Charles de Gaulle, *Le fil de l'épée* (Paris: Berger-Levrault, 1931); *Vers l'armée de métier* (Paris: Berger-Levrault, 1934); *La France et son armée* (Paris: Berger-Levrault, 1938).

29. See Young, 'The Strategic Dream: French Air Doctrine in the Inter-War Period, 1919–39', *Journal of Contemporary History*, ix, no. 4 (October 1974) 67–8.

30. For a succinct discussion of this issue, see Robert A. Doughty, *The Seeds of Disaster. The Development of French Army Doctrine, 1919–1939* (Hamden, Conn.: Archon Books, 1985) 14–39.

4. CONSENSUS AND DIVISION: POLITICS AND IDEOLOGY

1. See their respective memoirs, as well as their reports in the later volumes, second series, of the *Documents Diplomatiques Français*. André François-Poncet, *Souvenirs d'une ambassade à Berlin: septembre 1931 – octobre 1938* (Paris: Fayard, 1946); *Au Palais Farnèse. Souvenirs d'une ambassade à Rome, 1938–1940* (Paris: Flammarion, 1961); Léon Noel, *L'Agression allemande contre la Pologne* (Paris: Flammarion, 1946) and also *La guerre de 39 a commencé quatre ans plus tôt* (Paris: France-Empire, 1979).

2. A more detailed account of reporting practices in the foreign ministry can be found in the second chapter of Young *French Foreign Policy, 1918–1945. A Guide to Research and Research Materials* (Wilmington: Scholarly Resources, 1991). See in particular the organizational charts between 14–15, and the remarks on 17–18.

3. Cabinet minutes were not kept during the Third Republic, with the result that we are dependent on memoir accounts. For some remarks on the pitfalls associated with the latter, see my 'Partial Recall: Political Memoirs and Biography from the Third French Republic', in George Egerton (ed.) *Political Memoir. Essays on the Politics of Memory* (London: Cass, 1994) 62–75.

4. Further information on data gathering, assessment and interministerial communication can be found in my 'French Military Intelligence and Nazi Germany, 1938–1939', in Ernest May (ed.) *Knowing One's Enemies. Intelligence Assessment Before the Two World Wars* (Princeton: Princeton University Press, 1984) 271–309; and Peter Jackson, 'French Military Intelligence and Czechoslovakia, 1938', *Diplomacy and Statecraft*, vi, no. 1 (March 1994) 81–106.

5. Further information on the responsibilities and duties of the national defence secretariat, and of various interministerial committees, may be found in Young *In Command of France. French Foreign Policy and Military Planning, 1933–1940* (Cambridge: Harvard University Press, 1978) 24–6, and in Elisabeth Du Réau, 'L'Information du "décideur" et l'élaboration de la décision diplomatique française dans les dernières années de la IIIe République', *Relations Internationales*, no. 32 (Winter 1982) 525–41.

6. See Martin Alexander's affirmative answer to his question, 'Did the Deuxième Bureau Work?' in *Intelligence and National Security* (April 1991) 293–333.

7. For Premier Sarraut's speech of 10 March 1936, see *Journal Officiel*, Chambre des Députés, Débats, pp. 854–6, and Flandin's on 20 March, pp. 1063–5; see also Delbos'

speech to the Chamber on Spain and eastern Europe, 4 December 1936, pp. 3317–31, and 19 November 1937, pp. 2469–71; Daladier's speech on Munich was delivered on 4 October 1938, pp. 1526–29; and Bonnet gave a general exposé to the Chamber on 19 December, pp. 1943–4. In 1939 either Daladier or Bonnet spoke during the foreign policy debates of 20 and 26 January, 17 March, 11 May, 2 September.

Major foreign policy statements to the Senate, include that of Flandin, *Journal Officiel*, Sénat, Débats, 20 March 1936, pp. 388–90; Delbos and Blum, 23 June 1936, pp. 592–4, 25 June, pp. 619–21, 23 February 1937, pp. 188–90, 28 December 1937, pp. 1320–2; Daladier's statement on Munich, 4 October 1939, pp. 725–8; Bonnet on the general situation, 7 February 1939, pp. 103–5.

8. For example, see the unpublished minutes of the *audition* of Bonnet by the Chamber's Foreign Affairs Commission on 21 June 1939, *Assemblée Nationale*, dossier 2, pp. 66–7, and the more extensive *audition* of Daladier, on 4 October, pp. 7–83.

9. I have relied heavily here, and subsequently, upon the data provided by Alain Bomier-Landowski in his 'Les Groupes Parlementaires de l'Assemblée Nationale et de la Chambre des Députés de 1871 à 1940', in François Goguel and Georges Dupeux (eds.) *Sociologie Electorale* (Paris: Colin, 1951) 75–89. From Left to Right, those 17 'Groupes' are as follows: Communiste, Socialiste, Union Socialiste et Républicaine, Gauche Indépendante, Parti du Parti Camille Pelletan, Parti Frontiste, Parti de l'Unité Prolétarienne, Parti de la Jeune République, Républicain Radical et Radical-Socialiste, Gauche Démocratique et Radicale Indépendante, Alliance des Républicains de Gauche et des Radicaux Indépendants, Démocrate Populaire, Indépendant d'Action Populaire, Indépendants Républicains, Républicains Indépendants et d'Action Sociale, Agraire Indépendant, Fédération Républicaine de France, Indépendants d'Union Républicaine et Nationale.

10. The Radicals' position in the Senate was far more secure than in the Chamber. There were only 314 seats in the upper house, where Radical control started with the 152 senators who were registered under the 'Gauche démocratique'. See Annex to Report on the French Government, prepared by the Royal Institute of International Affairs for the Foreign Office, 14 September 1939, *PRO*, FO 371, 22918, C18749/25/17.

11. These readings and calculations derive from a collection of sources, including the September 1939 *PRO* report previously cited, Alain Bomier-Landowski, 'Les Groupes Parlementaires', Adamthwaite, *France and the Coming of the Second World War* (London: Cass, 1977) and Elisabeth Du Réau, *Edouard Daladier, 1884–1970* (Paris: Fayard, 1993).

12. The second largest block in the Chamber, with about 115 seats, the Radical and Radical Socialist 'party' is an historian's nightmare. As the name implies, it was plural rather than singular, an amalgam of related but disparate political tendencies, but tendencies grouped together by voluntary association rather than any kind of party discipline. Once 'radical' and 'leftist' only in its resistance to monarchy and Church, it had become a 'liberal' and 'centrist' influence by the 1930s, certainly in no way either 'radical' or 'socialist'. For a fuller characterization of the Radical Socialists, see my remarks on the Centre later in this chapter.

13. Young, *In Command of France*, 208–9, 298.

14. I have explored elsewhere the nature of the advice provided to the government by General Gamelin and by the chief of air staff, General Denain. See 'Le haut commandement français au moment de Munich', *Revue d'Histoire Moderne et Contemporaine*, 24 (January–March 1977) 110–29; and 'The Use and Abuse of Fear: France and the Air Menace in the 1930s', *Intelligence and National Security*, ii, no. 4 (October 1987) 88–109.

15. Exception can easily be taken to the political character attributed to some of these papers, as well as to their sales statistics and the obvious incompleteness of this

brief survey. Scholars are already far from unanimous on the first two counts, but will agree that my coverage is fragmentary. It is so only as a way of highlighting the debate, which itself is so central to my argument. For this purpose, I have relied principally on the table provided by Dominique Borne and Henri Dubief, *La crise des années 30* (Paris: Seuil, 1989) but have profited from the new work by Yvon Lacaze, *L'opinion publique française et la crise de Munich* (Berne: Peter Lang, 1991) and the older works by Jean Pierre Azéma, *De Munich à la Libération* (1979), Henri Noguères, *Munich, The Phoney Peace* (London: Weidenfeld and Nicolson, 1965) and Raymond Manévy, *La presse de la IIIe République* (Paris: Foret, 1955). A particularly useful treatment of the public debate over Munich can be found in James O. Safford, 'French Attitudes Toward Impending War' (Cornell University, 1976).

16. Adamthwaite records 535 votes for, and 75 against the Munich agreement. Du Réau records 331 votes for, 78 against the provision for special powers, with 203 abstentions. See *France and the Coming*, 127; *Edouard Daladier*, 290.

17. Recommended reading on this subject would include: André Guérin, *La Vie quotidienne au Palais-Bourbon à la fin de la IIIe République* (Paris: Hachette, 1978); Jean Estèbe, *Les Ministres de la République, 1871–1914* (Paris: FNSP, 1982); Pierre Guiral and Guy Thuillier, *La Vie quotidienne des députés en France de 1871 à 1914* (Paris: Hachette, 1980); René Rémond, Aline Coutrot and Isabel Boussard, *Quarante ans de cabinets ministériels* (Paris: FNSP, 1982); Catherine Durandin et al, *Histoire des élites en France* (Paris: Tallandier, 1991); Christophe Charle, *Les Elites de la République, 1880–1900* (Paris: Fayard, 1987); Robert Smith, *The Ecole Normal Supérieure and the Third Republic* (New York: SUNY Press, 1982); Jean-François Sirinelli, *Génération intellectuelle: Khâgneux et Normaliens dans l'entre-deux-guerres* (Paris: Fayard, 1988); Paul Gerbod, 'The Baccalauréate and its Roles in the Recruitment and Formation of French Elites in the Nineteenth Century', in Jolyon Howorth and Philip Cerny (eds) *Elites in France*, (New York: St. Martin's Press. 1981) 46–56.

18. See the older works of Charles Micaud, *The French Right and Nazi Germany, 1933–1939* (Durham: Duke University Press, 1943) and René Rémond, *La droite en France de 1815 à nos jours* (Paris: Aubier, 1954) and recent works by Oscar Arnal, *Ambivalent Alliance: The Catholic Church and the Action Française, 1899–1939* (Pittsburgh: University of Pittsburgh Press, 1985); Michael Sutton, *Nationalism, Positivism and Catholicism in the Politics of Charles Maurras* (Cambridge: Cambridge University Press, 1982); John Hellman, *The Knight-Monks of Vichy France. Uriage, 1940–1945* (Montreal: McGill-Queen's, 1993); Donald G. Wileman, 'L'Alliance Républicaine Démocratique, 1901–1947', (Unpublished doctoral dissertation, York University, 1988)

19. Recent work on the Popular Front includes: Martin Alexander and Helen Graham (eds) *The French and Spanish Popular Fronts* (Cambridge: Cambridge University Press, 1989); Julian Jackson, *The Popular Front in France* (Cambridge: Cambridge University Press, 1988); Nicole Jordan, *The Popular Front and Central Europe: The Dilemmas of French Impotence, 1918–1940* (Cambridge: Cambridge University Press, 1992).

20. On the controversial subject of French fascism, see Zeev Sternhell, *Neither Right Nor Left. Fascist Ideology in France* (Berkeley: University of California Press, 1986) and *The Birth of Fascist Ideology* (Princeton: Princeton University Press, 1994); Philippe Burrin, *La dérive fasciste. Doriot, Déat, Bergery, 1933–1945* (Paris: Seuil, 1986); Pierre Milza, *Fascisme français passé et présent* (Paris: Flammarion, 1987); Robert Soucy, *French Fascism: The First Wave, 1924–1933* (New Haven: Yale, 1986).

21. For a business critique of government economic and financial policy see the recent work of Richard Vinen, *The Politics of French Business, 1936–1945* (Cambridge: Cambridge University Press, 1991) 27–84.

22. See Azéma, *De Munich à la Libération*, 30.

23. See the older work by Daniel R. Brower, *The New Jacobins. The French Communist Party and the Popular Front* (Ithaca: Cornell University Press, 1968), and more recent

work by: Philippe Robrieux, *Histoire intérieure du part communiste, 1920–1945* (Paris: Fayard, 1981); Tony Judt, *Marxism and the French Left. Studies on Labour and Politics in France, 1830–1981* (Oxford: Clarendon Press, 1986); Edward Mortimer, *The Rise of the French Communist Party, 1920–1947* (London: Faber and Faber, 1984). A convenient survey of the interwar communist and socialist groups can be found in Maurice Agulhon et al *La France de 1914 à 1940* (Paris: Nathan, 1993).

24. See Christopher Andrew and A.S. Kanya-Forstner, *France Overseas: The Great War and the Climax of French Imperial Expansion, 1914–1924* (London: Thames and Hudson, 1981). For French intervention in Russia, see Michael J. Carley, *Revolution and Intervention. The French Government and the Russian Civil War, 1917–1919* (Montreal: McGill-Queen's, 1983). For a recent treatment of the Ruhr crisis of 1923, see Young, *Power and Pleasure. Louis Barthou and the Third French Republic* (Montreal: McGill-Queen's University Press, 1991).

25. There are several studies which discuss French policy during the Ethiopian crisis, including George W. Baer, *The Coming of the Italo-Ethiopian War* (Cambridge: Harvard University Press, 1967); *Test Case: Italy, Ethiopia, and the League of Nations* (Stanford: Hoover Institution Press, 1976); F.D. Laurens, *France and the Italo-Ethiopian Crisis, 1935–1936* (The Hague: Mouton, 1967); Young, *In Command of France* (1978); Shorrock, *From Ally to Enemy. The Enigma of Fascist Italy in French Diplomacy* (Kent, Onio: Kent State University Press, 1988).

26. See my earlier remarks in this chapter, Note 12. For further information on the Radicals, see the older work by P.J. Larmour, *The French Radical Party in the 1930s* (Stanford: Stanford University Press, 1964) and, more recently, Serge Berstein, *Histoire du parti radical*, 2 vols. (Paris: FNSP, 1980–2) and *Edouard Herriot, ou la République en personne* (Paris: FNSP, 1985).

27. On the subject of the President, see Leslie Derfler, *President and Parliament. A Short History of the French Presidency* (Boca Raton: University Press of Florida, 1983).

5. ECONOMIC PROPHECIES AND COUNTER-PROPHECIES

1. See Young, 'Reason and Madness: France, The Axis Powers and the Politics of Economic Disorder', *Canadian Journal of History*, xx (April 1985) 65–83.

2. Poncet to Bonnet, 27 June 1938, *Documents Diplomatiques Français D.D.F.*, 2e, x, no. 103, p. 200; and 13 October 1938, *ibid.*, xii, no. 105, p. 177. See also Robert Coulondre, *De Staline à Hitler* (Paris: Hachette, 1950) 205–6.

3. The Finance ministry in Paris was inclined to be more hopeful of some effective resistance to Nazi economic policies, more hopeful than the attachés in Berlin. See Nathalie Carré de Malberg, 'Les attachés financiers en 1938 – technocrates ou techniciens? – et la perception de la puissance de la France', *Relations Internationales*, no. 33 (Spring 1983) 43–64. For British doubts about imminent domestic resistance, see Bruce Strang, 'Two Unequal Tempers: Sir George Ogilvie-Forbes, Sir Nevile Henderson and British Foreign Policy, 1938–39', *Diplomacy and Statecraft*, v, no. 1 (March 1994) 119, 120, 122, 125.

4. For example, see Coulondre to Bonnet, 5 February 1939, *D.D.F.*, 2e, xiv, no. 18, p. 33. For Hitler's ability to turn the threat of an allied blockade into an argument for expansion in eastern Europe, see R.A.C. Parker, *Chamberlain and Appeasement. British Policy and the Coming of the Second World War* (New York: St. Martin's 1993) 268.

5. See André François-Poncet, *Souvenirs d'une ambassade à Berlin* (Paris: Flammarion, 1946) 319, 348; Coulondre, *Souvenirs* (Paris: Hachette, 1950) 319–325; Didelet to Daladier, 12 December 1938, *D.D.F.*, 2e, xiii, no. 103, p. 192, and his report of 11 April 1939, in the army archives *Service Historique de l'Armée de Terre* (S.H.A.T.) 7N2602.

6. According to Bernd-Jürgen Wendt, Nazi economic policy 'manoeuvred constantly on the brink of war, and . . . fully accepted the risk of war'. As such it was 'incompatible with a concept based on "economic reason" for which the preservation of peace was the basis for combatting national difficulties'. See 'Economic Appeasement – A Crisis Strategy', in W. Mommsen and L. Kettenacker (eds) *The Fascist Challenge and the Policy of Appeasement* (London: Allen and Unwin, 1983) 171.

7. De Montbas to Bonnet, 17 November 1938, *D.D.F.*, 2e, xii, no. 323, pp. 630–3; Coulondre to Bonnet, 8 February 1939, *ibid.*, xiv, no. 72, 130–1.

8. See the unpublished manuscript entitled 'Munich' by Edouard Daladier, in *Archives Daladier*, 2DA1, dossier 5, p. 45; and Young, 'French Military Intelligence,' in May (ed.) *Knowing One's Enemies: Intelligence Assessment Before the Two World Wars* (Princeton: Princeton University Press, 1984) 271–309.

9. While avoiding specific and concrete forecasts of attack, both military and civilian observers certainly kept the idea alive in the public consciousness by frequently, and publicly, hypothesizing about future German attacks. See Young, 'L'Attaque Brusquée and Its Use as Myth in Interwar France', *Historical Reflections / Réflexions Historiques*, viii, no. 1 (Spring 1981) 93–113.

10. See Robert Frank(enstein), *Le prix du réarmement français, 1935–1939* (Paris: Publications de la Sorbonne, 1982) 109. For the relationship between diplomatic and financial crisis in March 1936, when Germany reoccupied the Rhineland, see Stephen A. Schuker, 'France and the Remilitarization of the Rhineland, 1936', *French Historical Studies*, xiv, no. 3 (Spring 1986) 299–338.

11. On these devaluations, particularly that of 1936, see Frank(enstein), *Le prix du réarmement*, 129–43; Martin Wolfe, *The French Franc Between the Wars, 1919–1939* (New York: Columbia, 1951) 104–171; Kenneth Mouré, *Managing the Franc Poincaré: Economic Understanding and Political Constraint in French Monetary Policy, 1928–1936* (New York: Cambridge University Press, 1991).

12. Young, *In Command of France. French Foreign Policy and Military Planning, 1933–1940* (Cambridge: Harvard University Press, 1978), 18–19.

13. Jean-Louis Crémieux-Brilhac, *Les Français de l'An 40*, ii *Ouvriers et Soldats* (Paris: Gallimard, 1990) 35–53.

14. For evidence of innovation and adaptability on the part of French business, see Patrick Fridenson, 'Le patronat français', in René Rémond and Janine Bourdin (eds) *La France et les Français en 1938–1939* (Paris: FNSP, 1978) 139–56.

15. Richard Vinen identifies Daladier and the centre of the Radical party as the fortress of the small producer and investor, and Paul Reynaud, who came from the right of the Radicals, with big business. See his *The Politics of French Business, 1936–1945* (Cambridge: Cambridge University Press, 1991) 95, and also René Rémond and Janine Bourdin, 'Les Forces Adverses', in Pierre Renouvin and René Rémond (eds) *Léon Blum, Chef du Gouvernement, 1936–1937* (Paris: FNSP, 1981) 137–59.

16. See R. Frank(enstein), *Le prix du réarmement*, 95–111; Jean Bouvier, 'Contrôle des changes et politique économique extérieure de la S.F.I.O. en 1936,' *Relations Internationales*, 13 (Spring 1978) 111–15.

17. For French responses to the role of Anglo-American capital in the post-war period, see Jacques Bariéty, *Les relations franco-allemandes après la première guerre mondiale, 1918–1925* (Paris: Editions Pedone, 1977); and André Nouschi, 'L'Etat français et les pétroliers anglo-saxons: La naissance de la Compagnie Française des Pétroles (1923–1924),' *Relations Internationales*, 7 (1976) 241–59.

18. Billion, used here in the French and American sense of a thousand million. See Maurice Agulhon, André Nouschi, Ralph Schor *La France de 1914 à 1940* (Paris: Nathan, 1993) 158.

19. Jean Bouvier, René Girault, Jacques Thobie *L'Impérialisme à la française, 1914–1960* (Paris: Editions de la Découverte, 1986) 193.

NOTES 167

20. See Kenneth Mouré, *Managing the Franc Poincaré*, 275.

21. Bouvier et al, *L'Impérialisme*, 247.

22. See for example Gilbert Ziebura, 'Determinants of French Foreign Policy after 1932' in Eidlin (ed.) *Constitutional Democracy. Essays in Comparative Politics* (Boulder: Westview Press, 1983) 449–69; David E. Kaiser, *Economic Diplomacy and the Origins of the Second World War* (Princeton: Princeton University Press, 1980) 197–217, 284–315; and Georges Soutou, 'L'impérialisme du pauvre: la politique économique du gouvernement français en Europe Centrale et Orientale de 1918 à 1929', *Relations Internationales*, 7 (1976) 219–39.

23. See Richard Vinen, *The Politics of French Business, 1936–1945*, 16; and Agulhon et al, *La France de 1914 à 1940*, 167–8.

24. Serge Berstein, *La France des années 30* (Paris: Colin, 1988) 8–9.

25. The birthrate dropped between 1921 and 1936, reducing it for awhile to less than what it had been in 1911. In the latter year, 8.6 per cent of the population were older than 65; by 1936 that percentage had risen to 10. See Agulhon et al, *La France de 1914 à 1940*, 171; also, André Armengaud, 'La Population' in *Histoire Economique de la France entre les deux guerres*, by Alfred Sauvy, vol. 3 (Paris: Fayard, 1972) 17–46.

26. R. Frank(enstein), *Le prix du réarmement*, 190; René Girault, 'The Impact of the Economic Situation on the Foreign Policy of France, 1936–1939', in Mommsen and Kettenacker (eds) *The Fascist Challenge and the Policy of Appeasement* (London: Allen and Unwin, 1983) 220–1.

27. For an examination of Franco-German commercial exchanges between 1936 and 1939, see Gordon Dutter, 'Doing Business with the Nazis: French Economic Relations with Germany under the Popular Front', *Journal of Modern History* (1991) 296–326; Raymond Poidevin, 'La tentative de rapprochement économique entre la France et l'Allemagne, 1938–1939', in Jacques Bariéty, Alfred Guth and Jean-Marie Valentin (eds) *La France et l'Allemagne entre les deux guerres mondiales* (Nancy: Presses Universitaires de Nancy, 1987) 59–68.

28. For the connection between Bonnet's appeasement policy and the perceived weakness of the French economy and currency, see Robert Frank(enstein), 'The Decline of France and French Appeasement Policies, 1936–1939', in Mommsen and Kettenacker (eds) *The Fascist Challenge*, 242.

6. ALARM AND ASSURANCE: PUBLIC MOODS AND PERCEPTIONS

1. For a recent, succinct treatment of this subject see John Hellman's Introduction to his excellent wartime study, *The Knight-Monks of Vichy France. Uriage, 1940–1945* (Montreal: McGill Queen's, 1993).

2. Most of the information supplied here comes from Ralph Schor, *L'opinion française et les étrangers, 1919–1939* (Paris: Publications de la Sorbonne, 1985); Marianne Benteli, Daniel Jay and Jean-Pierre Jeancolas, 'Le cinéma français', in René Rémond and Janine Bourdin (eds) *La France et les Français en 1938–1939* (Paris: FNSP, 1978) 27–41; Richard Kuisel, *Seducing the French. The Dilemma of Americanization* (Berkeley: University of California Press, 1993); and Vicki Caron, 'Prelude to Vichy: France and the Jewish Refugees in the Era of Appeasement', *Journal of Contemporary History*, xx (1985) 157–76.

3. See Agulhon, Nouschi and Schor, *La France de 1914 à 1940* (Paris: Nathan, 1993) 171; Dudley Kirk, 'Population and Population Trends in Modern France', in E.M. Earle (ed.) *Modern France. Problems of the Third and Fourth Republics* (Princeton: Princeton University Press, 1951) 313–33; and Paul Monaco, 'The Popular Cinema as Reflection of the Group Process in France, 1919–1929', *History of Childhood Quarterly*, i, no. 4 (Spring 1974) 607–35.

4. The best book in English on French interwar pacifism, including feminist pacifists, is Norman Ingram, *The Politics of Dissent. Pacifism in France 1919–1939* (Oxford: Clarendon Press, 1991).

5. See Antoine Prost, 'Les anciens combattants français et l'Allemagne, 1933–1938', in *La France et l'Allemagne, 1932–1936* (Paris: Editions du CNRS, 1980) 131–48; and Janine Bourdin, 'Les anciens combattants et la célébration du 11 novembre 1938', in Rémond and Bourdin (eds) *La France et les Français en 1938–1939*, 95–114.

6. See Maurice Vaïsse, 'Le pacifisme français dans les années trente', *Relations Internationales* (1981) 46.

7. See Antoine Prost, *In the Wake of War: Les 'Anciens Combattants' and French Society* (Providence: Berg, 1992) 66–75; and Lacaze, *L'opinion publique française* et la crise de Munich (Berne: Peter Lang, 1991) 501–6.

8. Bourdin, 'Les anciens combattants' in Rémond and Bourdin (eds) *La France et les Français*, 95–114; and Jean Marie de Busscher, 'A l'ombre des monuments aux morts', in Olivier Barrot and Pascal Ory (eds) *Entre Deux Guerres* (Paris: Editions Bourin, 1990) 13–26.

9. See Barnett Singer, 'From Patriots to Pacifists: The French Primary School Teachers, 1880–1940', *Journal of Contemporary History*, xii, no. 3 (July 1977) 413–34.

10. See Isabel Boussard, 'Le pacifisme paysan', in Rémond and Bourdin (eds) *La France et les Français en 1938–1939*, 59–75.

11. Jean Giono, *Le grand troupeau* (1931); Jean Guéhenno, *Gonnet, déserteur* (1934); Gabriel Chevalier, *La Peur* (1930).

12. Georges Bourdon, *Les chaînes*, Henri Bataille, *L'Animateur*, Charles Méré, *La Captive*. The preceding section is very much indebted to the invaluable work of L. Mysyrowicz, *Autopsie d'une défaite* (Lausanne: Editions de l'Age d'Homme, 1973).

13. Mysyrowicz, *Autopsie d'une défaite*, 293; Julian Jackson, *Defending Democracy*, 139–45; Marianne Benteli et al, 'Le cinéma français' in Rémond and Bourdin (eds) *La France et les Français*, 27–41; Paul Monaco, 'The Popular Cinema as Reflection of the Group Process in France, 1919–1929', *History of Childhood Quarterly*, 607–35; Rémy Pithon, 'Opinions publiques et représentations culturelles face aux problèmes de la puissance. Le témoignage du cinéma français, 1938–1939', *Relations Internationales*, no. 33 (Spring 1983) 91–102.

14. For example, contrast Robert Frank(enstein)'s, *Le prix du réarmement français, 1935–1939* (Paris: Publications de la Sorbonne, 1982) with Alfred Sauvy's *Histoire économique de la France entre les deux guerres*, vol. 2 (Paris: Fayard, 1967).

15. Alfred Sauvy, 'L'évolution économique', in René Rémond and Janine Bourdin (eds) *Edouard Daladier, chef du gouvernement* (Paris: FNSP, 1977) 95–6; J.-B. Duroselle, *La Décadence*, 1932–1939 (Paris: Imprimerie nationale, 1979) 444; see also Patrick Fridenson, 'Le patronat français', in Rémond and Bourdin (eds) *La France et les Français en 1938–1939*, 139–56.

16. See Jean-Louis Crémieux-Brilhac, *Les Français de l'An 40*, vol. 2. (Paris: Gallimard, 1990), 54; Robert Frank(enstein), *Le prix du réarmement*, 26–9, and 'The Decline of France and French Appeasement Policies, 1936–9', in Mommsen and Kettenacker (eds) *The Fascist Challenge and the Policy of Appeasement* (London: Allen and Unwin, 1983) 238.

17. Frank(enstein), *Le prix du réarmement*, 311, 318.

18. Young, 'The Aftermath of Munich: The Course of French Diplomacy, October 1938 to March 1939', *French Historical Studies*, viii, no. 2 (Fall 1973) 317; 'La Guerre de Longue Durée', in A. Preston (ed.) *General Staffs and Diplomacy* (London: Croom Helm, 1978) 51.

19. See Maurice Mégret, 'Les origines de la propagande de guerre française', *Revue d'Histoire de le 2e Guerre Mondiale*, no. 41 (Jan. 1961) 3–27; Christine Sellin, 'L'Image de la puissance française à travers les manuels scolaires', *Relations Internationales* (1983)

NOTES 169

103–11; Claude Lévy, 'L'image de la puissance française dans un hebdomadaire dépolitisé: *Marianne*', *ibid.*, 113–21; André Tudesq, 'L'Utilisation gouvernementale de la radio', in Rémond and Bourdin (eds) *Edouard Daladier, chef du gouvernement*, 255–64; René Duval, 'Radio-Paris' in Barrot and Ory (eds) *Entre deux Guerres*, 129–46.

20 See Pascal Ory, 'La commémoration révolutionnaire en 1939', in Rémond and Bourdin (eds) *La France et les Français en 1938–1939*, 115–36. On the state visit to London, see the *Washington Post*, 21 March 1939, p. 4; 22 March, pp.1 and 5; 23 March, p.10.

21 See A. Anquetin, 'Symboles, mythes et stéréotypes nationaux dans les cinémas français et allemands', *Relations Internationales*, no. 24 (Winter 1980) 465–84; Rémy Pithon, 'Opinions publiques . . . Le témoignage du cinéma', *ibid.* (1983) 91–102; Marianne Benteli et al, 'Le cinéma français', in Rémond and Bourdin (eds) *La France et les Français*, 27–41.

22 *Ibid.*

23 Professor Adamthwaite has argued that France was in retreat from eastern Europe well in advance of the Franco-German accord. See his *France and the Coming of the Second World War* (London: Cass, 1977) 290–93; and 'The Franco-German Declaration of December 1938', in *Les relations franco-allemandes, 1933–1939* (Paris: CNRS, 1977) 395–409. Professor Du Réau denies that France had abandoned its eastern allies, either prior or subsequent to the December accord. See her 'Enjeux stratégiques . . .', *Relations Internationales* (1981) 328.

24 Du Réau, *ibid.*, 327.

25 See Young, 'The Aftermath of Munich', *French Historical Studies*, viii, no. 2 (Fall 1973) 305–22; Peter Jackson, 'France and the Guarantee to Romania, April 1939', *Intelligence and National Security* (forthcoming); Martin Alexander, *The Republic in Danger. General Maurice Gamelin and the Politics of French Defence, 1933–1940* (Cambridge: Cambridge University Press, 1992) 210–35; Dov B. Lungu, *Rumania and the Great Powers, 1933–1940* (Durham: Duke University Press, 1989) 170–3.

26 See Young, *In Command of France. French Foreign Policy and Military Planning, 1933–1940* (Cambridge: Harvard University Press, 1978) 236–40. See also Carley, 'End of the "Low, Dishonest Decade" ', *Europe-Asia Studies*, xlv, no. 2 (1993) 303–41, and 'Five Kopecks for Five Kopecks: Franco-Soviet Trade Negotiations 1928–1939', *Cahiers du monde russe et soviétique*, xxxiii, no. 1 (Jan–March 1992) 23–58.

27 See Du Réau, *Edouard Daladier, 1884–1970* (Paris: Fayard, 1993) 329–34; Shorrock, *From Ally to Enemy. The Enigma of Fascist Italy in French Diplomacy* (Kent, Ohio: Kent State University Press, 1988) 244–74; Young, 'French Military Intelligence and the Franco-Italian Alliance, 1933–1939', *Historical Journal*, xxviii, no. 1 (1985) 143–68; Paul Stafford, 'The French Government and the Danzig Crisis: The Italian Dimension', *International History Review*, vi, no. 1 (February 1984) 48–87.

28 See Alain Fleury, 'L'Image de l'Allemagne dans le journal *La Croix*, 1918–1940', in Jacques Bariéty, Alfred Guth and Jean-Marie Valentin (eds) *La France et l'Allemagne entre les deux guerres mondiales* (Nancy: Presses Universitaires de Nancy, 1987) 177–92; Antoine Prost, 'Les Anciens Combattants . . .', in *La France et l'Allemagne, 1932–1936* (1980) 131–48; Isabel Boussard, 'Le pacifisme paysan', in Rémond and Bourdin (eds) *La France et les Français*, 59–75.

29 Christel Peyrefitte reports that only 37 per cent of the respondents in April 1939 believed in the possibility of war that year. By July that figure had increased to 45 per cent, while as many as 67 per cent believed that war was possible after 1939. See her 'Les premiers sondages d'opinion', in Rémond and Bourdin (eds) *Edouard Daladier, chef du gouvernement*, 271–2. See also Maurice Vaïsse, 'Le pacifisme français dans les années trente', *Relations Internationales*, no. 53 (1988) 51.

30 Maurice Vaïsse, *ibid.*, 51. For the argument that the French were as disunited as ever, see Berstein, *La France des années 30* (Paris: Colin, 1988) 162–6, and Herrick

Chapman, *State Capitalism and Working Class Radicalism in the French Aircraft Industry* (Berkeley: University of California Press, 1991) 212–13.

31. See remarks under 'September' in Ambassador Campbell's quarterly report of 2 November, *PRO*, FO 371, 22918, C17813/25/17; and William Bullitt to Roosevelt, 8 September 1939, in Orville H. Bullitt (ed.) *For the President. Personal and Secret. Correspondence between Franklin D. Roosevelt and William C. Bullitt* (London: Deutsch, 1972) 368–9.

32. *Washington Post,* 25 August 1939, p. 11; Janet Flanner, *Paris Was Yesterday, 1925–1939* (New York: Viking, 1972) 222.

33. See his 'French Youth Takes Arms', and 'Vast Differences from 1914 . . .' in the *New York Times*, 27 August 1939, iv, p. 4, and 10 September, iv, p. 2.

34. See *Chicago Tribune*, 27 August 1939, p. 5.; and the two reports on this evacuation in Montreal's *Le Devoir*, 30 August, p. 10 and 31 August p. 10.

7. LINGERING DOUBTS AND CERTAIN DEFEAT

1. See Phipps to Halifax, 26 August 1939, *PRO*, FO 371, 22913, C12200/90/17; Campbell to Halifax, 23 August, *ibid.*, 22923, C11832/90/17; Bullitt to Washington, 22 August, *Foreign Relations of the United States* (F.R.U.S.) 1939, i, no. 1543, 301–4.

2. Frédéric Seager, 'Les buts de guerre alliés devant l'opinion (1939–1940)', *Revue d'Histoire Moderne et Contemporaine*, xxxii (Oct.–Dec. 1985) 617–38.

3. *Ibid.*, 629.

4. Royal Institute of International Affairs to Foreign Office, 20 November 1939, *PRO*, FO 371, 22918, C18749/25/17.

5. See Rossi-Landi, *La drôle de guerre. La vie politique en France 2 septembre 1939 – 10 mai 1940* (Paris: Colin, 1971) 96–100, 189.

6. See Duroselle, *L'Abîme, 1939–1945* (Paris: Imprimerie nationale, 1982) 62–63; Frank(enstein), *Le prix du réarmement français, 1935–1939* (Paris: Publications de la Sorbonne, 1982) 318–19; Chapman, *State Capitalism and Working Class Radicalism in the French Aircraft Industry* (Berkeley: University of California Press, 1991) 216–24.

7. Crémieux-Brilhac, *Les Français de l'an 40*, vol. 2 (Paris: Gallimard, 1990) 16.

8. See Crémieux-Brilhac, *Les Français de l'an 40*, i, 278–96; Duroselle, *L'Abîme*, 67–70; Young, 'In The Eye of the Beholder: The Cultural Representation of France and Germany by the *New York Times*, 1939–1940', *Historical Reflections/Réflexions Historiques* (in press).

9. Rossi-Landi, *La drôle de guerre*, 186–7.

10. I am again much indebted to the work of M. Crémieux-Brilhac, in this case especially to his chapter on the wartime industrial mobilization. See *Les Francais de l'an 40*, vol. 2, 83–99.

11. Duroselle, *L'Abîme*, 25.

12. For a serious reappraisal of Gamelin's capacities as wartime commander, see Martin S. Alexander, 'Maurice Gamelin and the Defeat of France, 1939–40', in Brian Bond (ed.) *Fallen Stars*, 107–40.

13. Apart from the keys works of Crémieux-Brilhac, Duroselle and Rossi-Landi, I remind readers of the recent books by Elisabeth Du Réau, Pierre Le Goyet, and Robert Doughty and some of the standard works by Bankwitz, Bond, Bell, Chapman, Gunsburg, Michel, and Shirer – to which reference is made in the notes for Chapters 1 and 2. The periodical literature is even more voluminous, but particular attention should be paid to: Martin Alexander, 'Maurice Gamelin and the Defeat of France, 1939–40', in B. Bond (ed.) *Fallen Stars. Eleven Studies of Twentieth Century Military Disasters* (London: Brassey's, 1991); John Cairns, 'Planning of *la guerre des masses*', in H.R. Borowski (ed.) *Military Planning in the Twentieth Century* (Washington, DC: United States

Air Force, 1986); and Bradford A. Lee, 'Strategy, Arms and the Collapse of France, 1930–1940', in R.T.B. Langhorne (ed.) *Diplomacy and Intelligence during the Second World War: Essays in Honour of F.H. Hinsley* (Cambridge: Cambridge University Press, 1985).

14. Statistics often produce paradox. No matter the differences which arise among those who generate them, the figures always have the ring of precision. 43 looks as solid as 39, even when it applies to the same subject. So I use them, here and elsewhere, only when I think they will be useful, often by finding some mean between rival figures – on the assumption that there are some grounds for each claim – and often with some kind of qualifier.

15. See Young, 'French Military Intelligence and Nazi Germany, 1938–1939', in Ernest May (ed.) *Knowing One's Enemies. Intelligence Assessment Before the Two World Wars* (Princeton: Princeton University Press, 1984), 271–309.

16. See R.H.S. Stolfi, 'Equipment for Victory in France in 1940', *History*, lv, no. 183 (February 1970) 1–20.

17. Duroselle, *L'Abîme*, 157.

18. The Germans had suffered 40 000 deaths in the same period. See Crémieux-Brilhac, *Les français de l'an 40*, vol. 2, 365; and Gunsburg, *Divided and Conquered. The French High Command and the Defeat of the West, 1940* (Westport, Conn.: Greenwood Press, 1979), 275–6.

19. For the personnel of the Daladier cabinet, and those who were retained in the Reynaud cabinet, see Appendix iv pp. 175–6.

20. Rossi-Landi, *La drôle de guerre*, 17, 171.

21. See Dossier 8, Commission des affaires étrangères, 15 November 1939, *Assemblée Nationale*, p. 113.

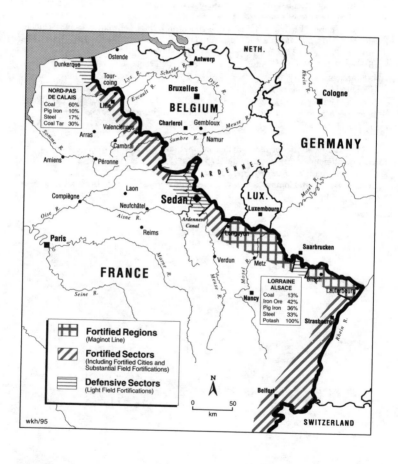

NETH.

Ostende
Dunkerque
Antwerp
Tour-
coing
Lys R. *Schelde R.*
Escaut R.
Bruxelles
Dyle R.
Lille
BELGIUM
Cologne
Rhein R.

NORD-PAS DE CALAIS
Coal	60%
Pig Iron	10%
Steel	17%
Coal Tar	30%

Valenciennes
Charleroi
Gembloux
Meuse R.
Namur
GERMANY

Arras
Cambrai
Sambre R.
ARDENNES

Somme R.
Amiens
Péronne

Compiègne
Laon
Sedan
LUX.
Mosel R.
Luxembourg

Oise R.
Neufchâtel
Ardennes Canal

Reims
Aisne R.
Verdun
Metz
Saarbrucken
Mosel R.

Paris
FRANCE
Marne R.
Meuse R.
Bitsch
Lauterbourg

Seine R.
Nancy

LORRAINE ALSACE
Coal	13%
Iron Ore	42%
Pig Iron	36%
Steel	33%
Potash	100%

Strasbourg
Rhein R.

Fortified Regions
(Maginot Line)

Fortified Sectors
(Including Fortified Cities and Substantial Field Fortifications)

Defensive Sectors
(Light Field Fortifications)

N

0   50
km

Belfort

SWITZERLAND

wkh/95

Appendix

Raymond Poincaré, 1913–20
Paul Deschanel, 1920
Alexandre Millerand, 1920–4
Gaston Doumergue, 1924–31
Paul Doumer, 1931–2
Albert Lebrun, 1932–40

II PRIME MINISTERS 1918–40

1. Georges Clemenceau, 16 November 1917 to 18 January 1920
2. Alexandre Millerand, 20 January 1920 to 18 February 1920
3. Alexandre Millerand, 18 February to 23 September 1920
4. Georges Leygues, 24 September 1920 to 12 January 1921
5. Aristide Briand, 16 January 1921 to 12 January 1922
6. Raymond Poincaré, 15 January 1922 to 26 March 1924
7. Raymond Poincaré, 29 March 1924 to 1 June 1924
8. François-Marsal, 9 June 1924 to 10 June 1924
9. Edouard Herriot, 14 June 1924 to 10 April 1925
10. Paul Painlevé, 17 April 1925 to 27 October 1925
11. Paul Painlevé, 29 October 1925 to 22 November 1925
12. Aristide Briand, 28 November 1925 to 6 March 1926
13. Aristide Briand, 9 March 1926 to 15 June 1926
14. Aristide Briand, 23 June 1926 to 17 July 1926
15. Edouard Herriot, 19 July 1926 to 21 July 1926
16. Raymond Poincaré, 23 July 1926 to 6 November 1928
17. Raymond Poincaré, 11 November 1928 to 27 July 1929
18. Aristide Briand, 29 July 1929 to 22 October 1929
19. André Tardieu, 3 November 1929 to 17 February 1929
20. Camille Chautemps, 21 February 1930 to 25 February 1930

21. André Tardieu, 2 March 1930 to 4 December 1930
22. Théodore Steeg, 13 December 1930 to 22 January 1931
23. Pierre Laval, 27 January 1931 to 13 June 1931
24. Pierre Laval, 13 June 1931 to 12 January 1932
25. Pierre Laval, 14 January 1932 to 16 February 1932
26. André Tardieu, 20 February 1932 to 10 May 1932
27. Edouard Herriot, 3 June 1932 to 14 December 1932
28. Joseph Paul-Boncour, 18 December 1932 to 28 January 1933
29. Edouard Daladier, 31 January 1933 to 24 October 1933
30. Albert Sarraut, 26 October 1933 to 23 November 1933
31. Camille Chautemps, 26 November 1933 to 27 January 1934
32. Edouard Daladier, 30 January 1934 to 7 February 1934
33. Gaston Doumergue, 9 February 1934 to 8 November 1934
34. Pierre-Etienne Flandin, 8 November 1934 to 31 May 1935
35. Fernand Bouisson, 1 June 1935 to 4 June 1935
36. Pierre Laval, 7 June 1935 to 22 January 1936
37. Albert Sarraut, 24 January 1936 to 4 June 1936
38. Léon Blum, 4 June 1936 to 21 June 1937
39. Camille Chautemps, 22 June 1937 to 14 January 1938
40. Camille Chautemps, 18 January 1938 to 10 March 1938
41. Léon Blum, 13 March 1938 to 8 April 1938
42. Edouard Daladier, 10 April 1938 to 20 March 1940
43. Paul Reynaud, 21 March 1940 to 16 June 1940
44. Philippe Pétain, 16 June 1940 to 12 July 1940

III FOREIGN MINISTERS 1918–40

Stéphen Pichon, 16 November 1917 to 18 January 1920
Alexandre Millerand, 20 January 1920 to 23 September 1920
Georges Leygues, 24 September 1920 to 12 January 1921
Aristide Briand, 16 January 1921 to 15 January 1922
Raymond Poincaré, 15 January 1922 to 1 June 1924
Edmond Lefebvre du Prey, 9 June 1924 to 14 June 1924
Edouard Herriot, 14 June 1924 to 10 April 1925
Aristide Briand, 17 April 1925 to 18 July 1926
Edouard Herriot, 19 July 1926 to 23 July 1926
Aristide Briand, 23 July 1926 to 12 January 1932
Pierre Laval, 13 January 1932 to 16 February 1932
André Tardieu, 20 February 1932 to 2 June 1932

Edouard Herriot, 3 June 1932 to 14 December 1932
Joseph Paul-Boncour, 31 December 1932 to 27 January 1934
Edouard Daladier, 30 January 1934 to 7 February 1934
Louis Barthou, 9 February 1934 to 9 October 1934
Pierre Laval, 13 October 1934 to 22 January 1936
Pierre-Etienne Flandin, 24 January 1936 to 4 June 1936
Yvon Delbos, 4 June 1936 to 10 March 1938
Joseph Paul-Boncour, 13 March 1938 to 8 April 1938
Georges Bonnet, 10 April 1938 to 13 September 1939
Edouard Daladier, 13 September 1939 to 20 March 1940
Paul Reynaud, 21 March 1940 to 18 May 1940
Edouard Daladier, 18 May 1940 to 5 June 1940
Paul Reynaud, 5 June 1940 to 16 June 1940
Paul Baudouin, 16 June 1940 to 12 July 1940

IV DALADIER CABINET 1938–40

Présidence du Conseil: Edouard Daladier, 10 April 1938 to 20
    March 1940
Vice-Présidence du Conseil: Camille Chautemps* Intérieur: Albert
    Sarraut*
Affaires étrangère: Georges Bonnet, 10 April 1938 to 13 September
    1939; Edouard Daladier*, 13 September 1939 to 20 March 1940
Finances: Paul Marchandeau, 10 April 1938 to 1 November 1938;
    Paul Reynaud*, 1 November 1938 to 20 March 1940
Défense nationale et guerre: Edouard Daladier*, 10 April 1938 to 20
    March 1940
Justice: Paul Reynaud, 10 April 1938 to 1 November 1938; Paul
    Marchandeau, 1 November 1938 to 13 September 1939; Georges
    Bonnet, 13 September 1930 to 20 March 1940
Travaux publics: L.-O. Frossard*, 10 April 1938; Anatole de Mon-
    zie*, 23 August 1938 to 20 March 1940
Travail: Paul Ramadier, 10 April 1938 to 23 August 1938; Charles
    Pomaret*, 23 August 1938 to 20 March 1940
Marine militaire: César Campinchi*
Air: Guy La Chambre
Colonies: Georges Mandel*

---

* for those who continued in the Reynaud Cabinet

Anciens Combattants: Auguste Champetier de Ribes*, 10 April 1938 to 13 September 1939; René Besse, 13 September 1939 to 20 March 1940

Education nationale: Jean Zay, 10 April 1938 to 13 September 1939; Yvon Delbos*, 13 September 1939 to 20 March 1940

Commerce: Fernand Gentin

Agriculture: Henri Queuille*

Santé publique: Marc Rucart

Postes, Télégraphes, Téléphones: Jules Julien*

Marine marchande: Louis de Chappedelaine, 10 April 1938 to 13 September 1939; Alphonse Rio*, 13 September 1939 to 20 March 1940

Blocus: Georges Pernot*, 13 September 1939 to 20 March 1940

Armement: Raoul Dautry*, 13 September 1939 to 20 March 1940

Economie nationale: Raymond Patenôtre, 10 April 1938 to 13 September 1939

Haut commissariat (Economie nationale): Daniel Serruys, 15 September 1939 to 20 March 1940

Commissariat général à l'Information: Jean Giraudoux, 29 July 1939 to 20 March 1940

Sous-Secrétariat d'Etat: Défense nationale et guerre: Hippolyte Ducos, 13 September 1939 to 20 March 1940

Sous-Secrétariat d'Etat: Affaires étrangères: Auguste Champetier de Ribes*, 13 September 1939 to 20 March 1940

Select Bibliography

For reasons of space, the following selections are confined to the works of historians which have been published since 1985, although *many* of my chapter notes contain references to older but indispensable works. For the same reason, I have included no memoirs, or works by contemporaries. Biographical works are confined to those whose subjects figure fairly prominently in the text. A more comprehensive bibliography will be found in my edited volume, *French Foreign Policy, 1918–1945*, as well as a convenient discussion of the French archives upon which so many of the following works are based.

GENERAL AND COLLECTIVE WORKS

Adamthwaite, Anthony *Grandeur and Misery. France's Bid for Power in Europe, 1914–1940* (London: Edward Arnold, 1995).

Agulhon, Maurice *The French Republic, 1879–1992* (London: Blackwell, 1993).

—— with Nouschi, André and Schor, Ralph *La France de 1914 à 1940* (Paris: Nathan, 1993).

Alexander, Martin S. and Graham, Helen (eds) *The French and Spanish Popular Fronts* (Cambridge: Cambridge University Press, 1989).

Barrot, Olivier and Ory, Pascal (eds) *Entre deux Guerres. La creation entre 1919 et 1939* (Paris: Editions Bourin, 1990).

Becker, Jean-Jacques and Audoin-Rouzeau, Stéphane (eds) *Les sociétées européennes et la guerre de 1914–1918* (Paris: Université de Paris X: Nanterre, 1990)

Bell, P.M.H. *The Origins of the Second World War in Europe* (London: Longman, 1986).

Berstein, Serge *La France des années 30* (Paris: Colin, 1988).

Bond, Brian (ed.) *Fallen Stars. Eleven Studies of Twentieth Century Military Disasters* (London: Brassey's, 1991).

Borowski, H.R. (ed.) *Military Planning in the Twentieth Century* (Washington: United States Air Force, 1986).

Bouvier, Jean, Girault, René and Thobie, Jacques *L'Impérialisme à la française* (Paris: Editions la Découverte, 1986).

Burrin, Philippe *La France à l'heure allemande, 1940–1944* (Paris: Seuil, 1995).

Delivet, Pierre and Le Béguec, Gilles *Henri Queuille et la République. Actes du colloque, 1984* (Limoges: Université de Limoges, 1987).

Doise, Jean and Vaïsse, Maurice *Diplomatie et Outil Militaire, 1871–1969* (Paris: Imprimerie nationale, 1987).

Dubief, Henri *Le Déclin de la Troisième, 1929–1938* (Paris: Seuil, 1979).

—— and Borne, Dominique *Les crises des années 30: 1929–1938* (Paris: Seuil, 1989)

Durand, Yves *Les Causes de la Deuxième Guerre Mondiale* (Paris: Colin, 1992).

Durandin, Catherine, et al *Histoire des élites en France du xvie siècle au xxe siècle* (Paris: Tallendier, 1991).

Egerton, George (ed.) *Political Memoir. Essays on the Politics of Memory* (London: Cass, 1994)

Fry, Michael G. (ed.) *Power, Personalities and Policies. Essays in Honour of Donald Cameron Watt* (London: Cass, 1992)

Girault, René and Frank, Robert *Turbulente Europe et nouveaux mondes, 1914–1941* (Paris: Masson, 1988).

Langhorne, R.T.B. (ed.) *Diplomacy and Intelligence During the Second World War: Essays in Honour of F.H. Hinsley* (Cambridge: Cambridge University Press, 1985)

Martel, Gordon (ed.) *The Origins of the Second World War Reconsidered* (London: Allen and Unwin, 1986).

Pyke, David Wingeate (ed.) *The Opening of the Second World War* (New York: Peter Lang, 1991).

Rioux, J.P., Prost, A., Azéma, J.P. *Les Communistes français de Munich à Chateaubriant* (Paris: FNSP, 1987).

Vaïsse, Maurice (ed.) *Le pacifisme en Europe des années 1930 aux années 1950* (Brussels: Bruylant, 1993)

Valentin, J.M., Bariéty, J. and Guth, A. *La France et l'Allemagne entre les deux guerres mondiales* (Nancy: Presses Universitaires de Nancy, 1987).

Watt, Donald Cameron *Too Serious A Business: European Armed Forces and the Approach to the Second World War* (London: Temple Smith, 1975).

—— *How War Came. The Immediate Origins of the Second World War, 1938–1939* (London: Heinemann, 1989).

Young, Robert J. (ed.) *French Foreign Policy, 1918–1945. A Guide to Research and Research Materials* (Wilmington: Scholarly Resources, 1991).

MONOGRAPHS

Alexander, Martin *The Republic in Danger. General Maurice Gamelin and the Politics of French Defence, 1933–1940* (Cambridge: Cambridge University Press, 1992).

Arnal, Oscar *Ambivalent Alliance: The Catholic Church and the Action Française, 1899–1939* (Pittsburgh: University of Pittsburgh Press, 1985)

Azéma, Jean-Pierre *1940, l'année terrible* (Paris: Seuil, 1990).

Baudouï, Rémi *Raoul Dautry, 1880–1951. Le Technocrate de la République* (Paris: Balland, 1992).

Beazley, Elizabeth N. 'André François-Poncet, Ambassador of France, and Franco-Italian Relations, November 1938–August 1939' (M.A. Thesis, Universities of Manitoba and Winnipeg, 1985).

Berstein, Serge *Edouard Herriot, ou la République en personne* (Paris: FNSP, 1985).

Blumenthal, Henry *Illusion and Reality in Franco-American Diplomacy, 1914–1945* (Baton Rouge, Louisiana State University Press, 1986).

Body, Jacques *Jean Giraudoux: The Legend and the Secret* (Cranbury NJ: Fairleigh Dickinson University Press, 1991).

Burrin, Philippe *La dérive fasciste. Doriot, Déat, Bergery. 1933–1945* (Paris: Seuil, 1986).

Chapman, Herrick *State Capitalism and Working Class Radicalism in the French Aircraft Industry* (Berkeley: University of California Press, 1991).

Cointet, Jean-Paul *Pierre Laval* (Paris: Fayard, 1993).

Crémieux-Brilhac, Jean Louis *Les Français de l'An 40*. vol. 1 *La guerre oui ou non?*, vol. 2 *Ouvriers et soldats* (Paris: Gallimard, 1990).

Crouy Chanel, Etienne de *Alexis Léger, l'autre visage de Saint John Perse* (Paris: Picollec, 1989).

Destremau, Bernard *Weygand* (Paris: Perrin, 1989).

Doughty, Robert A. *The Seeds of Disaster. The Development of French Army Doctrine, 1919–1939* (Hamden: Archon Books, 1985).

—— *The Breaking Point. Sedan and the Fall of France, 1940* (New York: Archon Books, 1990).

Dreifort, John E. *Myopic Grandeur: The Ambivalence of French Foreign Policy Toward the Far East, 1919–1945* (Kent, Ohio: Kent State University Press, 1991).

Du Réau, Elisabeth *Edouard Daladier, 1884–1970* (Paris: Fayard, 1993).

Duroselle, J.-B. *Clemenceau* (Paris: Fayard, 1988).

Farrar, Majorie M. *Principled Pragmatist: The Political Career of Alexandre Millerand* (Oxford: Berg, 1991).

Ferro, Marc *Pétain* (Paris: Fayard, 1987).

Fleury, Alain *La Croix et l'Allemagne, 1930–1940* (Paris: Editions du Cerf, 1986).

Hellman, John. *The Knight-Monks of Vichy France. Uriage, 1940–1945* (Montreal: McGill-Queen's University Press, 1993).

Hickok, James N. 'Anglo-French Military Cooperation, 1935–1940' (Ph.D. dissertation, University of Wisconsin, 1991).

Hood, Ronald Chalmers *Royal Republicans. The French Naval Dynasties Between the World Wars* (Baton Rouge: Louisiana State University Press, 1985).

Ingram, Norman *The Politics of Dissent. Pacifism in France, 1919–1939* (Oxford: Clarendon Press, 1991).

Jackson, Julian *The Politics of Depression in France, 1932–1936* (Cambridge: Cambridge University Press, 1985).

—— *The Popular Front in France Defending Democracy, 1934–38* (Cambridge: Cambridge University Press, 1988).

Jackson, Peter 'The Soldier as Statesman: The French Military Mission to Czechoslovakia and the Munich Crisis of 1938' (M.A. Thesis, University of Calgary, 1991).

Jeanneney, Jean-Noël. *Georges Mandel. L'homme qu'on attendait* (Paris: Seuil, 1991).

Jordan, Nicole *The Popular Front and Central Europe: The Dilemmas of French Impotence, 1918–1940* (Cambridge: Cambridge University Press, 1992).

Keeton, Edward David *Briand's Locarno Policy. French Economics, Politics and Diplomacy, 1925–1929* (New York: Garland, 1987).

Kiesling, Eugenia C. 'A Staff College for the Nation in Arms: The Collège des Hautes Etudes de Défense Nationale' (Ph.D. dissertation, Stanford University, 1988).

Kuisel, Richard *Seducing the French. The Dilemma of Americanization* (Berkeley: University of California Press, 1993).

Kupferman, Fred *Pierre Laval, 1883–1945* (Paris, Fayard, 1987).

Lacaze, Yvon *L'opinion publique française et la crise de Munich* (Berne: Peter Lang, 1991).

Lacouture, Jean *Charles de Gaulle*, 3 vols. (Paris: Seuil, 1984–1986).

Le Goyet, Pierre *Munich, un traquenard?* (Paris: France-Empire, 1988).

—— *La Défaite: 10 mai – 25 juin 1940* (Paris: Economica, 1990).

—— *France-Pologne, 1919–1939* (Paris: Editions France-Empire, 1991).

Lungu, Dov B. *Roumania and the Great Powers, 1933–1940* (Durham: Duke University Press, 1989).

Miller, Michael B. *Shanghai on the Métro. Spies, Intrigue and the French between the Wars* (Berkeley: University of California Press, 1994).

Milza, Pierre *Fascisme français passé et présent* (Paris: Flammarion, 1987).

Mouré, Kenneth *Managing the franc Poincaré:Economic understanding and political constraint in French monetary policy, 1928–1936* (New York: Cambridge University Press, 1991).

Oudin, Bernard *Aristide Briand. Biographie* (Paris: Laffont, 1987).

Parker, R.A.C. *Chamberlain and Appeasement. British Policy and the Coming of the Second World War* (New York: St. Martin's 1993).

Pitts, Vincent J. *France and the German Problem. Politics and Economics in the Locarno Period, 1924–1929* (New York: Garland, 1987).

Prost, Antoine *In the Wake of War. 'Les Anciens Combattants' and French Society* (Providence: Berg, 1992).

Rémond, René *Histoire de France*, tome vi *Notre Siècle, 1918–1988* (Paris: Fayard, 1988).

Schor, Ralph *L'opinion française et les étrangers, 1919–1939* (Paris: Publications de la Sorbonne, 1986).

Segal, Paul H. *The French State and French Private Investment in Czechoslovakia, 1918–1938: A Study of Economic Diplomacy* (New York: Garland, 1987).

Shorrock, William *From Ally to Enemy: The Enigma of Italy in French Diplomacy* (Kent, Ohio: Kent State University Press, 1988).

Sirinelli, Jean-François *Génération intellectuelle: Khâgneux et Normaliens dans l'entre-deux-guerres* (Paris: Fayard, 1988).

Soucy, Robert *French Fascism: The First Wave. 1924–1933* (New Haven: Yale University Press, 1986)

Soutou, Georges *L'or et le sang. Les buts économiques de la première guerre mondiale* (Paris: Fayard, 1989).

Sternhell, Zeev *Neither Right Nor Left. Fascist Ideology in France* (Berkeley: University of California Press, 1986)

—— with Sznajder, M. and Asheri, M. *The Birth of Fascist Ideology* (Princeton: Princeton University Press, 1994)

Vinen, Richard *The Politics of French Business, 1936–1945* (Cambridge: Cambridge University Press, 1991).

Wandycz, Piotr S. *The Twilight of French Eastern Alliances, 1926–1936. French–Czechoslovak–Polish Relations from Locarno to the Remilitarization of the Rhineland* (Princeton: Princeton University Press, 1988).

Wileman, Donald G. 'L'Alliance Républicaine Démocratique, 1901–1947' (Ph.D. dissertation, York University, 1988)

Young, Robert J. *Power and Pleasure. Louis Barthou and the Third French Republic* (Montreal: McGill-Queen's University Press, 1991).

HISTORICAL ARTICLES

Adamthwaite, Anthony 'French Military Intelligence and the Coming of War 1935–1939', in Christopher Andrew and Jeremy Noakes (eds) *Intelligence and International Relations 1900–1945* (Exeter: University of Exeter, 1987) 191–208.

Alexander, Martin S. 'Soldiers and Socialists: The French Officer Corps and Leftist Government 1935–1937', in Martin Alexander and Helen Graham (eds) *The French and Spanish Popular Fronts* (Cambridge: Cambridge University Press, 1987) 62–78.

—— 'The Fall of France, 1940', *Journal of Strategic Studies*, xii, no. 1 (March 1990) 10–44.

—— 'Did the Deuxième Bureau Work? The Role of Intelligence in French

Defence Policy and Strategy, 1919–1939', *Intelligence and National Security*, vi, no. 2 (April 1991) 293–333.

Alexander, Martin S. 'Safes and Houses: William C. Bullitt, Embassy Security and the Shortcomings of the US Foreign Service in Europe before the Second World War', *Diplomacy and Statecraft*, ii, no. 2 (July 1991) 187–210.

—— 'In Lieu of Alliance: The French General Staff's Secret Cooperation with Neutral Belgium, 1936–1940', *Jounrnal of Strategic Studies*, xiv, no. 4 (December 1991) 413–27.

—— 'Maurice Gamelin and the Defeat of France, 1939–40', in Brian Bond (ed.) *Fallen Stars. Eleven Studies of Twentieth Century Military Disasters* (London: Brassey's, 1991) 107–40.

Audoin-Rouzeau, Stéphane ' "Bourrage de crâne" et Information en France en 1914–1918', in J.J. Becker et al (eds) *Les Sociétés Européennes* (Paris: Université de Nanterre, 1990) 163–74.

Bariéty, Jacques 'Léon Blum, le prophète et l'action', *Politique Etrangère*, li (Spring 1986) 43–56.

—— 'Les partisans français de l'entente franco-allemande et la "prise du pouvoir" par Hitler, Avril 1932–Avril 1934', in Valentin, Bariéty, Guth (eds) *La France et l'Allemagne entre les deux guerres mondiales* (Nancy: Presses Universitaires, 1987) 21–30.

Becker, Jean-Jacques 'La Population française face à l'entrée en guerre', in Becker et al (eds) *Les Sociétées Européennes* (Paris: Université de Nanterre, 1990) 35–7.

Blatt, Joel 'France and the Washington Conference', *Diplomacy and Statecraft*, iv, no. 3 (November 1993) 192–219.

Busscher, Jean-Marie 'A l'ombre des monuments aux morts,' in Olivier Barrot and Pascal Ory (eds) *Entre deux Guerres. La creation entre 1919 et 1939* (Paris: Editions Bourin, 1990)., 13–26.

Cairns, John C. 'Planning for *la guerre des masses*: Constraints and Contradictions in France before 1940', in H.R. Borowski (ed.) *Military Planning in the Twentieth Century* (Washington, DC: United States Air Force, 1986) 37–66.

Carley, Michael Jabara 'Five Kopecks for Five Kopecks: Franco-Soviet Trade Negotiations 1928–1939', *Cahiers du monde russe et soviétique*, xxxiii, no. 1 (Jan.–March 1992) 23–58.

—— 'End of the "Low, Dishonest Decade": Failure of the Anglo-French-Soviet Alliance in 1939', *Europe–Asia Studies*, xlv, no. 2 (1993) 303–41.

—— 'Down a Blind-Alley: Anglo-Franco-Soviet Relations, 1920–1939', *Canadian Journal of History*, xxix (April 1994) 147–72.

—— 'Prelude to defeat: Franco-Soviet Relations, 1920–1939', *Historical Reflections/Réflexions Historiques* (in press).

Caron, Vicki 'Prelude to Vichy: France and the Jewish refugees in the Era of Appeasement', *Journal of Contemporary History*, xx (1985) 157–76.

Doughty, Robert A. 'The French Armed Forces, 1918–1940', in Allan R. Millet and Williamson Murray (eds) *Military Effectiveness*, vol. 2 (Boston: Allen and Unwin, 1988) 36–69.

Dreifort, John E. 'The French Role in the Least Unpleasant Solution', in *Reappraising the Munich Pact. Continental Perspectives* (Washington, DC: Woodrow Wilson Center Press and Johns Hopkins University Press, 1992) 21–46.

Dutter, Gordon 'Doing Business with the Fascists: French Economic Relations with Italy under the Popular Front', *French History*, iv, no. 2 (June 1990) 174–98.

—— 'Doing Business with the Nazis: French Economic Relations with Germany under the Popular Front', *Journal of Modern History*, lxiii (June 1991) 296–326.

Duval, René 'Radio-Paris,' in Barrot and Ory (eds) *Entre deux Guerres*, 129–46.

Fleury, Alain 'L'Image de l'Allemagne dans le journal *La Croix*, 1918–1940', in Valentin, Bariéty, Guth (eds) *La France et l'Allemagne* (Nancy: Presses Universitaires, 1987) 177–92.

Geyer, Michael 'The Crisis of Military Leadership in the 1930s', *Journal of Strategic Studies*, xiv, no. 4 (December 1991) 448–62.

Ingram, Norman 'Romain Rolland, Interwar Pacifism and the Problem of Peace', in Charles Chatfield and Peter van den Dungen (eds) *Peace Movements and Political Cultures* (Knoxville: University of Tennessee Press, 1988) 143–64.

Irvine, William D. 'Domestic Politics and the Fall of France in 1940', *Historical Reflections/Réflexions Historiques* (in press).

Jackson, Peter 'French Military Intelligence and Czechoslovakia, 1938', *Diplomacy and Statecraft*, v, no. 1 (March 1994) 81–106.

—— 'France and the Guarantee to Romania, April 1939', *Intelligence and National Security*, x, no. 2 (April 1995) 242–72.

—— 'La perception de la puissance aérienne allemande et son influence sur la politique extérieure Française pendant les crises internationales de 1938 à 1939'.

Jordan, Nicole 'Léon Blum and Czechoslovakia, 1936–1938', *French History*, v, no. 1 (March 1991) 48–73.

—— 'Maurice Gamelin, Italy and the Eastern Alliances', *Journal of Strategic Studies*, xiv, no. 4 (December 1991) 428–41.

Keeton, Edward D. 'Economics and Politics in Briand's German Policy, 1925–1931', in Carole Fink, Isabel V. Hull and MacGregor Knox (eds) *German Nationalism and the European Response, 1890–1945*, (Norman: University of Oklahoma Press, 1985) 157–80.

Keylor, William R. ' "How They Advertised France": The French Propaganda Campaign in the United States during the Breakup of the

Franco-American Entente, 1918–1923', *Diplomatic History*, xvii, no. 3 (Summer 1993) 351–73.

Kirkland, Farris R. 'Anti-Military Group Fantasies and the Destruction of the French Air Force, 1928–1940', *Journal of Psychohistory*, xiv, no. 1 (Summer 1986) 25–42.

Lacaze, Yvon 'L'opinion française et la crise de Munich', *Francia*, xix (1991) 73–83.

Lee, Bradford 'Strategy, Arms and the Collapse of France, 1930–1940', in R.T.B. Langhorne (ed.) *Diplomacy and Intelligence during the Second World War: Essays in Honour of F.H. Hinsley* (Cambridge: Cambridge University Press, 1985) 43–67.

Marks, Sally '1918 and After: The Postwar Era', in Gordon Martel (ed.) *The Origins of the Second World War Reconsidered* (London: Allen and Unwin, 1986) 17–48.

—— 'The Misery of Victory: France's Struggle for the Versailles Treaty', *Historical Papers* (Canadian Historical Association, 1986).

McKercher, Brian '"Our Most Dangerous Enemy": Great Britain Preeminent in the 1930s', *International History Review*, xiii, no. 4 (November 1991) 751–83.

Schuker, Stephen A. 'The End of Versailles', in Gordon Martel (ed.) *The Origins of the Second World War Reconsidered* (London: Allen and Unwin, 1986) 49–72.

—— 'France and the Remilitarization of the Rhineland, 1936', *French Historical Studies*, xiv, no. 3 (Spring 1986) 299–338.

Seager, Frédéric 'Les buts de guerre alliés devant l'opinion (1939–1940)', *Revue d'Histoire Moderne et Contemporaine*, xxxii (Oct.–Dec. 1985) 616–38.

Sirinelli, Jean-François 'Les Intellectuels français et la guerre', in Becker et al (eds) *Les Sociétées Européennes* (Paris: Université de Nanterre,1990) 145–61.

Soutou, Georges-Henri 'La France et l'Allemagne en 1919', in Valentin, Bariéty and Guth (eds) *La France et l'Allemagne* (Nancy: Presses Universitaires, 1987) 9–20.

Strang, Bruce 'Two Unequal Tempers: Sir George Ogilvie-Forbes, Sir Nevile Henderson and British Foreign Policy, 1938–1939', *Diplomacy and Statecraft*, v, no. 1 (March 1994) 107–37.

Vaïsse, Maurice 'L'adaptation du Quai d'Orsay aux nouvelle conditions diplomatiques, 1919–1939', *Revue d'Histoire Moderne et Contemporaine*, xxxii (Jan.–March 1985) 145–62.

—— 'Le pacifisme français dans les années trente', *Relations internationales*, liii (Spring 1988) 37–52.

Vivier, T. 'Pierre Cot at la naissance de l'armée de l'Air', *Revue historique des armées*, clxxxi (1990) 108–15.

Young, Robert J. 'Reason and Madness: France, the Axis Powers and the

Politics of Economic Disorder, 1938–1939', *Canadian Journal of History*, xx (April 1985) 65–83.

Young, Robert J. 'French Military Intelligence and the Franco-Italian Alliance, 1933–1939', *Historical Journal*, xxviii, no. 1 (1985) 143–168.

—— 'A.J.P. Taylor and the Problem with France', in Gordon Martel (ed.) *The Origins of the Second World War: Reconsidered* (London: Allen and Unwin, 1986) 97–118.

—— 'Louis Barthou, portrait intime', in *Barthou, un homme, une époque* (Pau: J. & D. Editions, 1986) 255–74.

—— 'The Use and Abuse of Fear: France and the Air Menace in the 1930s', *Intelligence and National Security*, ii, no. 4 (October 1987) 88–109.

—— 'Cultural Politics and the Politics of Culture: The Case of Louis Barthou', *French Historical Studies*, xvii, no. 2 (Fall 1991) 343–58.

—— 'The Making of a Foreign Minister: Louis Barthou (1862–1934)', in Michael G. Fry (ed.) *Power, Personalities and Policies: Essays in Honour of Donald Cameron Watt* (London: Cass, 1992) 83–106.

—— 'Partial Recall: Political Memoirs and Biography from the Third French Republic', in George Egerton (ed.) *Political Memoir: Essays on the Politics of Memory* (London: Cass, 1994) 62–75.

—— 'In The Eye of the Beholder: The Cultural Representation of France and Germany in the *New York Times*, 1939–1940', *Historical Reflections/Réflexions Historiques* (in press).

Index

DATE DUE